P9-EDU-105

# Why You Need This New Edition

1. Thoroughly updated, this fourth edition includes the most recent and relevant studies in the field of racial and ethnic relations.

2. New "Reality Check" features apply key concepts to the college experience and everyday life.

3. A new discussion of how the growing number of biracial Americans and higher birth rates among the foreign born are affecting American concepts about racial identity.

4. New cross-cultural examples are introduced in the "International Scene" feature.

5. End-of-chapter Internet Activities enable students to explore key topics more in-depth online.

6. A new section on residential segregation allows for fuller discussion on social and institutional discrimination.

7. Many new discussion questions at the end of chapters are designed to elicit personal experiences about, or reactions to, the content just read.

PEARSON

FOURTH EDITION

# Understanding Race and Ethnic Relations

**Vincent N. Parrillo**
*William Paterson University*

**Allyn & Bacon**
Boston   Columbus   Indianapolis   New York   San Francisco   Upper Saddle River
Amsterdam   Cape Town   Dubai   London   Madrid   Milan   Munich   Paris   Montreal   Toronto
Delhi   Mexico City   São Paulo   Sydney   Hong Kong   Seoul   Singapore   Taipei   Tokyo

**Publisher:** Karen Hanson
**Editorial Assistant:** Christine Dore
**Executive Marketing Manager:** Kelly May
**Marketing Assistant:** Janeli Bitor
**Production Assistant:** Caitlin Smith
**Production Manager:** Fran Russello
**Cover Administrator:** Jayne Conte
**Editorial Production and Composition Service:** Kalpana Venkatramani/PreMediaGlobal
**Cover Designer:** Suzanne Behnke
**Cover Image Credit:** Fotolia © tdoes

**Library of Congress Cataloging-in-Publication Data**

Parrillo, Vincent N.
    Understanding race and ethnic relations/Vincent N. Parrillo.—4th ed.
        p. cm.
Includes bibliographical references and index.
    ISBN-13: 978-0-205-79200-9 (alk. paper)
    ISBN-10: 0-205-79200-6 (alk. paper)
    1. Race relations.   2. Ethnic relations.   3. Minorities.   4. United States—Race relations.   5. United States—Ethnic relations.   I. Title.
    HT1521.P37 2012
    305.8—dc22

                                                                                    2010053560

10  9  8  7  6  5  4  3  2  1—CRS—15  14  13  12  11

**Allyn & Bacon**
**is an imprint of**

www.pearsonhighered.com

ISBN-10:     0-205-79200-6
ISBN-13: 978-0-205-79200-9

# CONTENTS

# PREFACE

Race and ethnic relations is an exciting, challenging, and dynamic field of study. It touches all of us, directly and indirectly, in many ways, and on personal, regional, national, and even global levels. Each generation thinks it lives through a unique situation, as shaped by the times or the "peculiarities" of a group's characteristics. In truth, each generation is part of a larger process that includes behavioral patterns inherited from past generations, who also thought their situation was unique.

Intergroup relations change continually, through alternating periods of quiet and turmoil, of entry of new groups of immigrants or refugees, and of problems sporadically arising between native-born racial or ethnic groups within the country. Often, we can best understand these changes within the context of discernible, recurring patterns that are influenced by economic, political, psychological, and sociological factors. This is partly what C. Wright Mills meant when he spoke of the intricate connection between the patterns of individual lives and the larger historical context of society, a concept we discuss in Chapter 1.

To understand both the interpersonal dynamics and the larger context of changing intergroup relations—particularly the reality of historical repetitions of behavior—we must utilize social science theory, research, and analysis. This volume provides the framework for such understanding, as adapted from my more comprehensive book *Strangers to These Shores*. I am grateful for the widespread adoptions of that book and the favorable response to it from colleagues and students throughout Asia, Canada, Europe, and the United States. I am equally pleased with the many similar positive responses from other students and colleagues to this book, which is intended as a concise but thorough sociological introduction to race and ethnic relations.

Following a presentation of some introductory concepts in Chapter 1—particularly that of the stranger as a social phenomenon and the concept of the Dillingham Flaw—the first group of chapters examines differences in culture, reality perceptions, social class, and power as reasons for intergroup conflict. These chapters also look at the dominant group's varying expectations about how minorities should "fit" into its society.

Chapters 2 and 3 include coverage of some middle-range conflict and interactionist theories. Chapters 4 and 5 explore the dimensions and interrelationships of prejudice and discrimination, and Chapter 6 covers the dominant–minority response patterns so common across different groups and time periods. This chapter presents middle-range conflict theories about economic exploitation too. Chapter 7 employs holistic sociological concepts in discussing ethnic consciousness; ethnicity as a social process; current racial and ethnic issues, fears, and reactions; and the various indicators of U.S. diversity in the twenty-first century.

Discussion questions and Internet activities appear at the end of each chapter, along with a list of key terms. At the end of the book, the reader will find an appendix giving immigration statistics for the period 1820–2009.

## What's New in the Fourth Edition

This new edition reflects a number of changes.

First, and most important, is the continuation of our policy to provide a thorough updating of all data and information, and the inclusion of the most recent and relevant studies not only in sociology but in many other related fields as well.

Second, each chapter contains a new boxed feature, "Reality Check," which applies key concepts to the college experience or everyday life to increase the relevance of the material.

Third, a slight restructuring moves the topics of social capital and segmented assimilation into Chapter 3 on ethnic and racial stratification to allow for a sharper focus on immigration issues in Chapter 7.

Fourth, a new section on residential segregation allows for fuller discussion on social and institutional discrimination (Chapter 5).

Fifth, a new section discusses the growing number of biracial Americans and how that and higher birth rates among the foreign born are affecting American concepts about racial identity (Chapter 7).

Sixth, new tables help the reader grasp major concepts more easily: racial and ethnic demographics in U.S. professional sports (Chapter 2); middle-range conflict theories (Chapter 3); and approaches to the study of prejudice (Chapter 4).

Seventh, new International Scene boxes offer cross-cultural examples of chapter content: cultural clashes in China (Chapter 2), ethnic stratification in Israel (Chapter 3), and economic competition in the Czech Republic (Chapter 4).

Eighth, many new discussion questions at the end of chapters are designed to elicit personal experiences about, or reactions to, the content just read.

Finally, each chapter ends with an Internet Activities section, giving new links that enable students either to read more on certain subjects or explore interactive sites that offer directly pertinent insights.

## Instructor Supplements

Instructor's Manual and Test Bank (ISBN 0205826504): This supplement offers an overview for each chapter followed by Essay, Multiple Choice, and True/False questions. The Instructor's Manual and Test Bank is available to adopters at www.pearsonhighered.com.

MyTest (ISBN 0205093868): This computerized software allows instructors to create their own personalized exams, to edit any or all of the existing test questions, and to add new questions. Other special features of this program include random generation of test questions, creation of alternate versions of the same test, scrambling question sequence, and test preview before printing. For easy access, this software is available at www.pearsonhighered.com.

PowerPoint Presentation (ISBN 0205093876): The Lecture PowerPoint slides provide an overview and outline of key topics for each chapter. They are available to adopters at www.pearsonhighered.com.

## Acknowledgments

I would like to thank the following reviewers for their helpful suggestions for this edition: Theresa Gilbertson—University of South Florida, Sarasota-Manatee, and Nekehia Quashie—University of Utah. I have also had the good fortune to work with a team at Pearson whose competence, cooperation, and dedication have made the production of this concise volume a most satisfying project. My special thanks go to Karen Hanson, Publisher, for signing the project and offering valuable input on the book's structure and features. I am also most appreciative of all the fine work done by Kalpana Venkatramani, Project Manager at PreMediaGlobal, in managing all the facets of this book's production. Finally, I want to express my gratitude to my family, friends, and colleagues worldwide for the support and encouragement they so generously provide in my writing endeavors.

Vincent N. Parrillo
William Paterson University
Wayne, New Jersey 07470
Email: parrillov@wpunj.edu

# CHAPTER 1

# The Study of Minorities

*"We may have different religions, different languages,*
*different colored skin, but we all belong to one human race.*
*We all share the same basic values."*

—KOFI ANNAN, FORMER UN SECRETARY GENERAL

Americans pride themselves as part of a nation of immigrants. Many still call the United States a great melting pot where people of all races, religions, and nationalities come to be free and to improve their lives. Certainly, a great number of immigrants offer living testimony to that ideal; their enthusiasm for their adopted country is evident in countless interviews found in oral histories at Ellis Island and elsewhere. As college students, regardless of how recently or long ago your family immigrated to the United States, most of you also provide evidence of the American Dream of freedom of choice, economic opportunity, and upward mobility.

Yet beneath the Fourth of July speeches, the nation's absorption of diverse peoples throughout the years, and the numerous success stories lies a disquieting truth. Native-born Americans have not always welcomed newcomers with open arms; indeed, they have often responded with overt acts of discrimination, ranging from avoidance to violence and murder. The dominant group's treatment of native-born Blacks and Native Americans disturbingly illustrates the persistence of subjugation and entrenched inequality. Today, serious problems remain in attitudes toward, and treatment of, Native Americans on reservations; poor Blacks in urban ghettos; large concentrations of Arab, Asian, Hispanic, and Muslim Americans struggling to

1

gain acceptance. For some, the American Dream becomes a reality; for others, blocked opportunities create an American nightmare.

Interethnic tensions and hostilities within a nation's borders are a worldwide reality dating from thousands of years ago to the present. In recent years, we have witnessed the horror of terrorist killings in Afghanistan, Indonesia, Iraq, the Philippines, Spain, Turkey, and the United States. Religious factions in India and the Middle East still harbor such animosity toward one another that violence continues to erupt sporadically.

In the past decade, more than 5.4 million have died in the armed conflict in the Democratic Republic of the Congo and more than 300,000 in Darfur, a vast region in the west of Sudan. In the 1990s, Orthodox Christian Serbians killed an estimated 60,000 Bosnian Muslims in the name of "ethnic cleansing," and Serbians killed thousands of ethnic Albanians in Kosovo, prompting military action by NATO. Tribal warfare between the Hutu and Tutsi in Rwanda led to the massacre of hundreds of thousands. In the 1980s, a bloody war raged among the Hausa, Ibo, and Yoruba tribes of Nigeria, and Iraq killed hundreds of Kurds with poisonous gas.

A few years earlier, appalling bloodbaths among Kampucheans (Cambodians), Chinese, Laotians, and Vietnamese horrified the world. Elsewhere, other minorities, such as West Indians in Britain, Algerians in France, Turks in Germany, Roma (Gypsies) in the Czech Republic, and Palestinians in Israel, have encountered prejudice, discrimination, and physical attacks. Within any society, groupings of people by race, religion, tribe, culture, or lifestyle can generate prejudices, tensions, and sporadic outbursts of violence.

On college campuses, which are microcosms of the larger society, intergroup relations are thankfully not as horrific as anything just described, but on a different level, they can sometimes be rather tense and occasionally even worse. Dorm life and social events may be marred by a level of discomfort with unlike roommates or by arguments, complaints, fights, vandalism, and verbal abuse that erupt out of strained intercultural or interracial interactions. Most common, however, are the self-segregated cafeteria tables or the clustering of specific minority groups at other campus locales, both illustrative of the sociological axiom "like likes to be with like." This seemingly harmless situation is, nevertheless, an indicator of a less-than-cohesive college community where avoidance and limited social interaction may produce social isolation and reduced acceptance of unlike others as equals.

Individuals of the dominant group usually absolve themselves of blame for a minority group's low status and problems, ascribing these instead to supposed flaws within the group itself (for example, slowness in learning the mainstream language or lack of a work ethic). Sociologists, however, note that interaction patterns among different groups transcend national boundaries, specific periods, or group idiosyncrasies. Opinions may vary as to the causes of these patterns of behavior, but a consensus does exist about their presence.

# The Stranger as a Social Phenomenon

To understand intergroup relations, we must recognize that differences among various peoples cause each group to view other groups as strangers. Among isolated peoples, the arrival of a stranger has always been a momentous occasion, often eliciting strong emotional responses. Reactions might range from warm hospitality to conciliatory or protective ceremonies to hostile acts. In an urbanized and mobile society, the stranger still evokes similar responses. From the Tiwi of northern Australia, who consistently killed intruders, to the nativists of any country or time, who continually strive to keep out "undesirable elements," the underlying premise is the same: The outsiders are not good enough to share the land and resources with the "chosen people" already there.

## Similarity and Attraction

At least since Aristotle (384–322 BCE) commented that we like "those like ourselves . . . of our own race or country or age or family, and generally those who are on our own level," social observers have been aware of the similarity-attraction relationship.[1] Numerous studies have explored the extent to which a person likes others because of similar attitudes, values, beliefs, social status, or physical appearance. Examining the development of attraction among people who are initially strangers to one another, an impressive number of these studies have found a positive relationship between the similarity of two people and their liking for each other. Most significantly, the findings show that people's perception of similarity between themselves is a more powerful determinant than actual similarity.[2] Cross-cultural studies also support this conclusion.[3] Thus a significant amount of evidence exists showing greater human receptivity to strangers who are considered as similar than to those who are viewed as different.

## Social Distance

One excellent technique for evaluating how perceptions of similarity attract closer interaction patterns consists of ranking **social distance**. In 1926, Emory Bogardus created a measurement device that has been used repeatedly since then.[4] In five comparable studies spanning 50 years, researchers obtained responses from a fairly evenly divided group of undergraduate and graduate students aged 18 to 35, about 10 percent of whom were Black.

These five national surveys measured students' preferences among 30 groups, most of them Europeans but also including Native Americans, Canadians, Blacks, and six Asian groups (Asian Indians, Chinese, Filipinos, Japanese, Japanese Americans, and Koreans). Some fluctuation occurred over the 50-year span of these surveys, most notably Blacks moving upward from near the bottom to the middle. Generally, the distribution showed White Americans, Canadians, northern and western Europeans in the top third, with southern, central, and eastern Europeans in the middle third, and racial minorities in the bottom third.

Generally, the consistent ranking in the three tiers illustrated the similarity-attraction relationship. In one exception, Italians moved up steadily, becoming the first group not from northwest Europe to break into the top ten. The leap upward by Blacks was even more dramatic, from near bottom to the midpoint. International politics or war usually caused groups to drop: Germans, Italians, and Japanese in 1946 and Russians after 1946 (Cold War, McCarthyism, Vietnam).[5] However, the end of both communism and the Soviet Union enabled Russians to rise to 14th place in a smaller 1993 study.[6]

In 2001, I updated the list of groups and conducted a larger national study.[7] I eliminated mostly assimilated groups (e.g., Armenians, Czechs, Finns, Norwegians, Scots, and Swedes) and added various Asian, Hispanic, and West Indian groups. In this national study, conducted in the six weeks following 9/11, the available choices were the same as in previous studies:

1. Would accept marrying into my family (1 point).
2. Would accept as a personal friend in my social circle (2 points).
3. Would accept as a neighbor on my street (3 points).
4. Would work in the same office (4 points).
5. Would only have as speaking acquaintances (5 points).
6. Would only have as visitors to my country (6 points).
7. Would bar from entering my country (7 points).

As expected, non-ethnic Whites remained in the top position as the most accepted group, with the other top ten slots filled by Canadians, British, Irish, French, Germans, and Dutch, essentially continuing a 70-year pattern. Particularly striking, though, was the dramatic rise of African Americans. By ranking ninth, they broke the racial barrier, entering the top sector and placing ahead of other White ethnic groups. Other significant changes were the rise of Italians into the second position—ahead of the previously dominating English, Canadians, and French—as well as the movement of Greeks into the seventh position. However, only one hundredth of a point separated a group from the next ranked group in positions 13 through 25. Therefore, in the middle part of the list in Table 1.1, the exact placement of a group in relation to those near it should not be given much importance because, due to the close scores, these rankings may be the result of sampling variability.

Although this analysis is not directly comparable with the 1977 data because of changes in the list of groups, some comparisons are still possible, and the findings are encouraging in many ways. The spread in social distance—despite (1) increased diversity in society, (2) a revised list reflecting that demographic reality, and (3) increased diversity among respondents—continues to shrink, from 1.93 in 1977 to 0.87 in 2001. Despite the removal of more assimilated groups and the addition of less assimilated groups

**TABLE 1.1    U.S. Social Distance Changes, 1977–2001**

| 1977 | | 2001 | |
|---|---|---|---|
| 1. Americans (U.S. Whites) | 1.25 | 1. Americans (U.S. Whites) | 1.07 |
| 2. English | 1.39 | 2. Italians | 1.15 |
| 3. Canadians | 1.42 | 3. Canadians | 1.20 |
| 4. French | 1.58 | 4. British | 1.23 |
| 5. Italians | 1.65 | 5. Irish | 1.24 |
| 6. Swedish | 1.68 | 6. French | 1.28 |
| 7. Irish | 1.69 | 7. Greeks | 1.32 |
| 8. Hollanders | 1.83 | 8. Germans | 1.33 |
| 9. Scots | 1.83 | 9. African Americans | 1.34 |
| 10. Indians (American) | 1.84 | 10. Dutch | 1.35 |
| 11. Germans | 1.87 | 11. Jews | 1.38 |
| 12. Norwegians | 1.93 | 12. Indians (American) | 1.40 |
| 13. Spanish | 1.98 | 13. Africans | 1.43 |
| 14. Finns | 2.00 | 14. Polish | 1.44 |
| 15. Jews | 2.01 | 15. Other Hispanic/Latino | 1.45 |
| 16. Greeks | 2.02 | 16. Filipinos | 1.46 |
| 17. Negroes | 2.03 | 17. Chinese | 1.47 |
| 18. Poles | 2.11 | 18. Puerto Ricans | 1.48 |
| 19. Mexican Americans | 2.17 | 19. Jamaicans | 1.49 |
| 20. Japanese Americans | 2.18 | 20. Russians | 1.50 |
| 21. Armenians | 2.20 | 21. Dominicans | 1.51 |
| 22. Czechs | 2.23 | 22. Japanese | 1.52 |
| 23. Chinese | 2.29 | 23. Cubans | 1.53 |
| 24. Filipinos | 2.31 | 24. Koreans | 1.54 |
| 25. Japanese | 2.38 | 25. Mexicans | 1.55 |
| 26. Mexicans | 2.40 | 26. Indians (from India) | 1.60 |
| 27. Turks | 2.55 | 27. Haitians | 1.63 |
| 28. Indians (from India) | 2.55 | 28. Vietnamese | 1.69 |
| 29. Russians | 2.57 | 29. Muslims | 1.88 |
| 30. Koreans | 2.63 | 30. Arabs | 1.94 |
| Arithmetic mean of 44,640 | | Arithmetic mean of 126,053 | |
| Racial reactions | 1.93 | Racial reactions | 1.44 |
| Spread in distance | 1.38 | Spread in distance | 0.87 |

*Sources:* Carolyn A. Owen, Howard C. Eisner, and Thomas R. McFaul, "A Half-Century of Social Distance Research: National Replication of the Bogardus Studies," *Sociology and Social Research* 66 (October 1981): 89; and Vincent N. Parrillo and Christopher Donoghue, "Updating the Bogardus Social Distance Studies: A New National Survey," *The Social Science Journal*, 42: 2 (2005): 257–71.

to the list, the downward trend in social distance continued. These results suggest that college students today have an increased level of acceptance of diverse groups, even though many are recent arrivals, racial minorities, and/or from non-Western lands (see the Reality Check box).

## Reality Check
## Cross-Racial College Friendships

Do college students actually have close friends in everyday life from outside their own racial or ethnic group? A recent study offers one insight into that question.

While measuring social distance among college students at a midsized state university in the northeastern United States, three researchers also examined friendship patterns between Blacks-Hispanics, Blacks-Whites, Hispanics-Blacks, Hispanics-Whites, Whites-Blacks, and Whites-Hispanics. Their sample consisted of 297 freshmen, 52 sophomores, 73 juniors, and 83 seniors, of whom 297 were Whites, 71 Blacks, and 80 Hispanics. No significant differences in responses existed among grade levels, but variances did occur among groups.

For Black students, 60 percent had White friends and 38 percent had Hispanic friends. About 37 percent of Hispanic students had Black friends, and 42 percent reported having White friends. Among White students, 42 percent had Black friends, and 36 percent had Hispanic friends.

In an academic setting with a diverse student body (about 12 percent each of Blacks and Hispanics), 3 of 5 Black students have at least one White friend, meaning 2 of 5 do not. In the other five friendship possibilities, on average, two of five students have a cross-racial friend but three of five do not. The good news is that cross-racial friendships have increased in recent years, but the bad news is that these generally do not exist yet for the majority of college students.

*Critical thinking question:*   What percentage of your friends is not part of your own racial or ethnic group? Why do you think it is that way?

*Source:* Adapted from Patricia Odell, Kathleen Korgen, and Gabe Wang, "Cross-Racial Friendships and Social Distance between Racial Groups on a College Campus," *Innovative Higher Education,* 29 (2005): 29–305.

---

Although relegating Muslims and Arabs to the bottom, respondents nevertheless gave them lower (i.e., more socially acceptable) mean scores than those received by 17 of the 30 groups in the 1977 study. This bottom ranking of Muslims and Arabs is hardly surprising as a repercussion of the terrorist attacks, but how do we explain their comparatively low social distance nonetheless? Perhaps the answer is the same as for the strong findings for African Americans and other groups as well. This study may well bear witness to a "unity syndrome," the coalescing of various groups against a common enemy who attacked on 9/11. Only time will tell how lasting this new spirit is, both in the bottom rankings of Muslims and Arabs and in the low social distance scores for all groups. This study only captured social acceptance of groups at a given moment in time. It is neither conclusive nor yet indicative of new patterns. Future social distance studies incorporating the new groups will ideally give a clearer picture of how tolerant Americans are in their ever-growing multiracial, multicultural society.

## Perceptions

By definition, the stranger is not only an outsider but also someone different and personally unknown. People perceive strangers primarily through **categoric knowing**—the classification of others on the basis of limited information obtained visually and perhaps verbally.[8] People make judgments and generalizations on the basis of scanty information, confusing an individual's characteristics with typical group-member characteristics. For instance, if a visiting Swede asks for tea rather than coffee, the host may incorrectly conclude that all Swedes dislike coffee.

Native-born Americans have in the past perceived immigrants—first-generation Americans of different racial and ethnic groups—as a particular kind of stranger: one who intended to stay. A common reaction pattern is an initial curiosity about the presence of immigrants, replaced by fear, suspicion, and distrust as their numbers increased. As a result, the strangers remain strangers as each group seeks its own kind for personal interaction.

The status of a stranger is consistent, whether we speak of the past, present, or future. German sociologist Georg Simmel (1858–1918) explained that strangers represent both *nearness*, because they are physically close, and *remoteness*, because they react differently to the immediate situation and have different values and ways of doing things.[9] The stranger is both inside and outside: physically present and participating but also outside the situation with a mindset influenced by a different culture.

The natives perceive the stranger in an abstract, typified way, and so the individual becomes the *totality*, or stereotype, of the entire group. In other words, because it is someone unknown or unfamiliar, someone not understood, the natives see the stranger only in generalized terms, as a representative member of a "different" group. In contrast, said Simmel, the stranger perceives the natives not in abstract but in specific, individual terms. Strangers are more objective about the natives because the strangers' geographical mobility enhances their mental mobility as well. The stranger—not caught up in taken-for-granted assumptions, habits, and traditions, and also not participating fully in society—has a certain mental detachment and so observes each situation more acutely.

## Interactions

Simmel approached the role of the stranger through an analysis of the formal structures of life. In contrast, Alfred Schutz (1899–1959)—an immigrant from Austria to the United States—analyzed the stranger as lacking "intersubjective understanding."[10] By this he meant that people from the same social world mutually "know" the language (including slang), customs, beliefs, symbols, and everyday behavior patterns that the stranger usually does not.

For the native, then, every social situation is a coming together not only of roles and identities but also of shared realities—the intersubjective structure of consciousness. What is taken for granted by the native is problematic to the stranger. In a familiar world, people live through the day by responding to daily routines without questions or reflection. To strangers, however, every situation is new and is therefore experienced as a crisis (see the International Scene box).

## The International Scene
## Enhancing German Interaction with Americans

CDS International, an organization that runs exchange programs, distributed a pamphlet, "An Information Guide for Germans on American Culture," to Germans working as interns in U.S. companies during the 1990s. The pamphlet was based on previous German interns' experiences and on their interviews with other colleagues; its intent was to provide insights into U.S. culture and to overcome ethnocentric reactions.

- Americans say "Hello" or "How are you?" when they see each other. "How are you?" is like "Hello." A long answer is not expected; just answer "Thank you, fine. How are you?"
- Using deodorant is a must.
- American women usually shave their legs and under their arms. Women who don't like to do this should consider wearing clothes that cover these areas.
- Expect to be treated like all other Americans. You won't receive special treatment because you are a German. Try not to talk with other Germans in German if Americans are around; this could make them feel uncomfortable.
- Please consider the differences in verbal communication styles between Americans and Germans. The typical German speaking style sounds abrupt and rude to Americans. Keep this in mind when talking to Americans.
- Be polite. Use words like "please" and "thank you." It is better to use these too often than not enough. Also, be conscious of your voice and the expression on your face. Your voice should be friendly, and you should wear a smile. Don't be confused by the friendliness and easygoing, nonexcitable nature of the people. They are deliberate, think independently, and do things their own way. Americans are proud of their independence.
- Keep yourself out of any discussions at work about race, sex, religion, or politics. Be open-minded; don't make judgments based on past experiences in Germany.
- Be aware that there are a lot of different cultures in the United States. There are also many different churches, which mean a great deal to their members. Don't be quick to judge these cultures; this could hurt people's feelings.
- Do it the American way and try to intermingle with the Americans. Think positive.

*Critical thinking question:*   What guidelines for avoiding ethnocentrism should Americans follow when traveling to or working in other countries?

Strangers experience a "lack of historicity"—a lack of the shared memories of those with whom they live. Human beings who interact together over a period of time "grow old together"; strangers, however, are "young"; as newcomers, they experience at least an approximation of the freshness of childhood. They are aware of things that go unnoticed by the natives, such as the natives' customs, social institutions, appearance, and lifestyle. Also existing within the natives' taken-for-granted world are social constructions of race and ethnicity that, to the stranger, are new realities. Race as a social construct can be illustrated by the case of Barack Obama. To many Whites, he is a Black. With a long-standing, rigid, racial classification system in the United States of White or non-White, perhaps this is understandable. Obama, however, had a Black Kenyan father and a White American mother, so he is actually biracial. This, however, led some Blacks to question if he was "black enough" to be their "authentic" representative when he sought his party's nomination for the presidency.[11] Within the racial divide, both Blacks and Whites are often strangers to each other, perceiving reality through different social constructs.

In time, however, strangers take on the natives' perspective; the strangers' consciousness decreases because the freshness of their perceptions is lost. At the same time, the natives' generalizations about the strangers become more concrete through social interaction. As Schutz said, "The vacant frames become occupied by vivid experiences." As acculturation takes place, the native begins to view the stranger more concretely, and the stranger becomes less questioning about daily activities. Use of the term *naturalized citizen* takes on a curious connotation when examined from this perspective because it implies that people are in some way odd or unnatural until they have acquired the characteristics of the natives.

Many strangers have come—and are still coming—to the United States in search of a better life. Others are strangers in their native land because of their minority status. Through an examination of sociological theory and the experiences of these many racial and ethnic groups, the story of how the stranger perceives the society and is received by it will continually be retold. The adjustment from stranger to neighbor may be viewed as movement along a continuum, but this continuum is not frictionless, and assimilation is not inevitable. Rather, it is the process of varying social interactions among different groups of people.

Before we proceed further, let us clarify three terms used extensively in this book. **Migration** is the general term that refers to the movement of people into and out of a specified area, which could either be within a country or from one country to another. Examples are the migration of people from one continent to another or the migration of U.S. Blacks from the South to the North. **Emigration** is a narrower term that refers to the movement of people *out of* a country to settle in another, while **immigration** refers to the movement of people *into* a new country to become permanent residents.

So we could speak, for example, of the *emigration* of people from Peru and their *immigration* into the United States. To the sending country, they are emigrants and to the receiving country, they are immigrants.

# A Sociological Perspective

Through scientific investigation, sociologists seek to determine the social forces that influence behavior as well as to identify recurring patterns that help them and others better understand that behavior. Using historical documents, reports, surveys, ethnographies, journalistic materials, and direct observation, sociologists systematically gather empirical evidence about intergroup relations. The sociologist then analyzes these data in an effort to discover and describe the causes, functions, relationships, meanings, and consequences of intergroup harmony or tension. Not all sociologists concur when interpreting the data, however. Different theories, ideas, concepts, and even ideologies and prejudices may influence a sociologist's conclusions too.

Disagreement among sociologists is no more unusual than in other areas of scientific investigation, such as physics debates about the creation of the universe, psychiatric debates on what constitutes a mental disorder, or genetic and social science debates on whether heredity or environment is more important in shaping behavior. Nonetheless, differing sociological theories play an important role in the focus of analysis and conclusions. In sociological investigation, three major perspectives shape analysis of the study of minorities: functionalist theory, conflict theory, and interactionist theory. The first two are **macrosocial theories** that focus on society itself, while the third one is a **microsocial theory** because it examines only one aspect within society. Each has a contribution to make, for each acts as a different lens providing a distinct focus on the subject.

## Functionalist Theory

Proponents of **functionalist theory** emphasize that the various parts of society have functions, or positive effects, that promote solidarity and maintain the stability of the whole. Sometimes called the *structural-functional paradigm* or model, it represents the core tradition of sociology, inspired by the writings of Auguste Comte (1798–1857), Herbert Spencer (1829–1905), and Emile Durkheim (1858–1917) in Europe, and developed further in the United States by Talcott Parsons (1902–1979) and Robert Merton (1910–2003).

Some components of the social structure have **manifest functions** (obvious and intended results), but they often have **latent functions** (hidden and unexpected results). For example, the obvious functions of the tourist visa program are to attract foreign visitors to build goodwill and to stimulate local economies at places they visit, thereby increasing the gross domestic product (GDP). One unintended result is thousands of visitors not returning after their visas expire and remaining here as illegal aliens.

Functionalists maintain that all the elements of a society should function together to maintain order and stability. Under ideal conditions, a society would be in a state of balance, with all its parts interacting harmoniously. Problems arise when parts of the social system become dysfunctional, upsetting the society's equilibrium. This system disorganization can occur for many reasons, but the most frequent cause is rapid social change. Changes in one part of the system necessitate compensatory adjustments elsewhere, but these usually do not occur fast enough, resulting in tensions and conflict.

Functionalists view dysfunctions as temporary maladjustments to an otherwise interdependent and relatively harmonious society. Because this perspective focuses on societal stability, the key issue in this analysis of social disorganization is whether to restore the equilibrium to its predisturbance state or to seek a new and different equilibrium. For example, how do we overcome the problem of undocumented aliens? Do we expel them to eliminate their exploitation; their alleged depression of regional wage scales; and their high costs to taxpayers in the form of health, education, and welfare benefits? Or do we grant them amnesty, help them enter the economic mainstream, and seal our borders against further undocumented entries? Whatever the solution—and these two suggestions do not exhaust the possibilities—functionalists emphasize that all problems regarding minorities can be resolved through adjustments to the social system that restore it to a state of equilibrium. Instead of major changes in the society, they prefer smaller corrections in the already functioning society.

Critics argue that this theoretical viewpoint focuses on order and stability and thus ignores the inequalities of gender, race, and social class that often generate tension and conflict. Those who see structural-functionalism as too conservative often favor the conflict perspective.

## Conflict Theory

Proponents of **conflict theory**, influenced by Karl Marx's socioeconomic view of an elite exploiting the masses, see society as being continually engaged in a series of disagreements, tensions, and clashes as different groups compete for limited resources. They argue that social structure fails to promote the society as a whole, as evidenced by existing social patterns benefiting some people while depriving others.

Rejecting the functionalist model of societal parts that usually work harmoniously, conflict theorists see disequilibrium and change as the norm. They examine the ongoing conflict between the dominant and subordinate groups in society, such as between Whites and people of color, between men and women, or between native born and foreign born. Regardless of the category studied, say conflict analysts, the pattern is usually that of those with power seeking to protect their privileges and those lower on the socioeconomic level struggling to gain a greater share than they have.

Conflict analysts focus on the inequalities that generate racial and ethnic antagonisms between groups. To explain why discrimination persists, conflict theorists ask this question: Who benefits? Those already in power—employers and holders of wealth and property—exploit the powerless, seeking additional profits at the expense of unassimilated minorities. Because lower wages allow higher profits, ethnic discrimination serves the interests of investors and owners by weakening workers' bargaining power.

By emphasizing economics, Marxist analysis offers penetrating insight into the problems associated with intergroup relations and racism. Conflict theorists insist that racism has much to do with maintaining power and controlling resources. In fact, racism is an **ideology**—a set of generalized beliefs used to explain and justify the interests of those who hold them.

In this sense, **false consciousness**—holding attitudes that do not accurately reflect the objective facts of the situation—exists, and it impels workers to adopt attitudes that run counter to their own real interests. If workers believe that the economic gains by workers of other groups would adversely affect their own living standards, they will not support actions to end discriminatory practices. If workers struggling to improve their situation

*Conflict theorists examine inequality in society and how existing social patterns benefit some people while depriving others. That contrast is evident in this photo of homeless men living on the streets of New York City keeping warm by lying on top of a warm air vent, while the store window behind them displays expensive and warm fur warm coats.*

believe other groups entrenched in better job positions are holding them back, they will view their own gains as possible only at the expense of the better established groups. In both cases, the wealthy and powerful benefit by pitting exploited workers of different racial and ethnic groups against each other, causing each to have strong negative feelings about the other. This distorted view foments conflict and occasional outbursts of violence between groups, preventing workers from recognizing their common bond of joint oppression and uniting to overcome it.[12]

Critics contend that this theoretical viewpoint focuses too much on inequality and thus ignores the achieved unity of a society through the social cement of shared values and mutual interdependence among its members. Those who see conflict theory as too radical often favor the functionalist perspective. Still other critics reject both of these macrosocial theories as too broad and favor instead an entirely different approach, as explained in the next section.

## Interactionist Theory

A third theoretical approach, **interactionist theory**, examines the microsocial world of personal interaction patterns in everyday life (e.g., social distance when talking and individual use of commonly understood terms) rather than the macrosocial aspects of social institutions and their harmony or conflict. **Symbolic interaction**—the shared symbols and definitions people use when communicating with one another—provides the focus for understanding how individuals create and interpret the life situations they experience. Symbols—our spoken language, expressions, body language, tone of voice, appearance, and images of television and other mass media—are what constitute our social worlds.[13] Through these symbols we communicate, create impressions, and develop understandings of the surrounding world. Symbolic interaction theories are useful in understanding race and ethnic relations because they assume that minority groups are responsive and creative rather than passive.[14]

Essential to this perspective is how people define their reality through a process called the **social construction of reality**.[15] Individuals create a background against which to understand their separate actions and interactions with others. Taken-for-granted routines emerge on the basis of shared expectations. Participants see this socially constructed world as legitimate by virtue of its "objective" existence. In other words, people create cultural products: material artifacts, social institutions, ideologies, and so on (*externalization*). Over time, they lose awareness of having created their own social and cultural environment (*objectification*), and subsequently, they learn these supposedly objective facts of reality through the socialization process (*internalization*).

The interactionist perspective can be particularly helpful in understanding some of the false perceptions that occur in dominant-minority relations. As we will discuss shortly, racism is a good example of the social construction of reality. In addition to its focus on shared understandings of members of the same group, this viewpoint also provides insight into misunderstandings about different groups. One example is the oft-heard complaint that today's immigrants don't want to learn English or assimilate. Those who so believe offer as evidence the presence of foreign-language media programs or signs in stores and other public places; they cite overheard conversations in languages other than English and/or differences in dress; or they point to residential ethnic clusters where "non-American" customs and practices, along with language, seemingly prevent assimilation. Critics often link such complaints with a comparison to previous immigrants, typically European, who were not like this and who chose to assimilate rather than remain apart from the rest of society.

In reality, such people fail to realize that they are simply witnessing a new version of a common pattern among all immigrants who come to the

*A November 2009 photo showing President Obama bowing to Japanese Emperor Akihito at the Imperial Palace in Tokyo led critics to complain about a U.S. President bowing to a foreign leader (he was not the first to do so). In Japanese culture though, this is an act of respect. Interactionists often study misunderstandings arising from cultural differences.*

United States. They create in their minds a reality about the newcomers' subculture as permanent instead of temporary, whereas their positive role model of past immigrant groups assimilating was actually seen by other nativists back then as also not assimilating, for the same reasons cited today. Interactionists would thus examine this reality that people create, the meaning they attach to that subjective reality, and how it affects their interactions with one another.

Critics complain that this focus on everyday interactions neglects the important roles played by culture and social structure, and the critical elements of class, gender, and race. Interactionists say they do not ignore the macro-elements of society but that, by definition, a society is a structure in which people interact, and why and how they do that needs investigation and explanation.

Perhaps it would be most helpful if you viewed all three theoretical perspectives as different camera lenses looking at the same reality. Whether a wide-angle lens (a macrosocial view) or a telephoto lens (a microsocial view), each has something to reveal, and together they offer a more complete understanding of society. Table 1.2 summarizes the three sociological perspectives just discussed.

**TABLE 1.2    Sociological Perspectives**

**Functionalist Theory**
- Focus is on a cooperative social system of interrelated parts that is relatively stable.
- Societal elements function together to maintain order, stability, and equilibrium.
- Societal dysfunctions result from temporary disorganization or maladjustment.
- Rapid social change is the most frequent cause of loss of societal equilibrium.
- Necessary adjustments will restore the social system to a state of equilibrium.

**Conflict Theory**
- Focus is on society as continually engaged in a series of disagreements, tensions, and clashes.
- Conflict is inevitable because there is always a societal elite group and an oppressed group.

- Disequilibrium and change are the norm because of societal inequalities.
- False consciousness allows the ruling elite to maintain power and benefit from exploitation.
- Group struggle against oppression is necessary to effect social change.

**Interactionist Theory**
- Focus is on the microsocial world of personal interaction patterns in everyday life.
- Shared symbols and definitions provide the basis for interpreting life experiences.
- An internalized social construction of reality makes it seem to be objective fact.
- Shared expectations and understandings, or the absence of these, explain intergroup relations.
- Better intercultural awareness will improve interaction patterns.

## Minority Groups

Sociologists use the term **minority group** to indicate a group's relative power and status in a society, not to designate its numerical representation. Although first used in the World War I peace treaties to protect approximately 22 million of 110 million people in east central Europe, the term's most frequent use has been as a description of biological features or national traits. Donald Young in 1932 thus observed that Americans make distinctions among people according to race and national origin.[16]

Louis Wirth (1897–1952) expanded Young's original conception of minority groups to include the consequences of those distinctions: group consciousness and differential treatment.[17] Wirth's contribution marked two important turning points in sociological inquiry. First, by broadening the definition of minority group to encompass any physical or cultural trait instead of just race or national origin, Wirth enlarged the range of variables to include also the aged, people with disabilities, members of various religions or sects, and groups with unconventional lifestyles. Second, his emphasis on the social consequences of minority status leads to a focus on prejudice, discrimination, and oppression. Not everyone agreed with this approach. Richard Schermerhorn, for example, noted that this "victimological" approach does not adequately explain the similarities and differences among groups or analyze relationships between majority and minority groups.[18]

A third attempt to define minority groups examines relationships between groups in terms of each group's position in the social hierarchy.[19] This approach stresses a group's social power, which may vary from one country to another as, for example, does that of the Jews in Russia and in Israel. The emphasis on stratification instead of population size explains situations in which a relatively small group subjugates a larger number of people (e.g., the European colonization of African and Asian populations).

### Minority-Group Characteristics

As social scientists reached some consensus on a definition of minority groups, anthropologists Charles Wagley and Marvin Harris identified five characteristics shared by minorities worldwide:

1. The group receives unequal treatment as a group.
2. The group is easily identifiable because of distinguishing physical or cultural characteristics that are held in low esteem.
3. The group feels a sense of group identity—that each of them shares something in common with other members.
4. Membership in the minority group has **ascribed status:** One is born into it.
5. Group members practice **endogamy:** They tend to marry within their group, either by choice or by necessity because of their social isolation.[20]

Although these five features provide helpful guidelines when discussing racial or ethnic minorities, the last two characteristics do not apply to other types of minority groups, such as the aged, gays, the disabled, or women. One is not born old, and people with disabilities are not always born that way. Only a small percentage of gays are easily identifiable by physical characteristics. Most women do not marry their own kind, nor necessarily do the aged or people with disabilities. In many states, gays are not permitted to marry at all. What all minority groups do have in common is their subordinate status to a more powerful, although not necessarily larger, group. Women outnumber men in U.S. society, for example, but numerous social indicators reveal they have not yet achieved full equality with men.

Therefore, we will use the term **dominant group** when referring to a minority group's relationships with the rest of society. A complication is that a person may be a member of both dominant and minority groups in different categories. For example, a White American Roman Catholic belongs to a prominent religious minority group but also is a member of the racially dominant group.

## Racial and Ethnic Groups

**Race** is a categorization in which a large number of people sharing visible biological characteristics regard themselves or are regarded by others as a single group on that basis. At first glance, race may seem an easy way to group people, but it is not. The nearly 7 billion humans inhabiting this planet exhibit a wide range of physical differences in body build, hair texture, facial features, and skin color. Centuries of migration, conquest, intermarriage, and evolutionary physical adaptation to the environment have caused these varieties. Anthropologists have attempted racial categorizations, ranging from three to more than a hundred. Some, such as Ashley Montagu, even argue that only one race exists—the human race.[21] Just as anthropologists apply different interpretations to biological groupings, so do most people. By examining these social interpretations, sociologists attempt to analyze and explain racial prejudice.

The social construction of race varies by culture and in history. The United States, for example, has had a rigid racial classification ("White" and "non-White"), unlike Latin America, which acknowledges various gradations of race, reflecting that region's multiracial heritage. U.S. purists have even subscribed to the "one-drop theory," that someone with even a tiny portion of non-White ancestry should be classified as Black. However, it is not only outsider classifications. Sometimes people will identify as, say, Black or Native American, when their DNA reveals higher percentage of a different race. Racial classifications are thus often arbitrary, with individuals or society placing undue emphasis on race. Indeed, some geneticists argue that race is a meaningless concept, that far more genetic variation exists within races than between them, and that many racial traits overlap without distinct boundaries.[22] Furthermore, with more than 7 million people of mixed racial parentage living in the United States, many social scientists have called for the "deconstruction of race," arguing against the artificial boundaries that promote racial prejudice.[23]

**Racism** is the linking of biological conditions with alleged abilities and behavior to assert the superiority of one race. When people believe that one race is superior to another because of innate abilities or specific achievements, racist thinking prevails. The subordinate group experiences prejudice and discrimination, which the dominant group justifies by reference to such undesirable perceptions. In addition to Blacks and Native Americans, Asians, Hispanics, and even White southern Europeans have encountered hostility because of social categorizations of their abilities based simply on physical appearance.

Racism is a human invention, a good example of the social construction of reality. It slowly evolved out of efforts to sort humans into distinctive categories based on skin color and facial features. These developments included philosophers such as Immanuel Kant (1724–1804) offering biological distinctions of the "races of mankind" and nineteenth-century Social Darwinists seeing human society as a "survival of the fittest" in which the naturally superior will win out. Some physical anthropologists suggested that physically distinctive groups fell into a hierarchy, with White Europeans (like themselves) at the top and Blacks at the bottom, as rationalized by their dark color, their supposedly primitive culture, and especially because Europeans then knew of Blacks as slaves. It was in this pseudo-scientific context that racism emerged as an ideology. Although most modern scientists and social scientists have debunked the "scientific" claims of racism, racist ideologies still attract many followers.[24]

While *race* deals with visible physical characteristics, **ethnicity** goes beyond a simple racial similarity to encompass shared cultural traits and/or national origin. People may be of the same race but different in language and cultural practices, such as Africans, Haitians, and Jamaicans. Conversely, people may be of different races but members of the same ethnic group, such as Hispanics. The complexities of social groupings by ethnicity don't stop there. People may be members of the same race and ethnic group, such as the Belgians, but speak different languages (Dutch, French, or Flemish) and so also be members of different subcultural ethnic groups. Moreover, if we add the element of social class, we will find even more differences within even these subcultural ethnic groups.

Religion is another determinant of ethnic group composition. Sometimes religion and national origin seem like dual attributes of ethnicity, such as Irish and Italian Catholics (although not all Irish or Italians are Catholic). Sometimes, too, what appear to be these dual attributes—Arab Muslims, for example—are not so; for example, the majority of Arabs in the United States are Christians, with 35 percent of the total Arab American population

Catholic.[25] Even here, though, we should refrain from generalizing about all members of any national origin group (or any racial group), because of the extensive differences within such groups.

The word *race* often is used incorrectly as a social rather than a biological concept. Thus, the British and Japanese are frequently classified as races, as are Hindus, Aryans, Arabs, Native Americans, Basques, and Jews.[26] Many people—even sociologists, anthropologists, and psychologists—use *race* in a general sense that includes racial and ethnic groups, thereby giving the term both a biological and a social meaning. Since the 1960s, *ethnic group* has been used more frequently to include the three elements of race, religion, and national origin.[27] Such varied use of these terms results in endless confusion because racial distinctions are socially defined categories based on physical distinctions.

Some groups, such as African Americans, cannot simply be defined on racial grounds, for their diversity as native-born Americans or African or Caribbean immigrants places them in ethnocultural groups as well. Similarly, Asians and Native Americans incorrectly get lumped together in broad racial categories despite their significant ethnic differences.

In this book, the word *race* refers to the common social distinctions made on the basis of physical appearance. The term *ethnic group* refers only to social groupings that are unique because of religious, linguistic, or cultural characteristics. Both terms are used in discussing groups whose racial and ethnic characteristics overlap.

## Ethnocentrism

Understanding the concept of the stranger is important to understanding **ethnocentrism**—a "view of things in which one's own group is the center of everything, and all others are scaled and rated with reference to it."[28] *Ethnocentrism* thus refers to people's tendency to identify with their own ethnic or national group as a means of fulfilling their needs for group belongingness and security. (The word is derived from two Greek words: *ethnos*, meaning "people," and *kentron*, meaning "center.")

As a result of ethnocentrism, people usually view their own cultural values as somehow more real than, and therefore superior to, those of other groups, and so they prefer their own way of doing things. Unfortunately for human relations, such ethnocentric thought is often extended until it negatively affects attitudes toward, and emotions about, those who are perceived as different. Fortunately, social scientists are making increasing numbers of people aware of a more enlightened and positive alternative to ethnocentrism. **Cultural relativism** evaluates beliefs and behavior in the context of that culture. The more widespread this perspective becomes known and applied, the more intergroup understanding and mutual acceptance grows.

Sociologists define an **ingroup** as a group to which individuals belong and feel loyal; thus, everyone—whether a member of a majority group or a minority group—is part of an ingroup. An **outgroup** consists of all people who are not members of one's ingroup. Studying majority groups as ingroups helps us understand their reactions to strangers of another race or culture entering their society. Conversely, considering minority groups as ingroups enables us to understand their efforts to maintain their ethnic identity and solidarity in the midst of the dominant culture.

From European social psychologists comes one of the more promising explanations for ingroup favoritism. **Social identity theory** holds that ingroup members almost automatically think of their group as being better than outgroups because doing so enhances their own social status or social identity and thus raises the value of their personal identity or self-image.[29]

Ample evidence exists about people from past civilizations who have regarded other cultures as inferior, incorrect, or immoral. This assumption that *we* are better than *they* are generally results in outgroups becoming objects of ridicule, contempt, or hatred. Such attitudes may lead to stereotyping, prejudice, discrimination, and even violence. What actually occurs depends on many factors, including structural and economic conditions; these factors will be discussed in subsequent chapters.

Despite its ethnocentric beliefs, the ingroup does not always view the outgroup as inferior. An outgroup may become a positive **reference group**—that is, it may serve as an exemplary model—if members of the ingroup think it has a conspicuous advantage over them. A good example would be immigrants who try to shed their ethnic identity and Americanize themselves as quickly as possible.

Ethnocentrism is an important factor in determining minority-group status in society, but because of many variations in intergroup relations, it alone cannot explain the causes of prejudice. For example, majority-group members may view minority groups with suspicion, but not all minority groups become the targets of extreme prejudice and discrimination.

Some social-conflict theorists argue that ethnocentrism leads to negative consequences when the ingroup feels threatened by the outgroup competing for scarce resources. Then the ingroup reacts with increased solidarity and exhibits prejudice, discrimination, and hostility toward the outgroup.[30] The severity of this hostility depends on several economic and geographic considerations. One counterargument to this view is that ethnocentric attitudes—thinking that because others are different, they are thus a threat—initially *caused* the problem. The primary difficulty with this approach, however, is that it does not explain variations in the frequency, type, or intensity of intergroup conflict from one society to the next or between different immigrant groups and the ingroup.

## In the United States

Often, an ethnocentric attitude is not deliberate but rather an outgrowth of growing up and living within a familiar environment. Even so, if recognized for the bias it is, it can be overcome. Consider, for example, that Americans have labeled their Major League Baseball championship games a *World Series*, although until recently not even Canadian teams were included in an otherwise exclusively U.S. professional sports program. *American* is another word we use—even in this book—to identify ourselves to the exclusion of people in other parts of North, Central, and South America. The Organization of American States (OAS), which consists of countries in North, Central, and South America, should remind us that others are equally entitled to call themselves Americans.

At one point in this country's history, many state and national leaders identified their expansionist goals as *Manifest Destiny*, as if divine providence had ordained specific boundaries for the United States. Indeed, many members of the clergy over the years preached sermons regarding God's special plans for this country, and all presidents have invoked the deity in their inaugural addresses for special assistance to this country.

## In Other Times and Lands

Throughout history, people of many cultures have demonstrated an ethnocentric view of the world. For example, British Victorians, believing their way of life superior to all others, concluded they were obliged to carry the "white man's burden" of cultural and intellectual superiority in colonizing and "civilizing" the non-Western world. Yet 2,000 years earlier, the Romans had thought natives of Britain were an especially inferior people, as indicated in this excerpt from a letter written by the orator Cicero to his friend Atticus: "Do not obtain your slaves from Britain because they are so stupid and so utterly incapable of being taught that they are not fit to form a part of the household of Athens."

The Greeks, whose civilization predated the Roman Empire, considered all those around them—Persians, Egyptians, Macedonians, and others—distinctly inferior and called them barbarians. (*Barbarikos*, a Greek word, described those who did not speak Greek as making noises that sounded like *bar-bar*.)

Religious chauvinism blended with ethnocentrism in the Middle Ages when the Crusaders, spurred on by their beliefs, considered it their duty to free the Holy Land from the control of the "infidels." They traveled a great distance by land and sea, taking with them horses, armor, and armaments, to wrest control from the native inhabitants because the "infidels" had the audacity to follow the teachings of Muhammad rather than Jesus. On their journey across Europe, the Crusaders slaughtered Jews (whom they falsely labeled "Christ killers"), regardless of whether they were men, women, or children, all in the name of the Prince of Peace. The Crusaders saw both Muslims and Jews not only as inferior peoples but also as enemies. Here are a few more examples of ethnocentric thinking in past times:

> The Roman, Vitruvius, maintained that those who live in southern climates have the keener intelligence, due to the rarity of the atmosphere, whereas "northern nations, being enveloped in a dense atmosphere, and chilled by moisture from the obstructing air, have a sluggish intelligence." . . . Ibn Khaldun argued that the Arabians were the superior people, because their country, although in a warm zone, was surrounded by water, which exerted a cooling effect. Bodin, in the sixteenth century, found an astrological explanation for ethnic group differences. The planets, he thought, exerted their combined and best influence upon that section of the globe occupied by France, and the French, accordingly, were destined by nature to be the masters of the world. Needless to say, Ibn Khaldun was an Arab, and Bodin a Frenchman.[31]

Anthropologists examining the cultures of other peoples have identified countless instances of ethnocentric attitudes. One frequent practice has been in geographic reference and mapmaking. For example, some commercially prepared Australian world maps depicted that continent in the center in relation to the rest of the world (see Figure 1.1). Throughout world history,

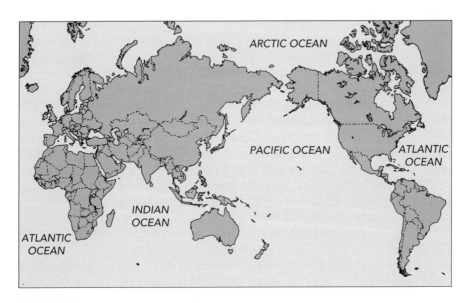

**FIGURE 1.1**

Unlike most U.S. maps of the world showing the American continents on the left side, this map—a common one in many Asian countries—puts the Americas on the right. The effect is to place these countries (such as Japan) in the center and not the edge, thus emphasizing the Pacific Rim rather than the Atlantic. Such repositioning is a form of ethnocentrism, shaping perceptions of the rest of the world.

we can find many examples of such nationalistic ethnocentrism. European map makers drew world maps with Europe at the center, and North Americans put their continent in the center. In Asia, the Chinese called their country the "Middle Kingdom," on the assumption their country was the center of the world. Beyond providing a group-centered approach to living, ethnocentrism is of utmost significance in understanding motivation, attitudes, and behavior when members of racially or ethnically distinct groups interact, for it often helps explain misunderstandings, prejudice, and discrimination.

## Eurocentrism and Afrocentrism

In recent years, many scholars and minority leaders have criticized the underrepresentation of non-European curriculum materials in the schools and colleges, calling this approach Eurocentric. **Eurocentrism** is a variation of ethnocentrism in which the content, emphasis, or both in history, literature, and other humanities primarily, if not exclusively, concern Western culture. Critics argue that this focus, ranging from the ancient civilizations of Greece and Rome to the writings of Shakespeare, Dickens, and other English poets and authors, ignores the accomplishments and importance of other peoples.

One counterforce to Eurocentrism is **Afrocentrism**, a viewpoint emphasizing African culture and its influence on Western civilization and the behavior of American Blacks. In its moderate form, Afrocentrism is an effort to counterbalance Eurocentrism and the suppression of the African influence in American culture by teaching African heritage as well.[32] In its bolder form, Afrocentrism becomes another variation of ethnocentrism. For example, a New York professor of African American Studies became embroiled in controversy when he asserted the superiority of African "sun people" over European "ice people." Others who argue that Western civilization merely reflects the Black African influence on Egyptian civilization find critics who charge them with excessively distorting history.[33]

For most advocates of pluralism, however, ethnocentrism in any form produces erroneous views. What is needed is a balanced approach that is inclusive, not exclusive, of the cultures, civilizations, and contributions of all peoples, both in the school curriculum and in our thinking (see the International Scene box for an example from abroad).

## Objectivity

When we are talking about people, usually those who differ from us, we commonly offer our own assumptions and opinions more readily than when we are discussing some other area, such as astronomy or biology. But if we are to undertake a sociological study of ethnicity, we must question our assumptions and opinions—everything we have always believed without question. How can we scientifically investigate a problem if we have already reached a conclusion?

Sociologists investigate many aspects of society and social behavior—including the study of minority groups, race, class, and gender—through the **scientific method**. This involves repeated objective observation, precise measurement, careful description, the formulation of theories based on the best possible explanations, and the gathering of additional information about the questions that followed from those theories. Although sociologists attempt to examine group relationships objectively, it is impossible to exclude their own subjectivity altogether. All human beings have **values**—socially shared conceptions of what is good, desirable, and proper, or bad, undesirable, and improper. Because we are human, we cannot be completely objective because these values influence our orientations, actions, reactions, and interpretations. For example, selecting intergroup relations as an area of interest and concern, emphasizing the sociological perspective of this subject, and organizing the material in this book thematically all represent value judgments regarding priorities.

Trying to be *objective* about race and ethnic relations presents a strong challenge. People tend to use selective perception, accepting only information that agrees with their values or interpreting data in a way that confirms their attitudes about other groups. Many variables in life influence people's subjectivity about minority relations. Some views may be based on personal or emotional considerations or even on false premises. Sometimes, however, reasonable and responsible people disagree on the matter in an unemotional way. Whatever the situation, the study of minority-group relations poses a challenge for objective examination.

The subject of race and ethnic relations is complex and touches our lives in many ways. As members of the groups we are studying, all readers of this book come to this subject with preconceived notions. Because many individuals have a strong tendency to tune out disagreeable information, you must make a continual effort to remain open-minded and receptive to new data.

## The Dillingham Flaw

Complaints about today's foreign-born presence in the United States often flow from critics' mistaken belief that they are reaching their judgments objectively. In comparing today's supposedly non-assimilating newcomers to past immigrants, many detractors fall victim to a fallacy of thinking that I call the **Dillingham Flaw**.[34]

Senator William P. Dillingham chaired a congressional commission on immigration that conducted extensive hearings between 1907 and 1911 on the massive immigration then occurring. In issuing its 41-volume report, the commission erred in its interpretation of the data by using simplistic categories and unfair comparisons of past and present immigrants by ignoring three important factors: (1) differences of technological evolution in the

**FIGURE 1.2    "Looking Backward"**

"They desire to ban the newest arrivals at the bridge over which they and theirs arrived." Five wealthy men—from left to right, an Englishman, a German Jew, an Irishman, a German, and a Scandinavian—prevent the new immigrants from coming ashore and enjoying the same privileges they now enjoy. The shadows of the five wealthy men are representations of their social status before immigration. The Englishman's shadow is a stableman, the German Jew's is a notions peddler, and the others' are peasant farm workers. (This cartoon by Joseph Keppler appeared in *Puck* on January 11, 1893.)

immigrants' countries of origin, (2) the longer interval during which past immigrants had time to acculturate, and (3) changed structural conditions in the United States wrought by industrialization and urbanization.[35]

The *Dillingham Flaw* thus refers to any inaccurate comparison based on simplistic categorizations and anachronistic judgments. This occurs any time we apply modern classifications or sensibilities to an earlier time, when either they did not exist or, if they did, they had a different form or meaning. To avoid the Dillingham Flaw, we must resist the temptation to use modern perceptions to explain a past that contemporaneous people viewed quite differently.

Here is an illustration of this concept. Anyone who criticizes today's immigrants as being slower to Americanize, learn English, and become a cohesive part of American society than past immigrants is overlooking the reality of the past. Previous immigrant groups went through the same gradual acculturation process and encountered the same complaints. Ethnic groups held up as role models and as studies in contrast to today's immigrants were themselves once the objects of scorn and condemnation for the same reasons.

To understand what is happening today, we need to view the present in a larger context—from a sociohistorical perspective. That is in part the approach taken in this book. By understanding past patterns in intergroup relations, we will better comprehend what is occurring in our times, and we will avoid becoming judgmental perpetrators of the Dillingham Flaw.

## Personal Troubles and Public Issues

Both ethnocentrism and subjectivity are commonplace in problems involving intergroup relations. In *The Sociological Imagination*, C. Wright Mills explained that an intricate connection exists between the patterns of individual lives and the larger historical context of society. Ordinary people do not realize this, however, and so view their personal troubles as private matters. Their awareness is limited to their "immediate relations with others" and "the social setting that is directly open to personal experience and to some extent [their] willful activity." Personal troubles occur when individuals believe their values are threatened.

However, said Mills, what we experience in diverse and distinct social settings often results from structural changes and institutional contradictions. The individual's local environment merely reflects the public issues of the larger structure of life. An issue is a public matter concerning segments of the public who believe that one of their cherished values is threatened.[36]

To illustrate, if a few undocumented aliens are smuggled into the United States and placed in a sweatshop in virtual slavery, that is their personal trouble, and we look for a resolution of that particular problem. But if large-scale smuggling of undocumented aliens into the country occurs, resulting in an underground economy of illegal sweatshops in many locales (as indeed happens), we need "to consider the economic and political institutions of the society, not just the personal situation and character of a scatter of individuals."[37]

Similarly, if a few urban African American or Hispanic American youths drop out of school, the personal problems leading to their quitting and the means by which they secure economic stability in their lives become the focus of our attention. But if their dropout rate in most U.S. cities is consistently far greater than the national average (and it is), we must examine the economic, educational, and political issues that confront our urban institutions. These are larger issues, and we cannot resolve them by improving motivation, discipline, and opportunities for a few individuals.

Throughout this book, and particularly in Chapters 2 and 3, we will examine this interplay of culture and social structure, ethnicity and social class. What often passes for assumed group characteristics—or for individual character flaws or troubles—needs to be understood within the larger context of public issues involving the social structure and interaction patterns.

Mills also wrote, "All sociology worthy of the name is 'historical' sociology."[38] Therefore, we should place all groups we study within a sociohistorical perspective so we can understand both historical and contemporary social structures that affect intergroup relations.

## The Dynamics of Intergroup Relations

The study of intergroup relations is both fascinating and challenging because relationships continually change. The patterns of relating may change for many reasons: industrialization, urbanization, shifts in migration patterns, social movements, upward or downward economic trends, and so on. However, sometimes the changing relationships also reflect changing attitudes as, for example, in the interaction between Whites and Native Americans. Whites continually changed the emphasis: exploitation; extermination; isolation; segregation; paternalism; forced assimilation; and more recently, tolerance for pluralism and restoration of certain (but not all) Native American ways. Similarly, African Americans, Asian Americans, Jews, Catholics, and other minority groups have all had varying relations with the host society.

Some recent world events also illustrate changing dominant-group orientations toward minority groups, such as Arabs and Muslims after 9/11. The large migrations of diverse peoples into Belgium, Denmark, France, Germany, the Netherlands, Sweden, and the United Kingdom triggered a backlash in each of those countries. Strict new laws enacted in most of these nations in the 1990s resulted in a marked increase in deportations. Violence also flared up, particularly in Germany and Italy, where neo-Nazi youths assaulted foreigners and firebombed their residences.

Elsewhere, intergroup relations fluctuate, as between Hindus and Muslims in India, Muslims and Christians in Lebanon, Arabs and Jews in the Middle East, Catholics and Protestants in Northern Ireland, and other groups as well. All go through varying periods of tumult and calm in their dealings with one another.

The field of race and ethnic relations has many theoreticians and investigators examining changing events and migration patterns. Each year, a vast outpouring of new research and information adds to our knowledge. New insights, new concepts, and new interpretations of old knowledge inundate the interested observer. What both the sociologist and the student must attempt to understand, therefore, is not a fixed and static phenomenon but a dynamic, ever-changing one, about which we learn more all the time.

## Retrospect

Human beings follow certain patterns when responding to strangers. Their perceptions of newcomers reflect categoric knowing; if they perceive that the newcomers are similar, people are more receptive to their presence. What makes interaction with strangers difficult are the varying perceptions of each to the other, occasioned by a lack of shared understandings and perceptions of reality.

In sociological investigation of minorities, three perspectives shape analysis: Functional theory stresses the orderly interdependence of a society and the adjustments needed to restore equilibrium when dysfunctions occur. Conflict theory emphasizes the tensions and conflicts that result from exploitation and competition for limited resources. Interactionist theory concentrates on everyday interaction patterns operating within a socially constructed perception of reality.

By definition, minority groups—regardless of their size—receive unequal treatment, possess identifying physical or cultural characteristics held in low esteem, are conscious of their shared ascribed status, and tend to practice endogamy. Racial groups are biologically similar groups, and ethnic groups are groups that share a learned cultural heritage. Intergroup relations are dynamic and continually changing.

Ethnocentrism—the tendency to identify with one's own group—is a universal human condition that contributes to potential problems in relating to outgroups. Examples of ethnocentric thinking and actions can be found in all countries throughout history. Eurocentrism and Afrocentrism are views emphasizing one culture or civilization over others.

The study of minorities presents a difficult challenge because our value orientations and life experiences can impair our objectivity. Even trained sociologists, being human, encounter difficulty in maintaining value neutrality. The Dillingham Flaw—using an inaccurate comparison based on simplistic categorizations and anachronistic judgments—seriously undermines the scientific worth of supposedly objective evaluations. Both ethnocentrism and subjectivity are commonplace in problems involving intergroup relations. Clearer understanding occurs by examining the larger context of how so-called personal troubles connect with public issues.

## KEY TERMS

| | |
|---|---|
| Afrocentrism | Dillingham Flaw |
| Ascribed status | Dominant group |
| Categoric knowing | Emigration |
| Conflict theory | Endogamy |
| Cultural relativism | Ethnicity |

Ethnocentrism
Eurocentrism
False consciousness
Functionalist theory
Ideology
Immigration
Ingroup
Interactionist theory
Latent functions
Macrosocial theory
Manifest functions
Microsocial theory

Migration
Minority group
Outgroup
Race
Racism
Reference group
Scientific method
Social construction of reality
Social distance
Social identity theory
Symbolic interaction
Values

## DISCUSSION QUESTIONS

1. Can you offer any examples of social distance or ethnocentrism from your own experiences and/or observations with family, friends, or neighbors, on campus or at work?

2. How does the similarity-attraction concept help us to understand intergroup relations?

3. What is ethnocentrism? Why is it important in relations between dominant and minority groups?

4. Why is objective study of racial and ethnic minorities difficult?

5. What about the Dillingham Flaw? Have you ever heard comments from anyone about other minorities that would illustrate this flawed thinking?

6. What are the main points of the functionalist, conflict, and interactionist theories?

## INTERNET ACTIVITIES

1. Read the Universal Declaration of Human Rights of the United Nations (http://www.un.org/rights/50/decla.htm). What similarities do you find in it with the U.S. Declaration of Independence and U.S. Constitution? Can you identify specific violations of any document in the situations of minorities in the United States?

2. To learn more about the social construction of race (pages 17–18), go to "Confusion about Human Races" for a forum on the subject sponsored by the Social Science Research Council (http://raceandgenomics.ssrc.org/Lewontin). Share with classmates something.

# CHAPTER 2

# The Role
# of Culture

*"No culture can live, if it attempts to be exclusive."*

—MAHATMA GANDHI

Understanding what makes people receptive to some, but not all, strangers requires knowledge of how culture affects perceptions and response patterns. Culture provides the guidelines for people's interpretations of situations they encounter and for the responses they consider appropriate. The distinctions and interplay between cultures are important to the assimilation process as well. For example, cultural orientations of both minority and dominant groups shape expectations about how a minority group should fit into the society.

This chapter first examines the various aspects of culture that affect dominant–minority relations, followed by an examination of varying cultural expectations about minority integration.

## The Concept of Culture

Human beings both create their own social worlds and evolve further within them. Adapting to the environment, to new knowledge, and to technology, we learn a way of life within our society. We invent and share rules and patterns of behavior that shape our lives and the way we experience the world about us. The shared products of society that we call *culture*, whether material or nonmaterial, make social life possible and give our lives meaning. **Material culture** consists of all physical objects created by members of a society and the meanings/significance attached to them (e.g., cars, cell phones, DVDs, iPods, jewelry, or clothing). **Nonmaterial culture** consists of abstract human creations and their meanings/significance in life (e.g., attitudes, beliefs, customs, ideas, languages, norms, social institutions, and values). **Culture**, then, consists of all of these elements shared by members of a society and transmitted to the next generation.

These cultural attributes provide a sense of peoplehood and common bonds through which members of a society can relate (see Table 2.1). Most sociologists therefore emphasize the impact of culture in shaping behavior.[1] Through language and other forms of symbolic interaction, the members of a society learn the thought and behavior patterns that constitute their commonality as a people.[2] In this sense, culture is the social cement that binds a society together.

Shared cultural norms encourage solidarity and orient the behavior of members of the ingroup. **Norms** are a culture's rules of conduct—internalized by the members—embodying the society's fundamental expectations. Through norms, ingroup members (majority or minority) know how to react toward the acts of outgroup members that surprise, shock, or annoy them or in any way go against their shared expectations. Anything contrary to this "normal" state is seen as negative or deviant. When minority-group members "act uppity" or "don't know their place," majority-group members often get upset and sometimes act out their anger. Violations of norms usually trigger strong reactions because they appear to threaten the social fabric of a community or society. Eventually, most minority groups adapt their distinctive cultural traits to those of the host society through a process called **acculturation**. Intragroup variations remain, though, because ethnic-group members use different reference groups as role models.

An important component of intragroup cultural variations, seldom a part of the acculturation process, is religion. Not only does religion have strong links to the immigrant experience in the United States, as well as to African American slavery and pacification efforts toward Native Americans, but it also has many other connections to prejudice and social conflict. Indeed, the Catholic and Jewish faiths of past European immigrants provoked nativist Protestant reactions, some quite violent and vicious. Similarly, recent immigrants who are believers of such religions as Hinduism, Islam, Rastafarianism, or Santería often experience prejudice and conflict because of their faith, as have the Amish, Mormons, Quakers, and many others in the United States in past years. Religious conflict is a sad reality in many parts of the world—the Balkans, India, the Middle East, and Northern Ireland, to mention just a few.

Professional sports are another part of culture that provide an area for the study of prejudice and racism. Long excluded from major league sports, people of color now are prominent participants in baseball, basketball, boxing, football, and track (see Table 2.2). In 2009, African Americans

**TABLE 2.1   Basic U.S. Values**

Within the United States' diverse society of racial, ethnic, and religious groups, each with a distinctive set of values, exists a common core of values. Sociologist Robin Williams, after decades of study, identified fifteen value orientations—the foundation of our beliefs, behaviors, definitions of social goals, and life expectations. Some are contradictory—freedom and individualism but external conformity; democracy and equality but racism and group superiority; nationalism but individualism—and these may spark divisions among people. Although other societies may subscribe to many of these values as well, this particular combination of values—virtually present from the nation's founding—have had and continue to have enormous impact in shaping our society.

1. **Achievement and success.** Competition-oriented, our society places much value on gaining power, prestige, and wealth.
2. **Activity and work.** We firmly believe that everyone should work, and we condemn as lazy those who do not work.
3. **Moral orientation.** We tend to moralize, seeing the world in absolutes of right and wrong.
4. **Humanitarian mores.** Through charitable and crisis aid, we lean toward helping the less fortunate and the underdog.
5. **Efficiency and practicality.** We try to solve problems by the quickest, least costly means.
6. **Progress.** We think technology can solve all problems, and we hold an optimistic outlook toward the future.
7. **Material comfort.** We share the American Dream of a high standard of living and owning many material goods.
8. **Equality.** We believe in the abstract ideal of equality, relating to one another informally as equals.
9. **Freedom.** We cherish individual freedom from domination by others.
10. **External conformity.** Despite our professed belief in individualism, we tend to join, conform, and go along; and we are suspicious of those who do not.
11. **Science and rationality.** We believe that through science we can gain mastery over our environment and secure a better lifestyle.
12. **Nationalism.** We think the American way of life is the best and we distrust "un-American" behavior.
13. **Democracy.** We believe that everyone has the right of political participation, that our government is highly democratic.
14. **Individualism.** We emphasize personal rights and responsibilities, giving the individual priority over the group.
15. **Racism and group superiority themes.** Through our attitudes and actions, we favor some racial, religious, and ethnic groups over others.

*Source:* Robin M. Williams, Jr., *American Society: A Sociological Interpretation*, 3d ed. (New York: Knopf, 1970).

Table 2.2    Racial and Ethnic Demographics in U.S. Professional Sports, by Percent

| | National Basketball Association | | National Football League | | Major League Baseball | |
|---|---|---|---|---|---|---|
| **Players** | 1999–2000 | 2009–2010 | 1999 | 2009 | 2000 | 2010 |
| White (%) | 22 | 18 | 32 | 30 | 60 | 59.8 |
| Black (%) | 78 | 77 | 67 | 67 | 13 | 9.1 |
| Latino (%) | <1 | 3 | <1 | 1 | 26 | 28.3 |
| Asian (%) | 0 | 1 | <1 | 2 | 0 | 2.4 |
| Other (%) | 0 | 1 | <1 | <1 | 1 | 0 |
| **Head Coach or Manager** | 1999–2000 | 2009–2010 | 2000 | 2010 | 2000 | 2010 |
| White (%) | 79 | 70 | 90 | 81 | 83 | 70.0 |
| Black (%) | 21 | 27 | 10 | 19 | 13 | 13.3 |
| Latino (%) | 0 | 0 | 0 | 0 | 3 | 13.3 |
| Asian (%) | 0 | 3 | 0 | 0 | 0 | 3.3 |

*Source:* The Institute for Diversity and Ethics in Sport, *The Racial and Gender Report Card*, 2010.

(13 percent of the U.S. population) account for 67 percent of National Football League (NFL) players and 77 percent of National Basketball Association (NBA) players. Nevertheless, the vast majority of owners, managers, and head coaches in all sports are White.[3] Still, many Blacks and Hispanics, and an increasing number of Asians, excel in athletics, serving as a source of racial and/or ethnic pride for many of their fellow group members.

## The Reality Construct

Our perception of reality is related to our culture: Through our culture, we learn how to perceive the world about us. Cultural definitions help us interpret the sensory stimuli from our environment and tell us how to respond to them. In other words, culture helps us "make sense" of what we encounter. It is the screen through which we "see" and "understand" (Figure 2.1).

*Language and Other Symbols.*    Culture is learned behavior, acquired chiefly through verbal communication, or language. A word is nothing more than a symbol—something that stands for something else. Whether it is

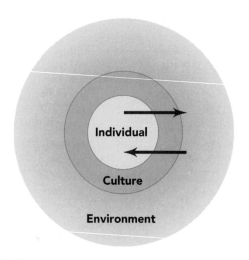

Each **Individual** observes the world through **Sense Perceptions**, which are evaluated in terms of **Culture** — values, attitudes, customs, and beliefs.

FIGURE 2.1    **Cultural Reality**

tangible (*chair*) or intangible (*honesty*), the word represents a mental concept that is based on empirical reality. Words reflect culture, however, and one word may have different meanings in different cultures. If you are *carrying the torch* in England, you are holding a flashlight, not yearning for a lost love; if you could use a *lift*, you want an elevator, not a ride or a boost to your spirits. Because words symbolically interpret the world to us, the **linguistic relativity** of language may connote both intended and unintended prejudicial meanings. For example, *black* is the symbol for darkness (in the sense of lightlessness) or evil, and *white* symbolizes cleanliness or goodness, and a society may subtly (or not so subtly) transfer these meanings to Black and White people.

Walter Lippmann, a prominent political columnist, once remarked, "First we look, then we name, and only then do we see." He meant that until we learn the symbols of our world, we cannot understand the world. A popular pastime in the early 1950s, called "Droodles," illustrates Lippmann's point. The object was to interpret drawings such as those in Figure 2.2. Many people were unable to see the meaning of the drawings until it was explained. They looked but did not see until they knew the "names." Can you guess what these drawings depict before looking up the correct names in the endnote?[4]

Interpreting symbols is not merely an amusing game; it is significant in real life. Human beings do not respond to stimuli but to their definitions of those stimuli as mediated by their culture.[5] The definition of beauty is one example. Beyond the realm of personal taste, definitions of beauty

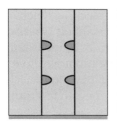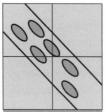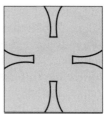

FIGURE 2.2    "Droodles"

have cultural variations. For instance, in different times and places, societies have based their appraisal of a woman's beauty on her having distended lips, scar markings, tattoos, or beauty marks or on how plump or thin she was.

Nonverbal communication—or body language—is highly important too. Body movements, gestures, physical proximity, facial expressions (there as many as 136 facial expressions, each of which conveys a distinct meaning[6]), and **paralinguistic signals** (sounds but not words, such as a sigh, a kiss-puckering sound, or the *m-m-m* sound of tasting something good) all convey information to the observer-listener. Body language is important in intergroup relations too, whether in conversation, interaction, or perception. Body language may support or belie one's words; it may suggest friendliness, aloofness, or deference.

Although some forms of body language are fairly universal (e.g., most facial expressions), many cultural variations exist in body language itself and in the interpretation of its meanings. Body movements such as posture, bearing, and gait vary from culture to culture. The degree of formality in a person's environment (both past and present) and other cultural factors influence such forms of nonverbal communication. Consider the different meanings one could attach to a student's being unwilling to look directly into the eyes of a teacher. In the United States, the teacher may assume that this behavior reflects embarrassment, guilt, shyness, inattention, or even disrespect. Yet, if the student is Asian or Hispanic, such demeanor is a mark of respect. The symbol's definition, in this case the teacher's interpretation of what the student's body language means, determines the meaning the observer ascribes to it.

A person who is foreign to a culture must learn both its language and the rest of its symbol system, as the members of the culture did through socialization. Certain gestures may be signs of friendliness in one culture but obscene or vengeful symbols in another. For example, in the United States, placing thumb and forefinger in a circle with the other fingers upraised indicates that everything is fine, but in Japan, this sign refers to money, and in Greece, it is an insulting anal expression.[7] Kisses, tears, dances, emblems, silence, open displays of emotions, and thousands of other symbols can and often do have divergent meanings in different cultures. Symbols, including language, help an ingroup construct a reality that may be unknown to or altogether different for an outgroup. Members of one group may then select, reject, ignore, or distort their sensory input regarding the other group because of cultural definitions.

*The Thomas Theorem.*   William I. Thomas once observed that, if people define situations as real, those situations become real in their consequences.[8] His statement, known as the **Thomas theorem**, relates directly to the *Dillingham Flaw*, discussed in Chapter 1. Whereas Thomas emphasized how definitions lead to actions that produce consequences to conform to the original, ill-founded definition, the Dillingham Flaw suggests the misguided thought process that may result in that definition in the first place.

The Thomas theorem is thus further testimony to the truth of reality constructs: Human beings respond to their definitions of stimuli rather than to the stimuli themselves. People often associate images (e.g., "terrorists" or "illegal aliens") with specific minority groups. They then behave according to the meaning they assign to the situation, and the consequences of their behavior serve to reaffirm the meaning; the definition becomes a self-fulfilling prophecy. For example, when Whites define Blacks as inferior and then offer them fewer opportunities because of that alleged inferiority, Blacks are disadvantaged, which in turn supports the initial definition.

Several variables contribute to the initial definition, but culture is one of the most important of them. Culture establishes the framework through which an individual perceives others, classifies them into groups, and assigns certain general characteristics to them. Because ethnocentrism leads people to consider their way of life as the best and most natural, their culturally defined perceptions of others often lead to suspicion and differential treatment of other groups. In effect, each group constructs myths about other groups and supports those myths through ingroup solidarity and outgroup hostility. In such instances, people create a culturally determined world of reality, and their actions reinforce their beliefs. Social interaction or social change may counteract such situations, however, leading to their redefinition.

Social scientists have long known how cultural definitions can influence perception. For example, more than half a century ago within a two-month interval, Gregory Razran twice showed the same set of 30 pictures of unknown young women to the same group of 100 male college students and 50 noncollege men.[9] Using a five-point scale, the subjects rated each woman's beauty, character, intelligence, ambition, and general likableness.

At the first presentation, the pictures had no ethnic identification, but at the second presentation, they were labeled with Irish, Italian, Jewish, and old American (English) surnames. All women were rated equally on the first presentation, but when the names were given, the ratings changed. The "Jewish" women received higher ratings in ambition and intelligence. Both "Jewish" and "Italian" women suffered a large decline in general likableness and a slight decline in beauty and character evaluations. This study is one of many illustrating how cultural definitions affect judgments about others.

Through **cultural transmission**, each generation transmits its culture to the next generation, which learns those cultural definitions at an early age. This fact is dramatically expressed in the Rodgers and Hammerstein musical *South Pacific*. The tragic subplot is the touching romance between Lieutenant Cable and the young Tonkinese woman Liat. Although Cable and Liat are sincerely in love, Cable's friends remind him that the couple's life would not be the same in the United States. Their differences in race and culture would work against a happy marriage for them and his own acceptance in Philadelphia high society. Miserable because of the choice his cultural values force him to make, he sings "Carefully Taught," a poignant song about how prejudice is taught to children. The lyrics tell how one must be continually taught to hate and fear people whose eyes are "oddly made" or "whose skin is a different shade." Other lines tell how this teaching must occur before it's too late, that before a child turns eight, he or she must learn to hate all the people one's relatives hate.

These lyrics reinforce the reality construct discussed earlier and illustrated in Figure 2.1. From family, friends, school, mass media, and all other sources of informational input, we learn our values, attitudes, and beliefs. Some of our learning reflects the prejudices of others, which we may incorporate in our own attitudes and actions.

# Cultural Change

Culture continually changes. Discoveries, inventions, technological advances, innovations, and natural disasters alter the customs, values, attitudes, and beliefs of a society. This section focuses on two common processes of cultural change: cultural diffusion within a whole society and changes within a particular subculture of that society.

## Cultural Diffusion

Even if members of a dominant culture wish to keep their society untainted by contact with foreign elements, cultures are inevitably influenced by other cultures—a phenomenon termed **cultural diffusion**. Ideas, inventions, and practices spread from one culture to another, but they may do so at different rates, depending on societal attitudes, conditions, and the distance between groups. Sometimes material objects get modified or reinterpreted, such as when some Latin Native American tribes of the early twentieth century showed a fondness for automobile tires, using them to make sandals, for they neither owned nor drove cars.[10]

***Borrowed Elements.***   U.S. anthropologist Ralph Linton calculated that any given culture contains about 90 percent borrowed elements. To demonstrate both the enormity and the subtlety of cultural diffusion, he offered a classic portrait of the "100 percent American" male:

> Our solid American citizen awakens in a bed built on a pattern which originated in the Near East but which was modified in Northern Europe before it was transmitted to America. He throws back covers made from cotton, domesticated in India, or linen, domesticated in the Near East, or wool, from sheep, also domesticated in the Near East, or silk, the use of which was discovered in China. All of these materials have been spun or woven by processes invented in the Near East. He slips into his moccasins, invented by the Indians of the Eastern woodlands, and goes to the bathroom,

*An excellent example of culture diffusion and cultural change is mobile phone texting, which only began in the 1990s and was widely used in Europe before it became popular in the United States. Even today, 80 percent of Europeans send text messages compared to about 60 percent in North America, although that gap is rapidly closing.*

whose fixtures are a mixture of European and American inventions, both of recent date. He takes off his pajamas, a garment invented in India, and washes with soap, invented by the ancient Gauls. He then shaves, a masochistic rite which seems to have been derived from either Sumer or ancient Egypt.

Returning to the bedroom, he removes his clothes from a chair of southern European type and proceeds to dress. He puts on garments whose form originally derived from the skin clothing of the nomads of the Asiatic steppes, puts on shoes made from skins tanned by a process invented in ancient Egypt and cut to a pattern derived from the classical civilizations of the Mediterranean, and ties around his neck a strip of bright-colored cloth which is a vestigial survival of the shoulder shawls worn by the seventeenth-century Croatians. Before going out for breakfast he glances through the window, made of glass invented in Egypt, and if it is raining puts on overshoes made of rubber discovered by the Central American Indians and takes an umbrella, invented in southeastern Asia. Upon his head he puts a hat made of felt, a material invented in the Asiatic steppes.

On his way to breakfast he stops to buy a paper, paying for it with coins, an ancient Lydian invention. At the restaurant a whole new series of borrowed elements confronts him. His plate is made of a form of pottery invented in China. His knife is of steel, an alloy first made in southern India, his fork a medieval Italian invention, and his spoon a derivative of a Roman original. He begins breakfast with an orange, from the eastern Mediterranean, a cantaloupe from Persia, or perhaps a piece of African watermelon. With this he has coffee, an Abyssinian plant, with cream and sugar. Both the domestication of cows and the idea of milking them originated in the Near East, while sugar was first made in India. After his fruit and first coffee, he goes on to waffles, cakes made by a Scandinavian technique from wheat domesticated in Asia Minor. Over these he pours maple syrup, invented by the Indians of the Eastern woodlands. As a side dish he may have the egg of a species of bird domesticated in Indo-China, or thin strips of the flesh of an animal domesticated in Eastern Asia, which have been salted and smoked by a process developed in northern Europe.

When our friend has finished eating he settles back to smoke, an American Indian habit, consuming a plant domesticated in Brazil in either a pipe, derived from the Indians of Virginia, or a cigarette, derived from Mexico. If he is hardy enough he may even attempt a cigar, transmitted to us from the Antilles by way of Spain. While smoking he reads the news of the day, imprinted in characters invented by the ancient Semites upon a material invented in China by a process invented in Germany. As he absorbs the accounts of foreign troubles he will, if he is a good conservative citizen, thank a Hebrew deity in an Indo-European language that he is 100 percent American.*

---

*Ralph Linton, *The Study of Man* (1936), 326–27. Reprinted by permission of Prentice Hall Inc., Upper Saddle River, N.J.

Typically, cultural diffusion is widespread in our pluralistic society. It can take many forms, including widened food preferences such as tacos or burritos, or use by U.S. corporations of the Japanese management technique of employee participation in setting work goals. Whatever its form, cultural diffusion is an ongoing process that influences a society and sometimes even alters our views of other cultures.

*Cultural Contact.*    Culture can also undergo change when people of different cultures come into contact with one another. Because people tend to take their own culture for granted, it operates at a subconscious level in forming their expectations. When people's assumptions are jolted through contact with an unfamiliar culture that supports different expectations, they often experience **culture shock**, characterized by feelings of disorientation and anxiety and a sense of being threatened.

Culture shock does not always occur. When people of two different cultures interact, many possible patterns can emerge. The two groups may peacefully coexist, with gradual cultural diffusion occurring. History offers some excellent examples of connections between migrations and innovations, wherein geographical conditions and native attitudes determined the extent to which a group resisted cultural innovations, despite invasions, settlements, or missionary work. The persistent pastoralism of Bedouin tribes and the long-sustained resistance to industrialization of Native Americans are two examples.

Some social scientists suggest that power alone determines the outcome, causing one group to become dominant and the other subservient.[11] If the native population becomes subordinate, the changes to its social organization can be devastating. No longer possessing the flexibility and autonomy it once enjoyed, it may suffer material deprivation and find its institutions undermined (see the International Scene box). If the migratory group finds itself in the subordinate position, it must adapt to its new environment to survive. Most commonly, this minority group draws from its familiar world as it attempts to cope with the prevailing conditions. Group members form a subculture with unique behavior and interests— neither completely those of the larger society nor fully those of their old culture. For example, both Catholicism and Judaism have undergone significant changes in form and expression since taking root in the United States. In other words, U.S. ethnic subcultures blend elements of their homeland and the dominant U.S. culture as group members adapt to their new environment.

## Subcultures

Usually, immigrants follow a pattern of **chain migration**, settling in an area already containing family, friends, or compatriots who located there earlier. An ethnic community evolves, providing an emotional support system to these strangers in a strange land as they strive to forge a better life for themselves.

## The International Scene
## Cultural Clashes in China

In July 2009, three days of ethnic violence broke out in the northwestern desert region of Xinjiang, which covers about one-sixth of China's land mass. The rioting broke out between the Han Chinese, the dominant ethnic group in the entire country, and the Uyghurs, a Turkic ethnic group that is predominantly Muslim. At least 197 people were killed and more than 1,700 injured, the deadliest ethnic violence to strike China in decades.

The violence began when police in Urumqi, the area's largest city (2.3 million), attempted to break up a peaceful march by at least 1,000 Uyghurs protesting the government's inaction over the killing of two Uyghur workers 10 days earlier. The ensuing ethnic brawl was the culmination of decades of resentment by Uyghurs over government policies that they believe threaten their culture and livelihoods.

Essentially, the Uyghurs illustrate the internal colonialism model. The Han have held power in Xinjiang since the 1949 communist takeover, even though they then only comprised six percent among the area's mostly Uyghur population. However, government incentives encouraged a massive migration and the Han proportion reached 40 percent in 2000, excluding the large number of Han migrant workers and military personnel stationed there with their families. The 10 million Uyghurs now constitute 45 percent of the region's total population.

The increased influx of Han, coupled with what the Uyghurs claim is "cultural imperialism," heightened ethnic tensions. The besieged minority points to the government's demolition of parts of the old town of Kashgar, phasing out Uyghur language instruction in the schools, restricting their religious practices, and compelling students and government workers to eat during the fasting period of Ramadan.

Uyghurs also complain about limited economic opportunities, job discrimination, and preferential treatment for the Han. The Han Chinese counter that the Uyghurs, like other ethnic minorities in China, have such advantages as an exemption from China's strict policy of one child per family or pay a fine, as well as extra points added to their standardized test scores to determine university placement. Uyghurs counter that these advantages do little for their primary concerns about their group identity, culture, dignity, fair treatment, equality, and economic well-being.

*Critical thinking questions:* What other persistent subcultures have faced harsh repressive actions? Are there common reasons for these government-endorsed actions?

*Sources:* Adapted from Edward Wong, "New Protests Flare in Chinese City After Deadly Ethnic Clashes," *New York Times* (July 8, 2009), p. A4; "Death Toll in Xinjiang Riot Rises to 156," China View, at http://news.xinhuanet.com/english/2009-07/07/content_11663866. htm; Wenran Jiang,"New Frontier, Same Old Problems for China," *The Globe and Mail* (January 9, 2010), at http://www.theglobeandmail.com/news/opinions/new-frontier-same-old-problems/article1208363/; and Tania Branigan, "New Mass Protests and Violence Break Out in Urumqi, Witnesses Claim," September 9, 2009 at http://www.guardian.co.uk/world/2009/sep/03/urumqi-china-new-violence-new-claims.

Part of this process of cultural insulation among others like themselves is the recreation in miniature of the world they left behind. Thus, **parallel social institutions**—their own clubs, organizations, newspapers, stores, churches, and schools duplicating those of the host society—appear, creating cohesiveness within the minority subculture, whether it is an immigrant or native-born grouping.

As **ethnic subcultures** among immigrants in the United States evolve in response to conditions within the host society, the immigrants sometimes develop a group consciousness unknown in their old countries. Many first-generation Americans possess a village orientation toward their homeland rather than a national identity. They may speak different dialects, feud with other regions, and have different values, but their common experience in the United States causes them to coalesce into a national grouping. One example is Italian Americans, who initially identified with their cities of origin: Calabria, Palermo, Naples, Genoa, Salerno, and so on. Within a generation, many came to view themselves as Italians, partly because the host society classified them as such.

Yet, even as a newly arrived group forges its community and subculture, a process called **ethnogenesis** occurs.[12] Shaped partly by the core culture in selectively absorbing some elements and modifying others, the group also retains, modifies, or drops elements from its cultural heritage as it adapts to its new country. The result is a distinctive new ethnic group unlike others in the host country, dominant or minority, but also somewhat different from the people who still live in the group's homeland. For example, first-generation German Americans differ from other ethnic groups and from native-born U.S. citizens, but they also possess cultural traits and values that distinguish them from nonmigrating Germans.

*Convergent Subcultures.*   Some ethnic subcultures are **convergent subcultures**; that is, they tend toward assimilation with the dominant society. Although recognizable by residential clustering and adherence to the language, dress, and cultural norms of their native land, these ethnic groups are nonetheless becoming assimilated. As the years pass—possibly across several generations—the distinctions between the dominant culture and the convergent subculture gradually lessen. Eventually, this form of subculture becomes completely integrated into the dominant culture.

Because the subculture is undergoing change, its members may experience problems of **marginality**—living under stress in two cultures simultaneously. The older generation may seek to preserve its traditions and heritage while the younger generation may be impatient to achieve full acceptance within the dominant society. Because of the impetus toward assimilation, time obviously favors the younger generation. The Dutch, German, and Irish subcultures are examples of once-prevalent ethnic subcultures that are barely visible today. Italian, Polish, and Slovak subcultures have also begun to converge more fully. These nationality groups still exhibit ethnic pride in many ways, but for the most part, they are no longer set apart by place of residence or subcultural behavior. Because of their multigenerational length of residence, these nationality groups are less likely to live in clustered housing arrangements or to display behavior patterns such as conflict, deviance, or endogamy to any greater degree than the rest of the majority group.

*Persistent Subcultures.*   Not all subcultures assimilate. Some do not even desire to do so, and others, particularly non-White groups, face difficulties in assimilating. These unassimilated subcultures are known as **persistent subcultures**. Some adhere as much as possible to their own way of life and resist absorption into the dominant culture. Religious groups such as the Amish, some Hutterites, and Hasidic Jews reject modernity and insist on maintaining their traditional ways of life; they may represent the purest form of a persistent subculture in U.S. society. Other ethnic groups adopt a few aspects of the dominant culture but adamantly preserve their own way of life; examples are most Native Americans who live on reservations and many *Hispanos* (Spanish Americans) in the Southwest. Chinatowns also support preservation of the Chinese way of life in many ways.

A minority group's insistence on the right to be different usually has not been well received among dominant-group members. This clash of wills sometimes leads to conflict; at the very least, it invites stereotyping and prejudice on both sides.

Just as convergent subcultures illustrate assimilation, persistent subcultures illustrate pluralism. We next examine these two forms of minority integration, as well as a third.

## Theories of Minority Integration

More than 75 million immigrants have come to the United States since its founding as a nation. Over the course of this extensive migration, three different theories have emerged regarding how these ethnically different peoples either should or did fit into U.S. society. These theories are (1) assimilation, or majority-conformity, theory; (2) amalgamation, or melting-pot, theory; and (3) accommodation, or pluralistic, theory.

The type of interaction between minority peoples and those of the dominant culture has depended partly on which ideology then prevailed among both groups. People formulate attitudes and expectations based on the values they hold. If those values include a clear image of how an "American" should look, talk, and act, people who differ from that model will find their adjustment to and acceptance by others more difficult. Conversely, if those values allow for diversity, a greater possibility exists that harmonious relationships will evolve.

## Assimilation (Majority-Conformity) Theory

Generally speaking, **assimilation (majority-conformity) theory** refers to the functioning within a society of racial or ethnic minority-group members who no longer possess any marked cultural, social, or personal differences from the people of the dominant group. Physical or racial differences may persist, but they do not serve as the basis for group prejudice or discrimination. In effect, these minority group members no longer appear to be strangers because they have abandoned their own cultural traditions and successfully blended into the dominant group. Assimilation thus may be described as $A + B + C = A$.[13]

*Anglo-Conformity.*   Because most of the people in power in the United States during the eighteenth century were of English descent, English influence on the new nation's culture was enormous—in language, institutional forms, values, and attitudes. By the first quarter of the nineteenth century, a distinct national consciousness had emerged, and many U.S. citizens wanted to deemphasize their English origins and influences. However, when migration patterns changed the composition of the U.S. population in the 1880s, the "Yankees" reestablished the Anglo-Saxon as the superior model.[14] Anglo-Saxonism remained dominant well into the twentieth century as the mold into which newcomers must fit.

To preserve their Anglo-Saxon heritage, people in the United States have often attempted, sometimes with success, to curtail the large numbers of non–Anglo-Saxon immigrants. Social pressures demanded that new arrivals shed their native culture and attachments as quickly as possible and be remade into "Americans" along cherished Anglo-Saxon lines. The schools served as an important socializing agent in promoting the shedding of cultural differences.

Sometimes insistence on assimilation reached feverish heights, as evidenced by the **Americanization movement** during World War I. The arrival of a large number of "inferior" people in the preceding 30 years and the participation of the United States in a European conflict raised questions about those who were not "100 percent American." Government agencies at all levels, together with many private organizations, acted to encourage more immediate adoption by foreigners of U.S. practices: citizenship, reverence for U.S. institutions, and use of the English language.[15] Other assimilation efforts have not been very successful—for example, with people whose ancestral history in an area predates the nation's expansion into that territory. Most Native American tribes throughout the United States as well as the *Hispanos* of the Southwest have resisted this cultural hegemony.

*Types of Assimilation.*   Milton Gordon that suggested assimilation has several phases.[16] One important phase is **cultural assimilation (acculturation)**—the change of cultural patterns to match those of the host society. **Marital assimilation (amalgamation)**—large-scale intermarriage with members of the majority society—and **structural assimilation**—large-scale entrance into the cliques, clubs, and institutions of the host society on a primary-group level—best reveal the extent of acceptance of minority groups in the larger society (see the Reality Check box).

## Reality Check
## Cultural Differentiation, Contact Hypothesis, and College Friendships

Do cultural differences affect college student friendships? Apparently so, according to a longitudinal study that tracked more than 1,000 male and female UCLA students from just before they began their freshmen year through to their senior spring quarter of classes. As freshmen, the mix was 36 percent Asian, 32 percent White, 18 percent Latino, 6 percent Black, 8 percent other, and changed only slightly by senior year.

Overall, students in all four racial/ethnic groups followed similar patterns throughout their college careers in their selection and maintenance of friends. Essentially, ingroup bias and intergroup anxiety were the determining factors. That is, students who held attitudes that were more favorable of their own group but felt more uneasy and less competent interacting with members of different groups, had fewer outgroup friends and more ingroup friends.

Although these results are hardly surprising given the similarity-attraction bond discussed in Chapter 1, another finding further lends support to the contact hypothesis (having outgroup friends is strongly associated with lower intergroup prejudice). In this study, the researchers found two equally significant causal paths. Students who had more outgroup friendships did indeed register lower ingroup bias and outgroup anxiety, but by the end of their college days, those with more ingroup friends in college had greater negative attitudes about other ethnic or racial groups.

Peer socialization may explain these differing effects. Students are likely to change their attitudes and behaviors to be consistent with those of their ingroup. If that group is heterogeneous, a higher level of mutual respect and acceptance occurs and reduces ethnocentric bias. A homogeneous group, if isolated from different attitudes and ideas, finds its views continually reinforced by friends and judges more negatively those outsiders with whom they have had no primary group contact.

*Critical thinking questions:*   Is your group of college friends any different racially and ethnically from those you had in high school? Are your views about other groups any different now than they were then?

*Source:* Adapted from Shana Levin, Colette van Laar, and Jim Sidanius, "The Effects of Ingroup and Outgroup Friendships on Ethnic Attitudes in College: A Longitudinal Study," *Group Processes & Intergroup Relations*, 6 (2003): 76–92.

Gordon believed that once structural assimilation occurred, all other types of assimilation—including the end an ethnic identity and residual ethnic prejudice—would follow.[17] Some researchers agree, offering evidence that migration generates similar consequences for successive generations, irrespective of ethnicity.[18] Other studies, however, suggest that cultural assimilation (English language and embeddedness in Anglo social contexts) is a necessary precondition to structural assimilation.[19] Similar to the primary and secondary labor markets (regulated and unregulated jobs), sociologists also divide structural assimilation into primary and secondary processes. **Secondary structural assimilation** typically involves the more impersonal public sphere of social interaction, such as intergroup mingling in civic, recreational, school, or work environments. **Primary structural assimilation** typically involves close, personal interactions between dominant- and minority-group members in small group settings, such as parties, social clubs, and other interactive gatherings.

Assimilation as a belief, goal, or pattern helps explain many aspects of dominant–minority relations, particularly acceptance and adjustment. For

**FIGURE 2.3** **"Uncle Sam's Troublesome Bedfellows"**

*This cartoon pictures Uncle Sam annoyed by groups that were seen as unassimilable. Both racial differences (Blacks, Chinese, and Native Americans) and religious differences (Catholics and Mormons) were cause for being kicked out of the symbolic bed. This cartoon appeared in a San Francisco illustrated weekly,* The Wasp, *on February 8, 1879.*

approximately three-fourths of this nation's existence, members of the dominant society interpreted the assimilation of minorities to mean their absorption into the White Anglo-Saxon Protestant mold. For physically or culturally distinct groups (Asians, Blacks, Catholics, Hispanics, Jews, Muslims, and Native Americans), this concept, at the time, raised a seemingly insurmountable barrier (see Figure 2.3). Even for those physically and culturally fitting the Anglo-Saxon role model, assimilation is preceded by a transitional period in which the newcomer gradually blends in with dominant-group members. During that process, the individual may encounter others' impatience at the pace and also may experience an identity crisis as well.

Because of the complexity of the assimilation process, peppered as it is by conflicting views on both sides on whether or not assimilation is even desirable, the dynamics of dominant–minority relations can vary from one group to another. Not all sociologists accept Gordon's view that the assimilation process is linear, that is, that all groups steadily move from a visible subculture to absorption into the dominant culture. Instead of this "one size fits all" approach, Alejandro Portes and Min Zhou suggested that assimilation is segmented and that several outcomes are possible, depending on a group's vulnerability and resources.[20] This perspective is popular among social scientists today and is one that we will apply throughout this book.

## Amalgamation (Melting-Pot) Theory

The democratic experiment in the United States fired many eighteenth-century imaginations in Europe. A new society had emerged, peopled by immigrants from different European nations and not traditionally bound by the customs and traditions of the past. Their bold initiatives generated a romantic notion of the United States as a melting pot. Conceptualized as the **amalgamation or melting-pot theory**, it holds that all the diverse peoples blend their biological and cultural differences (through intermarriage and creation of a new culture) into an altogether new breed—the American. This concept may be expressed as $A + B + C = D$.[21]

*Advocates.*   J. Hector St. John de Crèvecoeur, a French settler in New York, first popularized the idea of a melting pot. Envisioning the United States as more than just a land of opportunity, Crèvecoeur in 1782 spoke of a new breed of humanity emerging from the new society. That he included only White Europeans partly explains the weakness of this approach to minority integration:

> What is an American? He is either a European, or the descendant of a European; hence that strange mixture of blood which you will find in no other country. I could point out to you a man whose grandfather was an Englishman, whose wife was Dutch, whose son married a French woman, and

whose present four sons have now four wives of different nations. He is an American, who, leaving behind him all his ancient prejudices and manners, receives new ones from the new mode of life he has embraced, the new government he obeys and the new rank he holds. . . . Here individuals of all nations are melted into a new race of men, whose labors and posterity will one day cause great changes in the world.[22]

This idealistic concept found many advocates over the years. In 1893, Frederick Jackson Turner updated it with his frontier thesis, a notion that greatly influenced historical scholarship for half a century. Turner believed that the challenge of frontier life was the catalyst that fused immigrants into a composite new national stock within an evolving social order:

Thus the Middle West was teaching the lesson of national cross-fertilization instead of national enmities, the possibility of a newer and richer civilization, not by preserving unmodified or isolated the old component elements, but by breaking down the line-fences, by merging the individual life in the common product—a new product, which held the promise of world brotherhood.[23]

In 1908, the play *The Melting-Pot* by English author Israel Zangwill enthusiastically etched a permanent symbol on the assimilationist ideal:

There she lies, the great melting pot. Listen! Can't you hear the roaring and the bubbling? There gapes her mouth—the harbor where a thousand mammoth feeders come from the ends of the world to pour in their human freight. Ah, what a stirring and a seething—Celt and Latin, Slav and Teuton, Greek and Syrian. America is God's Crucible, the great Melting Pot where all the races of Europe are melting and reforming!—Here you stand good folk, think I, when I see you at Ellis Island, here you stand, in your fifty groups, with your fifty languages and histories, and your fifty hatreds and rivalries. But you won't be long like that, brothers, for these are the fires of God you come to—these are the fires of God! . . . Germans and Frenchmen, Irishmen and English, Jews and Russians, into the Crucible with you all! God is making the American! . . . the real American has not yet arrived . . . He will be the fusion of all races, perhaps the coming superman. . . . Ah, Vera, what is the glory of Rome and Jerusalem, where all races and nations come to worship and look back, compared with the glory of America, where all races and nations come to labor and look forward.[24]

Both the frontier thesis and the melting-pot concept have come under heavy criticism since. Although many still pay homage to the melting-pot concept, few social scientists accept this explanation of a minority integration that creates a new citizenry. Moreover, when U.S. citizens insist that others "blend in," they want ethnic groups to assimilate and have no desire that they themselves should be "blended" with the foreign-born.

*Did We Melt?*  Throughout several generations, intermarriages frequently occur between people of different nationalities, less frequently between people of different religions, and still less frequently between people of different races. Thus one could argue that a biological merging of previously distinct ethnic stocks, and to a lesser extent of different races, has taken place.[25] However, the melting-pot theory spoke not only of intermarriages among the different groups but also of a distinct new national culture evolving from elements of all other cultures. Here the theory has proved to be unrealistic. At its founding, the United States was dominated by an Anglo-Saxon population and thus by the English language and Anglo-Saxon institutional forms. Given the arrival of large numbers of non-British and non-Protestant arrivals, the definition of "Americanism" may have broadened, but Anglo-Protestant still defines the meaning of America more than any other.[26] Rather than various cultural patterns melting into a new U.S. culture, elements of minority cultures evolved into the Anglo-Saxon mold.

Only in the institution of religion did minority groups alter the national culture. From a mostly Protestant nation in its early history, the United States has become a land of four major faiths: Protestant, Catholic, Jewish, and Islam, with Hinduism, and other non-Western religions increasing as well. As ethnic differences disappeared among older immigrant groups, religious groupings became the primary foci of identity and interaction. Today, the high religious intermarriage rate is reshaping religious boundaries as, for some groups at least, assimilations blur previous distinctions of cultural differentiation.[27]

In other areas, the entry of diverse minority groups into U.S. society has not produced new social structures or institutional forms in the larger society. Instead, subcultural social structures and institutions have evolved to meet group needs, and the dominant culture has benefited from the labors and certain cultural aspects of minority groups within the already existing dominant culture. For example, minority influences are found in word usage, place names, cuisine, architecture, art, recreational activities, and music.

Sociologist Henry Pratt Fairchild offered a physiological analogy to describe how the absorption of various cultural components or peoples produces assimilation and not amalgamation. An organism consumes food and is somewhat affected (nourished) by it; the food, though, is assimilated in the sense that it becomes an integral part of the organism, retaining none of its original characteristics. This is a one-way process. In a similar manner, U.S. culture has remained basically unchanged, though strengthened, despite the influx of many minority groups.[28]

Most social scientists consider the melting-pot theory as a romantic myth. Its idealistic rhetoric continues to attract many followers, however.

In reality, the melting meant **Anglo-conformity**—being remade according to the idealized Anglo-Saxon mold:

> But it would be a mistake to infer from this that the American's image of himself—and that means the ethnic group member's image of himself as he becomes American—is a composite or synthesis of the ethnic elements that have gone into the making of the American. It is nothing of the kind; the American's image of himself is still the Anglo-American ideal it was at the beginning of our independent existence. The "national type" as ideal has always been, and remains, pretty well fixed. It is the *Mayflower*, John Smith, Davy Crockett, George Washington, and Abraham Lincoln that define the American's self-image, and this is true whether the American in question is a descendant of the Pilgrims or the grandson of an immigrant from southeastern Europe.[29]

The rejection of the melting-pot theory by many people, coupled with an ethnic consciousness, spawned a third ideology: the accommodation (pluralistic) theory.

## Accommodation (Pluralistic) Theory

The **accommodation (pluralistic) theory** recognizes the persistence of racial and ethnic diversity, as in Canada, where the government has adopted multiculturalism as official policy. Pluralist theorists argue that minorities can maintain their distinctive subcultures and simultaneously interact with relative equality in the larger society. In countries such as Switzerland and the United States, this combination of diversity and togetherness is possible to varying degrees because the people agree on certain basic values (see Table 2.1). At the same time, minorities may interact mostly among themselves, live within well-defined communities, have their own forms of organizations, work in similar occupations, and marry within their own group. Applying our descriptive equation, pluralism would be $A + B + C = A + B + C$.[30]

*Early Analysis.*    Horace Kallen is generally recognized as the first exponent of cultural pluralism. In 1915, he published "Democracy Versus the Melting Pot," in which he rejected the assimilation and amalgamation theories.[31] Not only did each group tend to preserve its own language, institutions, and cultural heritage, he maintained, but democracy gave each group the right to do so. To be sure, minority groups learned the English language and participated in U.S. institutions, but what the United States really had become was a "cooperation of cultural diversities." Seeing Americanization movements as a threat to minority groups and the melting-pot notion as unrealistic, Kallen believed that cultural pluralism could be the basis for a great democratic commonwealth. A philosopher, not a sociologist, Kallen nonetheless directed sociological attention to a long-standing U.S. pattern.

*Pluralistic Reality.*    From its colonial beginnings, the United States has been a pluralistic country. Early settlements were small ethnic enclaves, each peopled by different nationalities or religious groups. New Amsterdam and Philadelphia were exceptions; both were heavily pluralistic within their boundaries. Chain-migration patterns resulted in immigrants settling in clusters. Germans and Scandinavians in the Midwest, Poles in Chicago, Irish in New York and Boston, French in Louisiana, Chinese in California, Cubans in Miami, and many others illustrate how groups ease their adjustment to a new country by re-creating in miniature the world they left behind. Current immigrant groups and remnants of past immigrant groups are testimony to the pluralism in U.S. society.

    **Cultural pluralism**—two or more culturally distinct groups living in the same society in relative harmony—has been the more noticeable form of pluralism. **Structural pluralism**—the coexistence of racial and ethnic groups in subsocieties within social-class and regional boundaries—is less noticeable.

    As Gordon observed, "Cultural pluralism was a fact in American society before it became a theory—at least a theory with explicit relevance for the nation as a whole and articulated and discussed in the general English-speaking circles of American intellectual life."[32] Many minority groups lose their visibility when they acculturate. They may, however, identify with and take pride in their heritage and maintain primary relationships within their own racial/ethnic and social-class grouping. Despite this long-standing pluralistic reality, criticism of such self-segregating diversity remains a problem within U.S. society.

*Dual Realities.*    Although Americans give lip service to the concept of a melting pot, they typically expect foreigners to assimilate as quickly as possible. Mainstream Americans often tolerate pluralism only as a short-term phenomenon, believing that sustained pluralism is the enemy of assimilation, a threat to the cohesiveness of U.S. society.

    Assimilation and pluralism are not mutually exclusive, however; nor are they necessarily enemies. In fact, they have always existed simultaneously among different groups, at different levels. Whether as persistent subcultures or as convergent ones gradually merging into the dominant culture throughout several generations, culturally distinct groups have always existed. And even when their numbers have been great, they have never threatened the core culture, as we will see. Assimilation remains a powerful force affecting most minority groups, despite the assertions of anti-immigration fearmongers and radical multiculturalists. Although proponents of one position may decry the other, pluralism and assimilation have always been dual realities within U.S. society.

Assimilation occurs in different ways and to different degrees, and it does not necessarily mean the obliteration of all traces of ethnic origins. It can occur even as ethnic communities continue to exist in numerous cities and as many individuals continue to identify with their ethnic ancestry.

> [*Assimilation*] refers, above all, to long-term processes that have whittled away at the social foundations for ethnic distinctions. These processes have brought about a rough parity of opportunities to attain such socioeconomic goods as educational credentials and prestigious jobs, loosened the ties between ethnicity and specific economic niches, diminished cultural differences that serve to signal ethnic membership to others and to sustain ethnic solidarity, shifted residence away from central-city ethnic neighborhoods to ethnically intermixed suburbs, and finally, fostered relatively easy social intermixing across ethnic lines, resulting ultimately in high rates of ethnic intermarriage and ethnically mixed ancestry.[33]

Perhaps the dual realities of assimilation and pluralism may be appreciated more fully by realizing that acculturation occurs more quickly than assimilation. A group's acculturation gives supporting testimony to assimilationist theory, yet its accompanying lack of complete assimilation provides evidence in support of pluralist—or ethnic retention—theory. The existence of this twofold dynamic is the natural order of minority communities.

## Is There a White Culture?

In the mid-1990s, interest in White studies rose significantly. White studies essentially focus on how Whiteness has led to racial domination and hegemony, in which White American culture is simply called "American," thereby presuming that Black, Native American, Asian, or Hispanic cultures are not "American" but instead racial and/or ethnic subcultures. The idea that a White culture also exists is difficult for many people to grasp, say the White studies advocates, much like a fish is unaware of water until out of it, because of its environmental universality.

The premise for a White culture existing independent of an "American" culture is that all racial groups have large social/cultural characteristics that change over time. These White values, attitudes, shared understandings, and behavior patterns—like many aspects of culture—are often unrealized by group members because they are part of a taken-for-granted world. Yet even though White culture may not be identifiable among its members, it is nonetheless real and easily recognizable by non-Whites. For example, says Jeff Hitchcock in *Lifting the White Veil*, in Black culture feelings take precedence over sensibilities. He explains that when a feeling comes upon a person, Black culture says it is appropriate to express it, but White culture

> . . . works hard to keep the volume down, least we all go crazy from the demands we place on each other's capacity for self-control. Experience in the culture helps. We learn how not to step on toes, hurt other people's "feelings," to not make a scene, and all the other little social rules and practices of a lifetime. We rein it in, and trade spontaneity . . . for an orderly demeanor and generally predictable and controlled everyday existence.[34]

Lacking an understanding of the existence of White culture, say its proponents, results in the dominant group misinterpreting alternative cultural experiences as racial or else as the personal failings of someone of color. Recognizing its existence could be a first step toward building a truly multiracial society.

## Retrospect

Culture provides the normative definitions by which members of a society perceive and interpret the world about them. Language and other forms of symbolic interaction provide the means by which this accumulated knowledge is transmitted. Becoming acculturated requires learning both the language and the symbol system of the new society. Sometimes, though, situations become real in their consequences because people earlier defined them as real (the Thomas theorem). Unless it is isolated from the rest of the world, a society undergoes change through cultural contact and the diffusion of ideas, inventions, and practices. Within large societies, subcultures usually exist. They may gradually be assimilated (convergent subcultures), or they may remain distinct (persistent subcultures). The existence of a White culture, separate and distinct from American culture, is a debatable issue but one that offers intriguing talking points about intercultural interactions and understandings.

Three theories of minority integration have emerged. Assimilation, or majority-conformity, became a goal of many, both native-born and foreign-born; yet not all sought this goal or were able to achieve it. The romantic notion of amalgamation, or a melting pot, in which a new breed of people with a distinct culture would emerge, proved unrealistic. Finally, accommodation, or pluralism, arose as a school of thought recognizing the persistence of ethnic diversity in a society with a commonly shared core culture. Assimilation and pluralism are not mutually exclusive; both have always existed simultaneously, with assimilation exerting a constant, powerful force.

## KEY TERMS

Accommodation (pluralistic) theory
Acculturation
Amalgamation (melting-pot) theory
Americanization movement
Anglo-conformity
Assimilation (majority-conformity)
  theory
Chain migration
Convergent subcultures
Cultural assimilation (acculturation)
Cultural diffusion
Cultural pluralism
Cultural transmission
Culture
Culture shock
Ethnic subcultures

Ethnogenesis
Linguistic relativity
Marginality
Marital assimilation (amalgamation)
Material culture
Nonmaterial culture
Norms
Paralinguistic signals
Parallel social institutions
Primary structural assimilation
Persistent subcultures
Secondary structural assimilation
Structural assimilation
Structural pluralism
Thomas theorem

## DISCUSSION QUESTIONS

1. What is the relationship among culture, reality, and intergroup relations?

2. How does language affect our perception of reality?

3. How does the Thomas theorem help us understand problems in intergroup relations?

4. How would you answer someone who claims foreigners are changing American culture?

5. Do you belong to, or interact with, any subcultures? What have been your experiences with them?

6. Discuss the major theories of minority integration.

## INTERNET ACTIVITIES

1. Is the United States a melting pot? Most social scientists say this is a romantic myth that ignores the past and present realities of the United States. In "The Myth of the Melting Pot" (http://www.washingtonpost.com/wp-srv/national/longterm/meltingpot/melt0222.htm), the *Washington Post* offered an in-depth, six-part series (with graphs) that explored this issue. Take a look at any or all of these articles. Perhaps the most controversial is Part Three: Immigrants Shunning Idea of Assimilation. Do you agree with this claim? Why or why not? Feel free to comment on any part of any article as well.

2. To learn about the many ethnic subcultures in the United States, go to the Multiethnic America website (http://www.everyculture.com/multi/) and choose from among the dozens of listed groups.

# CHAPTER 3

# Ethnic and Racial Stratification

*"Poverty is a veil that obscures the face of greatness."*

—KHALIL GIBRAN

Relations between dominant and minority groups are influenced as much by structural conditions as by differences in culture. Social structure—the organized patterns of behavior among the basic components of a social system—establishes relatively predictable social relationships among the different peoples in a society.

The nature of the social structure influences not only the distribution of power resources (economic, political, and social) but also the accessibility of those resources to groups who seek upward mobility. An expanding economy and an open social system create increased opportunities for minority-group members, thereby reducing the likelihood that tensions will arise. In contrast, a stagnant or contracting economy thwarts many efforts to improve status and antagonizes those who feel most threatened by another group's competition for scarce resources. Such a situation may serve as a breeding ground for conflicts *among minority groups* even more than between majority and minority groups. This could occur because both minority groups may view the other as an economic threat.

The state of the economy is just one important structural factor influencing the opportunities for upward mobility. Another is the degree of change between a minority group's old society and the new one. A person who leaves an agrarian society for an industrial one is poorly prepared to enter any but the lowest social stratum in a low-paying position. Opportunities for upward mobility may exist, however, if the new land's economy is growing rapidly. In this sense, the structural conditions in the United States during the period from 1880 to 1920 were better for unskilled immigrants than are conditions today. Low-skill jobs are less plentiful today, and an unskilled worker's desire to support a family through hard work may not be matched by the opportunity to do so.

Meanwhile, technological advances have made the world smaller. Rapid transportation and communications (radios, televisions, telephones, computers, the Internet, fax machines, email, and FTP sites) permit stronger ties to other parts of the world than in the past.[1] Accessibility to their homeland, friends, or relatives may make people less interested in becoming fully assimilated in a new land. Befriending strangers in the new country becomes less necessary. In addition, people's greater knowledge of the world, the rising social consciousness of a society, and structural opportunities for mobility, all help to create a more hospitable environment for minority-group members.

## Stratification

**Social stratification** is the hierarchical classification of the members of society based on the unequal distribution of resources, power, and prestige. The word *resources* refers to such factors as income, property, and borrowing capacity. *Power* is the ability to influence or control others. *Prestige* relates to status, either *ascribed* (based on age, sex, race, or family background) or *achieved* (based on individual accomplishments).

Stratification may reduce or worsen any strains or conflicts between groups depending on how rigid and explicit or flexible and subtle are the class distinctions and discrimination based on race or ethnic group. Whether racial and ethnic groups face insurmountable barriers or minor obstacles in achieving upward mobility depends on the form of stratification. The more rigid the stratification, the more likely is the emergence of racial, religious, or other ideologies justifying the existing arrangements—as happened with the rise of racism during slavery in the United States.

Stratification also affects how groups within the various strata of society view one another. Some people confuse structural differentiation with cultural differentiation. For example, they may believe that a group's low socioeconomic status is due to its values and attitudes rather than to such structural conditions as racism, economic stagnation, and high urban unemployment. Racial or ethnic stratification can be an important determinant of the potential for intergroup conflict. In the United States, both the possibility of upward mobility and the existence of obstacles blocking that possibility have long co-existed. When the disparity between the ideal of the American Dream and the reality of its achievement grows too great, the possibility of conflict increases.

## Social Class

**Social class** designates people's place in the stratification hierarchy, identifying those in each grouping who share similar levels of income and status, amounts of property and power, and types of lifestyle. The individual's race and religion could also factor into one's status. Although no clearly defined boundaries exist between class groupings in the United States, people have a tendency to cluster together according to certain socioeconomic similarities. The concept or image of social-class results from socio-psychological distinctions people make about one another, including where they live and what they own as well as to interactions that occur because of those distinctions.

In the 1930s, W. Lloyd Warner headed a now-classic study of social-class differentiation in the United States.[2] Using the **reputational method**—asking people how they thought of others compared to them—Warner found a well-formulated class system in place. In "Yankee City"—actually Newburyport, Massachusetts, a small town at that time of about 17,000—Warner identified six classes: upper-upper, lower-upper, upper-middle, lower-middle, upper-lower, and lower-lower.

Although Warner reached several faulty conclusions because he failed to take a sociohistorical approach,[3] some of his findings have validity to our focus here. First, a significant relationship existed between an ethnic group's length of residence and class status; the more recent arrivals tended to be in the lower classes. In addition, an ethnic group tended to be less assimilated and less upwardly mobile if its population in the community was relatively large, if its homeland was close (such as in the case of immigrant French Canadians), if its members had a sojourner rather than a permanent-settler orientation, and if limited opportunities for advancement existed in the community.[4]

Social class becomes important in intergroup relations because it provides a basis for expectations and also serves as a point of reference in others' responses and in one's self-perception. As a result, social class helps shape an individual's world of reality and influences group interactions. Attitudes and behavior formed within a social-class framework are not permanent, however; they can change if circumstances change.

### Class Consciousness

Just how important are the ethnic factors that Warner and others reported in shaping an awareness of social class? The significance of ethnic factors depends on numerous variables, including economic conditions, mobility patterns, and prevailing attitudes.

Because ethnic minorities are disproportionately represented among the lower classes and because middle-class values dominate in the United States, it seems reasonable to conclude that at least some of the attitudes about a group may result from people's value judgments about social class. That is to say, the dominant group's criticism and stereotyping of the minority group probably rests in part on class distinctions. Such class-based views extend to racial groups as well. Researchers note that Whites tend to categorize lower-class Blacks by race but categorize middle-class Blacks by social class and react accordingly.[5]

Social-class status also plays an important role in determining a minority group's adjustment to, and acceptance by, society. For example, because the first waves of Cuban (1960s) and Vietnamese (1970s) refugees who arrived in the United States possessed the education and occupational experience of the middle class, they succeeded in overcoming early native concerns and did not encounter the same degree of negativism as did lower-class migrants from the same two countries in the 1980s. Whether generations ago or now, when unskilled and often illiterate peasants enter the lower-class positions in U.S. society, many U.S. citizens belittle, avoid, and discriminate against them because of their supposedly inferior ways. Frequently, these attitudes and actions reflect an awareness of class differences as well as cultural differences. Because the dominant group usually occupies a higher stratum in the social-class hierarchy, differences in social-class values and lifestyles—in addition to ethnic cultural differences—can be sources of friction.

## Ethnicity and Social Class

Differences in stratification among various groups cannot be explained by a single cause, although some social scientists emphasize one factor over another. For example, in *The Ethnic Myth*, Stephen Steinberg stressed the importance of social structure and minimized cultural factors.[6] For him, the success of Jews in the United States resulted more from their occupational skills in the urbanized country than from their values. Conversely, Thomas Sowell wrote in *Ethnic America* that the compatibility of a group's cultural characteristics with those of the dominant culture determines the level of a group's economic success.[7] Actually, structural and cultural elements intertwine. Emphasizing only social structure ignores important cultural variables such as values about education. Emphasizing only culture can lead to blaming people who do not succeed.

In a 1964 ground-breaking book, *Assimilation in American Life*, Milton Gordon first suggested that dominant–minority relations be examined within the larger context of the social structure.[8] Although he believed that all groups would eventually become assimilated, his central thesis about a pluralistic society was that four factors, or social categories, play a part in forming subsocieties within the nation: ethnicity (by which Gordon also meant race), social class, rural or urban residence, and regionalism.[9] These factors unite in various combinations to create a number of **ethclasses**—subsocieties resulting from the intersection of stratifications of race and ethnic group with stratifications of social class. Additional determinants are the rural or urban setting and the particular region of the country in which a group lives. Examples of ethclasses are lower-middle-class White Catholics in a northeastern city, lower-class Black Baptists in the rural South, and upper-class White Jews in a western urban area.

Numerous studies support the concept that race and ethnicity, together with social class, are important in social structures and intergroup conflicts.[10] For example, only by recognizing the intersection of race and class as a key element can we understand the continued existence of Black poverty.[11] Not only do ethclass groupings exist, but people tend to interact within them for their intimate primary relationships. To the extent that this is true, multiple allegiances and conflicts are inevitable. Both cultural and structural pluralism currently exist, with numerous groups presently coexisting in separate subsocieties based on social class and cultural distinctions. Even people whose families have been in the United States for several generations are affiliated with, and participate in, subsocieties. Even so, Gordon optimistically views assimilation as a linear process in which even **structural assimilation** (the large-scale entrance of minorities into mainstream social organization and institutions) will eventually occur.

## Blaming the Poor or Society?

In 1932, E. Franklin Frazier formulated his conception of a disorganized and pathological lower-class culture. This thesis served as the inspiration for the controversial **culture of poverty** viewpoint that emerged in the 1960s.[12] The writings of two men—Daniel P. Moynihan and Oscar Lewis—sparked an intense debate that continues to resonate today. In his 1965 government report, "The Negro Family: The Case for National Action," Moynihan used Frazier's observations as a springboard for arguing that a "tangle of pathology" so pervaded the Black community that it perpetuated a cycle of poverty and deprivation that only outside (government) intervention could overcome.[13]

*Family Disintegration.*    Moynihan argued that family deterioration was a core cause of the problems of high unemployment, welfare dependence, illegitimacy, low achievement, juvenile delinquency, and adult crime:

> At the heart of the deterioration of the fabric of Negro society is the deterioration of the Negro family. It is the fundamental source of weakness of the

Negro community at the present time. . . . The white family has achieved a high degree of stability and is maintaining that stability. By contrast, the family structure of the lower class Negroes is highly unstable, and in many urban centers is approaching complete breakdown.[14]

Moynihan described Black males as occupying an unstable place in the economy, which prevented them from functioning as strong fathers and husbands. This environment, he said, served as a breeding ground for a continuing vicious circle: The women often not only raised the children but also earned the family income. Consequently, the children grew up in a poorly supervised, unstable environment; they often performed poorly or dropped out of school; they could secure only low-paying jobs—and so the cycle began anew.[15] The Moynihan Report called for federal action to create, among other things, jobs for Black male heads of household in the inner city:

> At the center of the tangle of pathology is the weakness of the family structure. Once or twice removed, it will be found to be the principal source of most of the aberrant, inadequate, or anti-social behavior that did not establish but now serves to perpetuate the cycle of poverty and deprivation. . . .
> What then is the problem? We feel that the answer is clear enough. Three centuries of injustice have brought about deep-seated structural distortions in the life of the Negro American. At this point, the present tangle of pathology is capable of perpetuating itself without assistance from the white world. The cycle can be broken only if these distortions are set right.[16]

In 1990, Moynihan reaffirmed his view that a link existed between specific cultural values and deteriorating conditions in lower-class Black family life. Citing further social deterioration since the 1960s, he noted in particular the startling rise in out-of-wedlock births from 3 percent of White births and 24 percent of Black births in 1963 to 16 percent and 63 percent, respectively, in 1987.[17] These distressing statistics led Moynihan to repeat a statement from his 1965 report:

> From the wild Irish slums of the nineteenth-century Eastern seaboard, to the riot-torn suburbs of Los Angeles, there is one unmistakable lesson in American history: a community that allows a large number of young men to grow up in broken families, dominated by women, never acquiring a stable relationship to male authority, never acquiring any set of rational expectations about the future—that community asks for and gets chaos. Crime, violence, unrest, disorder—most particularly the furious, unrestrained lashing out at

the whole social structure—that is not only to be expected; it is very near to inevitable.[18]

***Perpetuation of Poverty.*** Moynihan's position shared the same premises as Oscar Lewis's theory about a subculture of poverty, detailed in *The Children of Sanchez* (1961) and *La Vida* (1966):[19]

> The culture of poverty, however, is not only an adaptation to a set of objective conditions of the larger society. Once it comes into existence it tends to perpetuate itself from generation to generation because of its effect on the children. By the time slum children are age six or seven they have usually absorbed the basic values and attitudes of their subculture and are not psychologically geared to take full advantage of changing conditions or increased opportunities which may occur in their lifetime.[20]

Politically, Lewis was a leftist, and he did not blame the poor as some critics misinterpreted. Rather, he emphasized the institutionalized tenacity of their poverty, arguing that the system damaged them.[21] Edward Banfield, a conservative, recast Lewis's position to assert that poverty continues because of subcultural patterns. Whereas Lewis held that the mechanics of capitalist production for profit caused poverty, Banfield found its cause in the folkways of its victims. Banfield argued that good jobs, good housing, tripled welfare payments, new schools, quality education, and armies of police officers would not stop the problem. He added:

> If, however, the lower classes were to disappear—if, say, their members were overnight to acquire the attitudes, motivations, and habits of the working class—the most serious and intractable problems of the city would all disappear. . . . The lower-class forms of all problems are at bottom a single problem: the existence of an outlook and style of life which is radically present-oriented and which therefore attaches no value to work, sacrifice, self-improvement, or service to family, friends, or community.[22]

Another form of the "blame game" occurs during the political wrangling that goes on whenever welfare measures are considered. For example, when Congress passed the welfare reform act in 1996, its title was the Personal Responsibility and Work Opportunity Act, a not-too-subtle implication that the poor must change their ways if they want to escape poverty. The act's key provisions were a time limit on welfare payments and a requirement that welfare recipients, after two years, must work. No doubt some lazy people preferred living off a government handout than working, but that was only an extremely small percentage of the welfare recipients. Then, as now, the heavy majority of those living in poverty *do* work, but their limited education and job skills restrict them to low-paying, often unstable, work.[23]

*This single, homeless mother of four children works as an administrative assistant for a high-tech company in California, but the family lives in a church-supported shelter because of her limited income. Living in a homeless shelter not only can be stressful on both the children and mother, but also may lead to multigenerational poverty.*

***Criticism.*** Although they were not saying the same thing, Moynihan, Lewis, and Banfield all came under heavy criticism during the 1960s and 1970s—the height of the civil-rights movement—from commentators who felt that they were blaming the victim. Critics argued that intergenerational poverty results from discrimination, structural conditions, or stratification rigidity. Fatalism, apathy, low aspirations, and other similar orientations found in lower-class culture are thus situational responses within each generation and not the result of cultural deficiencies transmitted from parents to children.

To William Ryan, blaming the victim results in misdirected social programs. If we rationalize away the socially acquired stigma of poverty as being the expression of a subcultural trait, we ignore the continuing effect of current victimizing social forces. As a result, we focus on helping the "disorganized" Black family instead of on overcoming racism, or we strive to develop "better" attitudes and skills in low-income children rather than revamping the poor-quality schools they attend.[24]

Charles A. Valentine led an attack on the culture of poverty thesis and on Lewis. He argued that many of Lewis's "class distinctive traits" of the poor are either "externally imposed conditions" (unemployment, crowded and deteriorated housing, and lack of education) or "unavoidable matters of situational expediency" (hostility toward social institutions and low expectations and self-image).[25] Only by changing the total social structure and the resources available to the poor can we alter any subcultural traits of survival.

Yet Lewis was also saying the same thing.[26] Michael Harrington, whose *The Other America* (1963) helped spark the federal government's "War on Poverty" program, defended Lewis.[27] Harrington—like Lewis—said that society was to blame for the culture of poverty: "The real explanation of why the poor are where they are is that they made the mistake of being born to the wrong parents, in the wrong section of the country, in the wrong industry, or in the wrong racial or ethnic group."[28]

Like Lewis, Valentine, and Harrington, others argued that all people would desire the same things and cherish the same values if they were in an economic position to do so. Because they are not, they adopt an alternative set of values to survive.[29] Eliot Liebow, in a participant-observer study of lower-class Black males, concluded that they try to achieve many of the goals of the larger society but fail for many of the same reasons their fathers did: discrimination, unpreparedness, lack of job skills, and self-doubt.[30] The similarities between generations are due not to cultural transmission but to the sons' independent experience of the same failures. What appears to be a self-sustaining cultural process is actually a secondary adaptation to an adult inability to overcome structural constraints, such as racism, for example.

The debate continues over whether the culture of poverty results from **economic determinism** (structural barriers and discrimination) or from **cultural determinism** (transmission of cultural inadequacies). Some scholars continue to advance arguments about power relations and racial subjugation as the primary culprits, while others insist that cultural values and beliefs primarily explain a group's self-perpetuating world of dependence.[31]

Whatever the cause, most people's attitudes toward welfare and the urban poor (who are predominantly racial and ethnic minorities) reflect a belief in one position or the other.

Is poverty the result of personal deficiencies? Does long-term poverty result in the development of negative values passed from one generation to the next? Are personal characteristics of the poor the result of long-term poverty, or are they simply adjustments to conditions of poverty? Such questions of blaming the poor and/or existing socioeconomic systems for the existence of poverty, particularly among minority groups, evoke different answers depending on one's perspective. How would we answer the larger question: Is inequality an inevitable part of society?

## Intergroup Conflict

Is conflict inevitable when culturally distinct groups interact? Do structural conditions encourage or reduce the probability of conflict? In this section we examine the major factors that may underlie such conflict: cultural differentiation and structural differentiation.

### Cultural Differentiation

When similarities between the arriving minority group and the indigenous group exist, the relationship tends to be relatively harmonious and assimilation is likely to occur eventually.[32] Conversely, the greater and more visible the **cultural differentiation**, the greater the likelihood that conflict will occur. When large numbers of German and Irish Catholics came to the United States in the mid-nineteenth century, Protestants grew uneasy. As priests and nuns arrived and Catholics built churches, convents, and schools, Protestants became alarmed at what they feared was a papal conspiracy to gain control of the country. Emotions ran high, resulting in civil unrest and violence.

Religion has often been a basis for cultural conflict in the United States as is demonstrated by the history of discriminatory treatment suffered by Mormons, Jews, and Quakers. Yet many other aspects of cultural visibility also can serve as sources of strife as well. Cultural differences may range from clothing (e.g, Sikh turbans and Hindu saris) to leisure activities (e.g., Hispanic cockfights). Americans once condemned the Chinese as opium smokers, even though the British had introduced opium smoking into China, promoted it among the lower-class Chinese population, and even fought wars against the Chinese government to maintain the lucrative trade.

Cultural differentiation does not necessarily cause intergroup conflict. A partial explanation of variances in relations between culturally distinct groups comes from interactionist theory, which holds that the extent of

*In this ESL class these Latino immigrants, like many other newcomers, seek to master English to ease their entry into the societal mainstream. Nationwide, there is a shortage of such classes in this important step in the acculturation process that helps reduce cultural differentiation and enhances opportunities for occupational mobility.*

shared symbols and definitions between intercommunicating groups determines the nature of their interaction patterns. Although actual differences may support conflict, interactionists state that the key to harmonious or disharmonious relations lies in the definitions or interpretations of those differences. Tolerance or intolerance—acceptance or rejection of others—thus depends on whether others are perceived as threatening or nonthreatening, assimilable or nonassimilable, worthy or unworthy.

## Structural Differentiation

Because they offer macrosocial analyses of a society, both functionalist and conflict theorists provide bases for understanding how structural conditions (**structural differentiation**) affect intergroup relations. Functionalists seek explanations for the dysfunctions in the social system and the adjustments needed to correct them. Conflict theorists emphasize the conscious, purposeful actions of dominant groups to maintain systems of inequality.

Functionalists explain how sometimes economic and technological conditions facilitate minority integration. When the economy is healthy and jobs are plentiful, newcomers find it easier to get established and work their way up the socioeconomic ladder. In the United States today, however, technological progress has reduced the number of low-status, blue-collar jobs and increased the number of high-status, white-collar jobs, which require more highly skilled and educated workers. As a result, fewer jobs are available for unskilled, foreign, marginal, or unassimilated people.

Perhaps because of the importance of a job as a source of economic security and status, **occupational mobility**—the ability of individuals to improve their job position—seems to be a key factor in affecting the level of prejudice. Numerous studies have shown that a fear of economic insecurity increases ethnic hostility. One study of U.S. workers found that a perceived threat to either their cultural norms or economic well-being led to more negative attitudes toward immigrants.[33] Other researchers found that worsening economic circumstances intensify prejudicial stereotypes and attitudes about immigration.[34] In addition, upwardly mobile people are generally more tolerant than non-mobile individuals. Loss of status and prestige appear to increase hostility toward outgroups, whereas upward gains enable people to feel more benevolent toward others.

American scholar Thomas F. Pettigrew and five European colleagues (2008) reported similar findings from extensive data collected from France, Germany, Great Britain, and the Netherlands. They found a direct correlation between intergroup prejudice and group relative deprivation (comparative income, education, and housing). Specifically, respondents from a lower socioeconomic background were more likely to express prejudicial attitudes toward immigration and various ethnic groups. However, they denied any discrimination against such outgroups, instead placing responsibility for their problems on the outgroups themselves, a classic example of blaming the victim.[35]

## Ethnic Stratification

If one group becomes dominant and another becomes subservient, obviously one group has more power than the other. Social-class status partly reflects this unequal distribution of power, which also may fall along racial or ethnic lines. **Ethnic stratification** is the structured inequality of different groups with different access to social rewards as a result of their status in the social hierarchy. Because most Americans associate ethnicity with anything different from the mainstream, they don't realize that ethnicity also exists at the top. Ashley W. Doane, Jr., reminds us that dominant group ethnicity lies "hidden" because its status results in the taken-for-granted nature of dominant group identity.[36]

Stratification is a normal component of all societies, but it typically falls along racial and ethnic lines in diverse societies. How does ethnic stratification continue in a democracy where supposedly all have an equal opportunity for upward mobility? Functionalists suggest that the ethnocentrism of those in the societal mainstream leads to discrimination against those in outgroups, as determined by their racial or cultural differences. Conflict analysts instead stress the subordination of minorities by the dominant group because they benefit from such ethnic stratification. Two middle-range conflict theories offer helpful insights into this perspective. The power-differential theory helps explain the initial phases of domination and conflict, whereas the internal-colonialism theory examines the continuation of such subordination (Table 3.1).

## The Power-Differential Theory

Stanley Lieberson suggested a **power-differential theory** in which intergroup relations depend on the relative power of the migrant group and the indigenous group.[37] Because the two groups usually do not share the same culture, each strives to maintain its own institutions. Which group becomes dominant and which becomes *subordinate* governs subsequent relations.

If the newcomers possess superior technology (particularly weapons) and a cohesive social organization, conflict may occur at an early stage, with a consequent native population decline due to warfare, disease, or disruption of sustenance activities. Finding their institutions undermined or co-opted, the local inhabitants may eventually participate in the institutions of the dominant group. In time, a group consciousness may arise, and sometimes the indigenous group even succeeds in ousting the formerly dominant migrant group. When this happened in many former African colonies and in Southeast Asia, interethnic fighting among the many indigenous groups led to new forms of dominance and subordination within countries (as with the Hutu and Tutsi peoples in Burundi and Rwanda, respectively).

Lieberson maintained that neither conflict nor assimilation is an inevitable outcome of racial and ethnic contact. Instead, the particular relationship between the two groups involved determines which alternative will occur. Conflict between a dominant migrant group and a subordinate indigenous group can be immediate and violent. If the relationship is the reverse, and the indigenous group is dominant, conflict will be limited and sporadic, and the host society will exert a great deal of pressure on the subordinate migrant group to assimilate, acquiesce, or leave.

In addition, a dominant indigenous group can limit the numbers and groups entering to reduce the threat of demographic or institutional imbalance. Restrictive U.S. immigration laws against the Chinese in 1882 and against all but northern and western Europeans in 1921 and 1924 illustrate this process. Labor union hostility against African American and Asian workers, government efforts to expel foreigners (e.g., Indians, Japanese, and Filipinos), and planned attempts to revolutionize the social

## The International Scene
## Ethnic Stratification in Israel

Ethnic stratification, which exists worldwide, can be measured in many ways. In Israel—where home ownership is significantly higher than in Australia, Canada, and the United States—one study found a patterned distribution among owners and renters by ethnic groups, even when controlled for length of residence and intention to live permanently in Israel.

Immigrants from the United States and Western Europe were more affluent and concentrated on the upper rungs of the socioeconomic ladder. This apparently gave them an economic advantage in the purchase of homes over immigrants from Eastern Europe and Asia/northern Africa. However, some groups—mostly from former Soviet republics—were more likely eventually to own a home, even though most were renters in their countries of origin. This appears to result from a cultural disposition to accept the dominant value orientation of home ownership, together with the efforts of several family units to pool their money—including savings, salaries, and government aid—to make it easier to purchase a private home.

With the exception of many Jewish immigrants from Iraq, Egypt, and Iran who reportedly managed to smuggle their personal savings out of their countries of origin, most immigrant groups from Asia and northern Africa were less likely to own homes. Educationally and culturally at odds with prevailing societal norms, they often were labeled as backward and apathetic. Such negative stereotypes, particularly of northern Africans, affected their interpersonal relations with the non-immigrant population. Differences in sympathy and relations with settlement authorities in turn affected the range of choices for permanent housing and assistance, thereby contributing to the formation of ethnic gaps in housing characteristics.

Numerous factors may explain the differences in home ownership among groups. These may include lack of economic resources and/or a reluctance to take out a loan; lack of knowledge about how to get economic assistance; a preference for other residential arrangements, such as the rental of a spacious home in a good neighborhood instead of a self-owned small dwelling in a less developed area. Also, some larger groups, particularly from Eastern Europe, benefited from assistance from organizations composed of veteran immigrants from similar countries of origin, creating differentiations in social and economic mobility to the disadvantage of other immigrant groups.

Race seems to be another factor in some groups lagging behind others in purchasing homes. Most noticeable are the Ethiopian immigrants, regardless of many personal and household-level characteristics. Some studies suggest that visible physical characteristics play a role in the spatial integration of immigrants into Israeli society and that Ethiopian Israelis experience systematic discrimination in obtaining immigrant benefits relative to Soviet immigrants.

*Source:* Derived from Uzi Rebhun, "Immigration, Ethnicity, and Housing—Success Hierarchies in Israel," *Research in Social Stratification and Mobility* 27 (2009): 219–43.

order (Native American boarding schools and the Americanization movement) all illustrate the use of institutional power against minority groups.

Another sociologist, William J. Wilson, suggested that power relations between dominant and subordinate groups differ in paternalistic and competitive systems.[38] With **paternalism** (the system that once governed South Africa and the Old South of the United States), the dominant group exercises almost absolute control over the subordinate group and can direct virtually unlimited coercion to maintain societal order. In a competitive system (such as the United States today), some degree of power reciprocity exists, so the dominant group in society is somewhat vulnerable to political pressures and economic boycotts.

Rapid social change—industrialization, unionization, urbanization, migration, and political change—usually loosens the social structure, leading to new tensions as both groups seek new power resources. If the minority group increases its power resources through protective laws and improved economic opportunities, it may foresee even greater improvement in its condition. This heightened awareness is likely to lead to conflict unless additional gains are forthcoming. For example, the civil rights movement of the mid-1960s brought about legislation ensuring minority rights and opportunities in jobs, housing, education, and other aspects of life, but this led to new tensions. The 1960s were marked by urban riots and burnings, protest demonstrations and human barricades to stop construction of low-income housing sites, school-busing controversies, and challenges to labor discrimination.

## The Internal-Colonialism Theory

In analyzing the Black militancy of the late 1960s, Robert Blauner attempted to integrate the factors of caste and racism, ethnicity, culture, and economic exploitation.[39] His major point was that U.S. treatment of its Black population resembled past European subjugation and exploitation of non-Western peoples in their own lands. Although he focused on Black–White relations in the United States, he suggested that Mexican Americans might also fit his **internal-colonialism theory** and that Native Americans could be added as another suitable example:

> Of course many ethnic groups in America have lived in ghettoes. What makes the Black ghettoes an expression of colonized status are three special features. First, the ethnic ghettoes arose more from voluntary choice, both in the sense of the choice to immigrate to America and the decision to live among one's fellow ethnics. Second, the immigrant ghettoes tended to be a one- and two-generation phenomenon; they were actually way-stations in the process of acculturation and assimilation. When they continue to persist as in the case of San Francisco's Chinatown, it is because they are big business for the ethnics themselves and there is a new stream of immigrants.

The Black ghetto on the other hand has been a more permanent phenomenon, although some individuals do escape it. But most relevant is the third point. European ethnic groups like the Poles, Italians and Jews generally only experienced a brief period, often less than a generation, during which their residential buildings, commercial stores, and other enterprises were owned by outsiders. The Chinese and Japanese faced handicaps of color prejudice that were almost as strong as the Blacks faced, but very soon gained control of their internal communities, because their traditional ethnic culture and social organization had not been destroyed by slavery and internal colonization. But Afro-Americans are distinct in the extent to which their segregated communities have remained controlled economically, politically, and administratively from the outside.[40]

Several of these statements need to be modified. Chinatowns long persisted not because of any business advantage but because of racial discrimination. In proportion to the Chinatown population, only a few Chinese benefit from the tourist trade. Also, the Chinese and Japanese *always* had "control of their internal communities," although they differ greatly from each other in their structure and cohesiveness.

Blauner considers the exploitation phase that was temporary for other groups to be more nearly permanent for Blacks and possibly Chicanos. He believes that conflict and confrontation, as well as real or apparent chaos and disorder, will continue, because this may be the only way an internally colonized group can deal with the dominant society. This conflict orientation suggests that the multigenerational exploitation of certain groups creates a unique situation and a basis for the often violent conflict that sporadically flares up in our cities (Table 3.1).

## Origins of Ethnic Stratification

For ethnicity to become a basis for stratification, several factors seem necessary:

> Ethnic stratification will emerge when distinct ethnic groups are brought into sustained contact only if the groups are characterized by a high degree of ethnocentrism, competition, *and* differential power. Competition provides the motivation for stratification; ethnocentrism channels the competition along ethnic lines; and the power differential determines whether either group will be able to subordinate the other.[41]

This power differential is of enormous importance in race and ethnic relations. If the stratification system is rigid, as in a slave or caste system, so that people have no hope or means of improving their status, intergroup relations may remain stable despite perhaps being far from mutually satisfactory. Dominant power, whether expressed in legalized ways or through structural discrimination, intimidation, or coercion, maintains the social system.

TABLE 3.1    Middle-Range Conflict Theories

**The Power-Differential Theory**

1. Neither conflict nor assimilation is inevitable.
2. The relative power of indigenous and migrant groups determines events.
3. If the migrant group is dominant, early conflict and colonization will occur.
4. If the indigenous group is dominant, occasional labor and racial strife, legislative restrictions, and pressures to assimilate are common.
5. In a paternalistic society, the dominant group has almost absolute power.
6. A competitive society is vulnerable to political pressures and economic boycotts.

**The Internal-Colonialism Theory**

1. U.S. treatment of its Black population resembles past European subjugation and exploitation of non-Western peoples.
2. Black ghettos are more nearly permanent than immigrant ghettos.
3. Black ghettos are controlled economically, politically, and administratively from the outside.
4. Continual exploitation produces conflict and confrontation.
5. Mexican Americans and Native Americans may also fit this model.

---

*Challenges to the Status Quo.*    Even if the stratification system allows for upward mobility, some members of the dominant group may believe that the lower-class racial and ethnic groups are challenging the social order as they strive for their share of the "good life." If the dominant group does not feel threatened, the change will be peaceful. If the minority group meets resistance but retains hope and a sense of belonging to the larger society, the struggle for more power will occur within the system (perhaps through demonstrations, boycotts, voter-registration drives, or lobbying) rather than through violence. The late-nineteenth-century race-baiting riots on the West Coast against Chinese and Japanese workers and the 1919 Chicago race riots against Blacks attempting to enter the meat-packing industry illustrate violent responses of a dominant group against a minority group over power resources. Similarly, the Black–Korean violence in several urban neighborhoods during the late twentieth century, including the 1992 Los Angeles riots and the violence between Blacks and Cubans in Miami in 1988, typifies minority-group clashes over limited resources.

*Social-Class Antagonisms.*    Conflict theorists argue that class-based prejudice, oppression, and violence are to be expected in a competitive, capitalist system.[42] A connection exists between a group's economic position and the intensity of its conflict with the dominant society. The greater the deprivation in economic resources, social status, and social power, the likelier the weaker group will resort to violent conflict to achieve gains in any of these three areas (see The International Scene box). As the social-class position of a group increases, intergroup conflict becomes less intense and less violent.

Conflict occurs not only because a lower-class group seeks an end to deprivation but also because the group next higher on the socioeconomic ladder feels threatened. Often, the working-class group displays the greatest hostility and prejudice of all established groups in the society toward the upward-striving minority group. Other factors may be at work as well, but status competition is a significant source of conflict.

Social-class antagonisms influence people's perceptions of racial and ethnic groups too.[43] Some social scientists suggest parallels between Irish, Italian, and Polish immigrants and southern Blacks who migrated to northern cities (the Chinese, some Japanese, and others also fit this model). All immigrated from agrarian poverty to urban industrial slums. Encountering prejudice and discrimination, some sought alternative routes to material success: crime, ethnic politics, or stable but unskilled employment.[44] Other social scientists, however, argue that the Black experience does not equate with that of European immigrants. They hold, as did the Kerner Commission investigating the urban riots of the late 1960s, that the dominant society's practice of internal colonialism toward Blacks deprived them of the strong social organizations that other groups had. Moreover, they believe that today's labor market offers fewer unskilled jobs for Blacks than it offered other immigrant groups in earlier times, thereby depriving poor urban Blacks of a means to begin moving upward.[45]

Whether race or social class is the primary factor in assessing full integration of Blacks in the United States is a still-continuing debate, particularly among Black social scientists.

## Labor Market Outcomes

Regardless of whether one is native-born, or a legal immigrant, or an undocumented immigrant, integration into the societal mainstream and placement within the socioeconomic layers of society is heavily dependent on education, job skills, and social networks. The occupational patterning found among some groups (e.g., Greeks as restaurateurs, Asian Indians owning convenience stores, or Koreans as green grocers) is partly reflective of the social capital within these groups that enabled such ventures to occur on a widespread basis, and also why some groups are able to assimilate more easily than others.

### Social Capital

The term **social capital** refers to actual or virtual resources available to an individual or a group through social relationships, networks, and institutions

*Multigenerational occupational patterning often occurs among working-class ethnic Americans, as son joins father in the same line of work to carry on the tradition. A good example is found among the miners in the Appalachian coal regions, where men from families of Slavic ancestry have worked in the mines for three or more generations.*

that "facilitate cooperation and collective action for mutual benefits."  Social capital thus is a collective asset in terms of shared norms and values, mutual trust and norms of reciprocity, information, social support, and personal connections inherent in social network relationships that are indispensable for achieving social, economic, and political goals.[46]

When we examine ethnic communities in terms of social capital, we can determine how community-based support systems and cultural orientations do or do not assist first- and second-generation Americans in their quest to share in the American Dream. Social capital is not a fixed object but rather a socially constructed, episodic, and value-based means that facilitates access to benefits and resources that best suit the goals of specific immigrant groups.[47]

Essentially, social capital offers resources to racial or ethnic minorities that are beyond their individual reach by creating connections and support. The presence of these networks cultivates hope, trust, communication, mutual assistance, and problem solving through cooperative, collective action. Although the presence of strong social capital does not guarantee a minority group's successful integration into the economic and political mainstream, it certainly makes life easier than in a community lacking it.

Ethnic communities with strong social capital can offer help to new arrivals in securing informal sources of credit, insurance, child support, English language training, and job referrals. Ethnic resources feed on supportive ethnic social structures though. For example, although Koreans and Latinos share the same neighborhood in Los Angeles's Koreatown, they live within two entirely different social environments. Unlike the Latinos, Korean children benefit from a cultural emphasis on the value of education, various after-school institutions, and a strong social network in which coethnic friends reinforce academic goals. As a result, more graduate high school and go on to college.[48]

## Segmented Assimilation

Building on the concept that immigrant groups possess different levels of social capital is the theory of **segmented assimilation**. As its name implies, this hypothesis suggests a variety of outcomes among, and even within, contemporary immigrant streams. Instead of a uniform adaptation process that becomes more successful with longer residence in the United States, new immigrant groups may follow different assimilation paths than did previous immigrants. Besides the variants in available social capital, such factors as country of origin, settlement area, social class, race, and education also play an important role.[49]

In a positive scenario, those groups that are received favorably and possess high levels of human capital may quickly move up the socioeconomic ladder and integrate into the societal mainstream. In contrast, a second scenario depicts groups with limited resources as unable to find stable employment to earn enough income to support their children's education. Moreover, longer residence in an inner-city environment may result in their children's acculturation to other minority peers, leading to lower educational aspirations and downward mobility, somewhat of a "new rainbow underclass."[50] Yet a third scenario is limited assimilation where immigrant parents support their children's educational success but reinforce traditional cultural values and thus limit their acculturation into the American youth subculture.[51]

The segmented-assimilation hypothesis provides a lens for understanding the discrepancy in research findings on the educational enrollment of recent immigrants and the children of immigrants in the United States. One study, for example, reported significant intergenerational progress in educational attainment for many second-generation groups. Indeed, some surpassed those of third-generation or higher Whites and African Americans. However, those of Mexican and Puerto Rican heritage languished behind the other groups.[52] A downward mobility pattern for Hispanic Caribbean youths, found in another study, was consistent with the second possible outcome of the segmented-assimilation hypothesis, whereas Afro-Caribbean youths appeared to illustrate the third type of

## Reality Check
## The Second Generation: Assimilation and Integration

How well do immigrants integrate into U.S. society? Research findings vary, as per segmented assimilation theory, but generally they report positive findings. Perhaps the most encouraging insights come from a definitive, 10-year study, *Inheriting the City: The Children of Immigrants Come of Age* (2008), that examined five immigrant groups—Chinese, Dominicans, Russian Jews, South Americans, and West Indians—living in metropolitan New York. Importantly, the authors also conducted companion studies on native-born Blacks, Puerto Ricans, and whites for a comparison.

Their study included a survey and in-person interviews of a random sample of second-generation residents ages 22 to 32 in four New York City boroughs and the inner suburbs, either in their residence, college, or workplace. What they learned contradicted the fears of some experts that these young adults would not do as well as previous waves of immigrants due to lack of high-paying manufacturing jobs, poor public schools, and an entrenched racial divide. Far from descending into an urban underclass, the children of immigrants are using their cultural and social capital to avoid some of the obstacles that native minority groups cannot.

Repeating the pattern of the children of earlier European immigrants, this new second generation has exceeded its parents' success. The degree to which this has occurred varies, though. The children of Chinese and Russian Jewish immigrants have achieved higher levels of education and earnings than native-born Whites. Those of South American and Dominican ancestry earn about as much as white Americans and have a higher education level than that of African Americans and Puerto Ricans, but their level of educational attainment is lower than that of Whites. West Indians encounter the same systemic racial barriers that their darker-skinned native counterparts also face.

Overall though, the second generation is rapidly moving into the mainstream—speaking English and working in jobs that resemble those held by native New Yorkers their age. Still, the second generation has not followed the traditional immigration model in all areas. Unlike their parents, who found economic success within ethnic enclaves, many of the second generation immigrants have moved into the mainstream economy. Yet even as they successfully integrate into U.S. society, they are able to preserve their cultural identities without feeling torn between the two cultures.

Despite their relatively high level of education and income, many have not yet become politically and civically engaged. This study, however, does leave open the question of whether New York, with its long history of incorporating immigrants into an already diverse population, provides a different context of reception than might be true elsewhere.

*Source:* Derived from Philip Kasinitz, John H. Mollenkopf, Mary C. Waters, and Jennifer Holdaway, *Inheriting the City: The Children of Immigrants Come of Age.* Cambridge, MA: Harvard University Press, 2008.

outcome.[53] Similarly, a study of the Vietnamese community in New Orleans revealed that those more successful in school were those who were able to retain their mother tongue and traditional values.[54] Yet another study found that Caribbean immigrants often pass along to their children an immigrant or ethnic identity that retards acculturation into the African American community.[55]

If, therefore, we are to understand more completely the acculturation patterns among today's immigrants, the segmented-assimilation hypothesis informs us that one model does not fit all groups or even all members of any group. Groups differ in their incorporation into the U.S. stratification system, and this theory attempts to explain how and why they do.

### Nonimmigrant Workers

A common worldwide pattern is a labor force partly comprised of foreign workers who do not intend to stay in the host country. Such was the case in the United States, for example, of many nineteenth-century Chinese railroad workers, twentieth-century Italian and Polish factory laborers, and twenty-first-century Mexican agricultural workers. In 2009 alone, a total of 1.7 million temporary workers and their families came to the United States, including 302,000 Mexicans, 263,000 Asian Indians, 165,000 Canadians, 144,000 Japanese, 127,000 British, 74,000 Germans, 62,000 French, 41,000 South Koreans, and 25,000 Australians.[56]

Only about 10 percent of those with temporary visas are seasonal agricultural workers. About 20 percent are intra-company transferees and another 20 percent of workers with highly specialized knowledge, such as architects, engineers, and scientists. A few other categories include athletes, artists and entertainers, and treaty traders and investors.[57]

Like Americans temporarily working abroad for a multinational corporation, foreigners in the United States on a work visa contribute to the economy through their labor and as consumers. They sightsee and take in the cultural lifestyle but do not seek assimilation, knowing they will be returning to their own country and culture in the near future.

# Retrospect

Structural conditions influence people's perceptions of the world—whether they live in an industrialized or agrarian society, a closed or open social system, a growing or contracting economy, a friendly or unfriendly environment, and whether their homeland, friends, and relatives are accessible or remote. Distribution of power resources and compatibility with the existing social structure greatly influence majority–minority relations as well. Interactionists concentrate on perceptions of cultural differences as they affect intergroup relations. Functionalists and conflict theorists emphasize structural conditions.

The interplay between the variables of race, ethnic group, and social class is important for understanding how some problems and conflicts arise. A feature interpreted as an attribute of a race or ethnic group may in fact be a broader aspect of social class. Because many attitudes and values are situational responses to socioeconomic status, a change in status or opportunities will bring about a change in those attitudes and values. Investigative studies have not supported the culture-of-poverty hypothesis of family disintegration and a self-perpetuating poverty value orientation.

Stratification along racial and ethnic lines is common in a diverse society. Functionalists think ethnocentrism leads to discrimination to cause this. One middle-range conflict perspective focuses on the power differential. Whether the indigenous group or migrant group possesses superior power determines the nature of subsequent intergroup relations. Another factor is whether the social system is paternalistic or competitive. Considering Black and Hispanic ghettos or Native American reservations as examples of internal colonialism offers a second conflict perspective.

Social capital, the resources available through contacts and relationships, and segmented assimilation, the integration outcome dependent on that social capital, are important factors in the labor endeavors of any minority group. Nonimmigrants are another important element in the labor force, but their tenure is limited as is their integration into the host society.

## KEY TERMS

Cultural determinism
Cultural differentiation
Culture of poverty
Economic determinism
Ethclasses
Ethnic stratification
Internal-colonialism theory
Occupational mobility

Paternalism
Power-differential theory
Reputational method
Social class
Social stratification
Social structure
Structural differentiation

## DISCUSSION QUESTIONS

1. What economic factors can affect intergroup relations?

2. Does social class awareness affect ethnic self-consciousness?

3. What is the relationship between ethnicity and social class?

4. What is meant by the *culture of poverty*? What criticisms exist about this thinking?

5. What is the difference between cultural differentiation and structural differentiation?

6. How do the functional and conflict perspectives approach the factors likely to contribute to intergroup conflict?

## INTERNET ACTIVITIES

1. How much do you know about inequality? Take the interactive quiz of the Center for the Study of Inequality at Cornell University (http://inequality.cornell.edu/).

2. For a wide range of readings on stratification, primarily from the conflict perspective, go to the Sociosite readings under "Inequalities" at www.sociosite.net/topics/inequality.php#INEQUALITY.

# CHAPTER 4

# Prejudice

*"Prejudices are what fools use for reason."*

—Voltaire

When strangers from different groups come into contact with one another, their interaction patterns may take many forms. So far, we have discussed the roles that ethnocentrism, social distance, culture, and social structure play in shaping perceptions of any outgroup. Prejudice and discrimination also emerge as major considerations in understanding intergroup relations. Why do they exist? Why do they persist? Why do certain groups become targets more frequently? How can we eliminate prejudicial attitudes?

The word *prejudice*, derived from the Latin word *praejudicium*, originally meant "prejudgment." Thus, some scholars defined a prejudiced person as one who hastily reached a conclusion before examining the facts.[1] This definition proved inadequate, however, because social scientists discovered that prejudice often arose *after* groups came into contact and had at least some knowledge of one another. For that reason, Louis Wirth described prejudice as "an attitude with an emotional bias."[2]

Because feelings shape our attitudes, they reduce our receptivity to additional information that may alter those attitudes. Ralph Rosnow had this fact in mind when he broadened the definition of prejudice to encompass "any unreasonable attitude that is unusually resistant to rational influence."[3] In fact, a deeply prejudiced person is almost totally immune to information. Gordon Allport offered a classic example of such an individual in the following dialogue:

> MR. X: The trouble with the Jews is that they only take care of their own group.

MR. Y:   But the record of the Community Chest campaign shows that they gave more generously, in proportion to their numbers, to the general charities of the community, than did non-Jews.

MR. X:   That shows they are always trying to buy favor and intrude into Christian affairs. They think of nothing but money; that is why there are so many Jewish bankers.

MR. Y:   But a recent study shows that the percentage of Jews in the banking business is negligible, far smaller than the percentage of non-Jews.

MR. X:   That's just it; they don't go in for respectable business; they are only in the movie business or run night clubs.*

It is almost as if Mr. X is saying, "My mind is made up; don't confuse me with the facts." He does not refute the argument; rather, he ignores each bit of new and contradictory information and moves on to a new area in which he distorts other facts to support his prejudice against Jews.

Prejudicial attitudes may be either positive or negative. Sociologists primarily study the latter, however, because only negative attitudes can lead to turbulent social relations between dominant and minority groups. Therefore, a good working definition of **prejudice** is that it is an attitudinal system of negative beliefs, feelings, and action-orientations regarding a certain group or groups of people. The status of the strangers is an important factor in the development of such negative attitudes. Moreover, prejudicial attitudes exist among members of both dominant and minority groups. Thus, in the relations between dominant and minority groups, the antipathy felt by one group for another is quite often reciprocated.

Psychological perspectives on prejudice—whether behaviorist, cognitive, or psychoanalytic—focus on the subjective states of mind of individuals. In these perspectives, a person's prejudicial attitudes may result from imitation or conditioning (behaviorist), perceived similarity–dissimilarity of beliefs (cognitive), or specific personality characteristics (psychoanalytic). In contrast, sociological perspectives focus on the objective conditions of society as the social forces behind prejudicial attitudes and behind racial and ethnic relations. Individuals do not live in a vacuum; social reality affects their states of mind.

Both perspectives are necessary to understand prejudice. As psychologist Gordon Allport argued, besides needing a close study of habits, perceptions, motivation, and personality, we need an analysis of social settings, situational forces, demographic and ecological variables, and legal and economic trends.[4] Psychological and sociological perspectives complement each other in providing a fuller explanation of intergroup relations.

*Gordon W. Allport, *The Nature of Prejudice*, 25th anniversary ed. (New York; Basic Books, 1979), pp. 13–14.

# The Psychology of Prejudice

The psychological approach to prejudice is to examine individual behavior. We can understand more about prejudice among individuals by focusing on four areas of study: levels of prejudice, self-justification, personality, and frustration.

## Levels of Prejudice

Prejudice exists on three levels: cognitive, emotional, and action orientation.[5] The **cognitive level of prejudice** encompasses a person's beliefs and perceptions of a group as threatening or nonthreatening, inferior or equal (e.g., in terms of intellect, status, or biological composition), seclusive or intrusive, impulse-gratifying, acquisitive, or possessing other positive or negative characteristics. Mr. X's cognitive beliefs are that Jews are intrusive and acquisitive. Other illustrations of cognitive beliefs are that the Irish are heavy drinkers and fighters, African Americans are rhythmic and lazy, and the Poles are thick-headed and unintelligent.

Generalizations shape both ethnocentric and prejudicial attitudes, but there is a difference. *Ethnocentrism* is a generalized rejection of all outgroups on the basis of an ingroup focus, whereas *prejudice* is a rejection of certain people solely on the basis of their membership in a particular group.

In many societies, members of the majority group may believe that a particular low-status minority group is dirty, immoral, violent, or law-breaking. In the United States, the Irish, Italians, African Americans, Mexicans, Chinese, Puerto Ricans, and others have at one time or another been labeled with most, if not all, of these adjectives. In most European countries and in the United States, the group lowest on the socioeconomic ladder has often been depicted in caricature as also lowest on the evolutionary ladder. The Irish and African Americans in the United States and the peasants and various ethnic groups in Europe have all been depicted in the past as apelike:

> The Victorian images of the Irish as "white Negro" and simian Celt, or a combination of the two, derived much of its force and inspiration from physiognomical beliefs . . . [but] every country in Europe had its equivalent of "white Negroes" and simianized men, whether or not they happened to be stereotypes of criminals, assassins, political radicals, revolutionaries, Slavs, gypsies, Jews or peasants.[6]

The **emotional level of prejudice** encompasses the feelings that a minority group arouses in an individual. Although these feelings may be based on stereotypes from the cognitive level, they represent a more intense stage of personal involvement. The emotional attitudes may be negative or positive, such as fear/envy, distrust/trust, disgust/admiration, or contempt/empathy. These feelings, based on beliefs about the group, may be triggered by social interaction or by the possibility of interaction. For example, Whites might react with fear or anger to the integration of their schools or neighborhoods, or Protestants might be jealous of the lifestyle of a highly successful Catholic business executive.

An **action-orientation level of prejudice** is the positive or negative predisposition to engage in discriminatory behavior. A person who harbors strong feelings about members of a certain racial or ethnic group may have a tendency to act for or against them—being aggressive or nonaggressive, offering assistance or withholding it. Such an individual would also be likely to want to exclude or include members of that group both in close, personal social relations and in peripheral social relations. For example, some people would want to exclude members of the disliked group from doing business with them or living in their neighborhood. Another manifestation of the action-orientation level of prejudice is the desire to change or maintain the status differential or inequality between the two groups. Note that an action orientation is a predisposition to act, not the action itself.

## Self-Justification

**Self-justification** involves denigrating a person or group to justify maltreatment of them. In this situation, self-justification leads to prejudice and discrimination against members of another group.

Some philosophers argue that we are not so much rational creatures as we are rationalizing creatures. We require reassurance that the things we do and the lives we live are proper and that good reasons for our actions exist. If we can convince ourselves that another group is inferior, immoral, or dangerous, we may feel justified in discriminating against its members, enslaving them, or even killing them.

History is filled with examples of people who thought their maltreatment of others was just and necessary: As defenders of the "true faith," the Crusaders killed "Christ killers" (Jews) and "infidels" (Muslims). Participants in the Spanish Inquisition imprisoned, tortured, and executed "heretics," "the disciples of the Devil." Similarly, the Puritans burned witches, whose refusal to confess "proved they were evil"; pioneers exploited or killed Native Americans who were "heathen savages"; and Whites mistreated, enslaved, or killed African Americans, who were "an inferior species." According to U.S. Army officers, the civilians in the Vietnamese village of My Lai were "probably" aiding the Vietcong; so in 1968, U.S. soldiers fighting in the Vietnam War felt justified in slaughtering more than 300 unarmed people there, including women, children, and the elderly. In recent years, suicide bombers and terrorists have killed innocent civilians, also justifying their actions through their religious fanaticism. Another example of self-justification serving as a source of prejudice is the dominant group's assumption of an attitude of superiority over other groups. In this respect, establishing a prestige hierarchy—ranking the status of various ethnic groups—results in differential association. To enhance or maintain self-esteem, a person may avoid social contact with groups deemed inferior and associate only with those identified as being of high status. Through such behavior, self-justification may come to intensify the social distance between groups. As discussed in Chapter 1, *social distance* refers to the degree to which ingroup members do not engage in social or primary relationships with members of various outgroups.

## Personality

In a famous 1950 study, T. W. Adorno and his colleagues reported a correlation between individuals' early childhood experiences of harsh parental discipline and their development of an **authoritarian personality** as adults.[7] If parents assume an excessively domineering posture in their relations with a child, exercising stern measures and threatening to withdraw love if the child does not respond with weakness and submission, the child tends to be insecure and to nurture much latent hostility against the parents. When such children become adults, they may demonstrate **displaced aggression**, directing their hostility against a powerless group to compensate for their feelings of insecurity and fear. Highly prejudiced individuals tend to come from families that emphasize obedience.

The authors identified authoritarianism by the use of a measuring instrument called an F scale (the *F* stands for potential fascism). Other tests included the A-S (anti-Semitism) and E (ethnocentrism) scales, the latter measuring attitudes toward various minorities. One of their major findings was that people who scored high on authoritarianism also consistently showed a high degree of prejudice against all minority groups. These highly prejudiced persons were characterized by rigidity of viewpoint, dislike for ambiguity, strict obedience to leaders, and intolerance of weakness in themselves and others.

No sooner did *The Authoritarian Personality* appear than controversy began. Critics challenged the methodology, questioned the assumptions that the F scale responses represented a belief system, and argued that social factors (e.g., ideologies, stratification, mobility, intelligence, and education) relate far more to prejudice than one's personality. Others complained that the authors were interested only in measuring authoritarianism of the political right while ignoring such tendencies in those on the political left.

Although studies of authoritarian personality have helped us understand some aspects of prejudice, they have not provided a causal explanation. Most of the findings in this area show a correlation, but the findings do not prove, for example, that harsh discipline of children causes them to become prejudiced adults. Perhaps the strict parents were themselves prejudiced, and the child learned those attitudes from them.

For some people, prejudice may indeed be rooted in subconscious childhood tensions, but we simply do not know whether these tensions directly cause a high degree of prejudice in the adult or whether other powerful social forces are the determinants. Whatever the explanation, authoritarianism is a significant phenomenon worthy of continued investigation. Recent research, however, has stressed social and situational factors, rather than personality, as primary causes of prejudice and discrimination.[8]

Yet another dimension of the personality component is the role of self-esteem. Those with high self-esteem tend to evaluate an outgroup more positively than those with low self-esteem.[9] Also, individuals' awareness of potential discrimination against themselves can provide self-esteem protection, in contrast to the lower self-esteem experienced by those less aware of such external factors.[10] Thus it would appear that the level of one's self-esteem affects attitudes both about oneself and others.

## Frustration

Frustration is the result of relative deprivation in which expectations remain unsatisfied. **Relative deprivation** is a lack of resources, or rewards, in one's standard of living in comparison with those of others in the society. A number of investigators have suggested that frustrations tend to increase aggression toward others.[11] Frustrated people may easily strike out against the perceived cause of their frustration. However, this reaction may not be possible because the true source of the frustration is often too nebulous to be identified or too powerful to act against. In such instances, the result may be displaced aggression; in this situation, the frustrated individual or group usually redirects anger against a more visible, vulnerable, and socially sanctioned target that is unable to strike back. Minorities meet these criteria and are thus frequently the recipients of displaced aggression by the dominant or even another minority group.

Blaming others for something that is not their fault is known as **scapegoating**. The term comes from the ancient Hebrew custom of using a goat during the Day of Atonement as a symbol of the sins of the people. In an annual ceremony, a priest placed his hands on the head of a goat and listed the people's sins in a symbolic transference of guilt; he then chased the goat out of the community, thereby freeing the people of sin.[12] Since those times, the powerful group has usually punished the scapegoat group rather than allowing it to escape.

Throughout world history, minority groups often served as scapegoats, including the Christians in ancient Rome, the Huguenots in France, the Jews in Europe and Russia, and the Puritans and Quakers in England. Certain characteristics are necessary for a group to become a suitable scapegoat.

The group must be (1) highly visible in physical appearance or observable customs and actions; (2) not strong enough to strike back; (3) situated within easy access of the dominant group and, ideally, concentrated in one area; (4) a past target of hostility for whom latent hostility still exists; and (5) the symbol of an unpopular concept.[13]

Some groups fit this typology better than others, but minority racial and ethnic groups have been a perennial choice. Irish, Italians, Catholics, Jews, Quakers, Mormons, Chinese, Japanese, Blacks, Puerto Ricans, Chicanos, and Koreans have all been treated, at one time or another, as the scapegoat in the United States. Especially in times of economic hardship, societies tend to blame some group for the general conditions, which often leads to aggressive action against the group as an expression of frustration. For example, in the South between 1882 and 1930, cotton prices declined and the number of lynchings of Blacks increased.[14]

A growing number of studies show that unanticipated failure to reach a desired goal is more unpleasant than an expected failure. Frustrations will then generate aggressive inclinations to the extent of how bad individuals feel about not getting what they wanted. Confronted with unexpected frustrating situations, highly prejudiced individuals are more likely to seek scapegoats than are unprejudiced individuals. Another intervening variable is that personal frustrations (marital failure, injury, or mental illness) make people more likely to seek scapegoats than do shared frustrations (dangers of flood or hurricane).[15]

Frustration–aggression theory, although helpful, is not completely satisfactory. It ignores the role of culture and the reality of actual social conflict and fails to show any causal relationship. Most of the responses measured in these studies were of people already biased. Why did one group rather than another become the object of aggression? Moreover, frustration does not necessarily precede aggression, and aggression does not necessarily flow from frustration.

## The Sociology of Prejudice

The sociological approach to prejudice is not to examine individual behavior, as psychologists do, but rather to examine behavior within a group setting. Sociologist Talcott Parsons provided one bridge between psychology and sociology by introducing social forces as a variable in frustration–aggression theory. He suggested that both the family and the occupational structure may produce anxieties and insecurities that create frustration.[16] According to this view, the growing-up process (gaining parental affection and approval, identifying with and imitating sexual role models, and competing with others in adulthood) sometimes involves severe emotional strain. The result is an adult personality with a large reservoir of repressed aggression that becomes *free-floating*—susceptible to redirection against convenient scapegoats. Similarly, the occupational system is a source of frustration: Its emphasis on competitiveness and individual achievement, its function of conferring status, its requirement that people inhibit their natural impulses at work, and its ties to the state of the economy are among the factors that generate emotional anxieties. Parsons pessimistically concluded that minorities fulfill a functional "need" as targets for displaced aggression and therefore will remain targets.[17]

Perhaps most influential in staking out the sociological position on prejudice was Herbert Blumer, who suggested that prejudice always involves the "sense of group position" in society. Echoing other social scientists about the three levels of prejudice we discussed earlier, Blumer argued that prejudice can include beliefs, feelings, and a predisposition to action, thus motivating behavior that derives from the social hierarchy.[18] By emphasizing historically established group positions and relationships, Blumer shifted the focus away from the attitudes and personality compositions of individuals. As a social phenomenon, prejudice rises or falls according to issues that alter one group's position in relation to that of another group.

## Socialization

In the **socialization process**, individuals acquire the values, attitudes, beliefs, and perceptions of their culture or subculture, including religion, nationality, and social class. Generally, the child conforms to the parents' expectations in acquiring an understanding of the world and its people. Being impressionable and knowing of no alternative conceptions of the world, the child usually accepts these concepts without questioning. We thus learn the prejudices of our parents and others, which then become part of our values and beliefs. Even when based on false stereotypes, prejudices shape our perceptions of various peoples and influence our attitudes and actions toward particular groups. For example, if we develop negative attitudes about Jews because we are taught that they are shrewd, acquisitive, and clannish—all-too-familiar stereotypes—as adults we may refrain from business or social relationships with them. We may not even realize the reason for such avoidance; so subtle has been the prejudice instilled within us.

People may learn certain prejudices because of their pervasiveness. The cultural screen that we develop and through which we view the surrounding world is not always accurate, but it does permit transmission of shared values and attitudes, which are reinforced by others. Prejudice, like cultural values, is taught and learned through the socialization process. The prevailing prejudicial attitudes and actions may be deeply embedded in custom or law (e.g., the **Jim Crow laws** of the 1890s and the early twentieth century establishing segregated public facilities throughout the South, which

*No one is born prejudiced. Through the socialization process, children learn the values and attitudes of their parents, no matter whether those are positive or negative. Brought to this hate-laden demonstration and given a sign to hold, such continuing exposure may develop this boy into becoming part of the next generation's bigots and hate mongers.*

subsequent generations accepted as proper and maintained in their own adult lives).

Although socialization explains how prejudicial attitudes may be transmitted from one generation to the next, it does not explain their origin or why they intensify or diminish over the years. These aspects of prejudice must be explained in another way.

## Economic Competition

People tend to be more hostile toward others when they feel that their security is threatened; thus, many social scientists conclude that economic competition and conflict breed prejudice. Certainly, considerable evidence shows that negative stereotyping, prejudice, and discrimination increase markedly whenever competition for available jobs increases (see the International Scene box).

An excellent illustration relates to the Chinese sojourners in the nineteenth-century United States. Prior to the 1870s, the transcontinental railroad was being built, and the Chinese filled many of the jobs made

## The International Scene
## Economic Competition in the Czech Republic

The 70,000 Vietnamese currently living in the Czech Republic are mostly first- and second-generation families who came since the 1970s, as well as 20,000 low-skilled migrants who came as a second wave in the 2007 booming economy. While times were good, the Vietnamese quietly prospered and the Czechs ignored their presence. Then came the severe 2008–2009 economic downturn and high unemployment, driving many Czechs to seek the low-paying work they once left to foreigners. Polls revealed that two-thirds of Czechs no longer wanted the Vietnamese in their country.

That attitude led to an outpouring of bitterness against minorities, particularly the Vietnamese. Verbal taunts, physical attacks, denial of access to discos and restaurants, and public expressions that the Vietnamese should "go home" became common. In 2009, the government initiated a voluntary policy for any unemployed foreign worker wanting to go home, offering free one-way air or rail fare and about $700 in cash. However, many workers, saddled with debt and ashamed to return home with so little money, decided to wait for the economy to improve.

Many Vietnamese are store owners, speak Czech fluently, and send their children to the public schools, where they typically are among the highest academic achievers. However, the backlash against the newer Vietnamese workers, whether employed or jobless, has threatened even the decades-old coexistence of the longer-residing Vietnamese and the host society. Until the economy improves, tensions likely will remain.

*Critical thinking question:*   What parallels do you see in dominant–minority relations in the Czech Republic and the United States?

Source: Based on the observations of Vincent N. Parrillo, a former Fulbright scholar in the Czech Republic and frequent visitor.

---

available by this project in the sparsely populated West. Although they were expelled from the region's gold mines and schools and could seek, but not obtain, justice in the courts, they managed to convey to some Whites the image of being a clean, hardworking, law-abiding people. The completion of the railroad, the flood of former Civil War soldiers into the job market, and the economic depression of 1873 worsened their situation. The Chinese became more frequent victims of open discrimination and hostility. Their positive stereotype among some Whites was widely displaced by a negative one: They were now "conniving," "crafty," "criminal," "the yellow menace." Only after they retreated into Chinatowns and entered specialty occupations that minimized their competition with Whites did the intense hostility abate.

One pioneer in the scientific study of prejudice, John Dollard, demonstrated how prejudice against the Germans, which had been virtually nonexistent, arose in a small U.S. industrial town when times got bad:

> Local Whites largely drawn from the surrounding farms manifested considerable direct aggression toward the newcomers. Scornful and derogatory opinions were expressed about the Germans, and the native Whites had a satisfying sense of superiority toward them. . . . The chief element in the permission to be aggressive against the Germans was rivalry for jobs and status in the local woodenware plants. The native Whites felt definitely crowded for their jobs by the entering German groups and in case of bad times had a chance to blame the Germans who by their presence provided more competitors for the scarcer jobs. There seemed to be no traditional pattern of prejudice against Germans unless the skeletal suspicion of all out-groupers (always present) be invoked in this place.[19]

Both experimental studies and historical analyses have provided support for the economic-competition theory. In an oft-cited classic study, Muzafer Sherif directed several experiments showing how intergroup competition at a boys' camp led to conflict and escalating hostility.[20] On a much larger scale, throughout U.S. history, in times of high unemployment and thus intense job competition, nativist movements against minorities have flourished.[21] This pattern has held true regionally—against Asians on the West Coast, Italians in Louisiana, and French Canadians in New England—and nationally, with the anti-foreign movements always peaking during periods of depression. So it was with the Native American Party in the 1830s, the Know-Nothing Party in the 1850s, the American Protective Association in the 1890s, and the Ku Klux Klan after World War I.

In recent times, one group's pressure of job competition on another group continues to be a factor in its becoming a target of prejudice. For example, one study conducted in the southern United States found that although both Blacks and non-Blacks perceived a potential economic threat from continued Latino immigration, Blacks were more concerned about its effects on them than were Whites.[22] It appears they may have some cause for concern. Studies show that many employers view Latinos as far more desirable employees than Blacks, in part, because they see immigrants as more easily controllable.[23] In an urban labor market where limited low-skill jobs exist, such a situation can generate hostility between the two groups.

Once again, a theory that offers some excellent insights into prejudice—in particular, that economic competition sparks increased hostility toward or between minorities—also has some serious shortcomings. Not all groups that have been objects of hostility (e.g., Quakers and Mormons) have been economic competitors. Moreover, why is hostility against some groups greater than against others? Why do the negative feelings in some communities run against groups whose numbers are so small that they cannot possibly pose an economic threat? Evidently, values besides economic ones cause people to be antagonistic to a group perceived as an actual or a potential threat.

## Social Norms

Many social scientists insist that a relationship exists between prejudice and a person's tendency to conform to societal expectations.[24] **Social norms**—the cultural guidelines—form the generally shared rules defining what is and is not proper behavior. By learning and unknowingly accepting the prevailing prejudices, an individual is simply conforming to those norms.

This theory holds that a direct relationship exists between degree of conformity and degree of prejudice. If so, people's prejudices should decrease or increase significantly when they move into areas where the prejudicial norm is different. An abundance of research, both classical and current, offers evidence to support this view.

John Dollard's study, *Caste and Class in a Southern Town*, provided an in-depth look at the emotional adjustment of Whites and Blacks to rigid social norms in the 1930s.[25] Intimidation—sometimes even severe reprisals for going against social norms—ensured compliance. However, reprisals usually were unnecessary. The advantages Whites and Blacks gained in personal security and stability set in motion a vicious circle. They encouraged a way of life that reinforced the rationale of the social system in this community. Later, Thomas Pettigrew found that Southerners in the 1950s became less prejudiced against Blacks when they interacted with them in the army, where the social norms were less prejudicial.[26] Another researcher found that people moving into an anti-Semitic neighborhood in New York City became more anti-Semitic.[27]

In recent years, researchers have further documented how ingroup norms influence attitudes and behavior.[28] As individuals conform to the norms and prejudices of a desirable group, they begin to identify with this group and internalize its norms.[29] Further, in a majority-group controlled setting such as the workplace, members of a stigmatized minority group are likely to adopt a pragmatic strategy of stigmatizing a different minority group both to conform to the majority group's recognized prejudicial norms and to deflect prejudice from itself. In time, their repeated accommodation to these norms for self-preservation could lead to internalization or conversion of their own beliefs to prejudicial attitudes.[30]

Although the social-norms theory explains prevailing attitudes, it does not explain either their origins or the reasons new prejudices develop when other groups move into an area. In addition, the theory does not explain why prejudicial attitudes against a particular group rise and fall cyclically over the years.

Although many social scientists have attempted to identify the causes of prejudice, no single factor provides an adequate explanation. Prejudice is

TABLE 4.1   **Approaches to the Study of Prejudice**

| Approach | Concept | Example |
|---|---|---|
| **Psychological** | | |
| Self-Justification | We blame others to justify our mistreatment of them. | "They asked for it!" |
| Personality | Strict child rearing results in an intolerant adult. | "I can't stand people who aren't neat!" |
| Frustration | Unmet expectations lead to finding a scapegoat. | "She didn't deserve that promotion! I did!" |
| **Sociological** | | |
| Socialization | We learn tolerance or intolerance from others. | "They're just not like us. They're lazy!" |
| Economic Competition | We become hostile when we think others are a threat. | "Immigrants take jobs away from Americans!" |
| Social Norms | We learn to conform to prevailing attitudes. | "Don't be seen talking to those people." |

a complex phenomenon, and it is most likely the product of more than one causal agent (see Table 4.1). Sociologists today tend either to emphasize multiple-cause explanations or to stress social forces encountered in specific and similar situations—forces such as economic conditions, stratification, and hostility toward an outgroup.

# Stereotyping

One common reaction to strangers is to categorize them broadly. Prejudice at the cognitive level often arises from false perceptions that are enhanced by cultural or racial stereotypes. A **stereotype** is an oversimplified generalization by which we attribute certain traits or characteristics to a group without regard to individual differences. Sometimes stereotypes are positive—for example, that African Americans are good athletes and that Asians excel in mathematics. Even here, however, they can create pressures and problems—for example, for African Americans who are not athletic or for Asians who are weak in math. Stereotypes may distort reality, but they nevertheless are images one group may hold about another.[31]

Stereotypes easily can become embedded within everyday thinking and serve to enhance a group's self-esteem and social identity by favorably comparing oneself to outgroups. Even if an outgroup is economically successful, stereotyping it as clannish, mercenary, or unscrupulous enables other groups to affirm their own moral superiority.

**FIGURE 4.1** **"Mutual: Both Are Glad There Are Bars Between 'Em!"**

*This visual stereotype of an apelike Irishman reinforced prevailing beliefs that the Irish were emotionally unstable and morally primitive. This cartoon appeared in* Judge *on November 7, 1891, and is typical of a worldwide tendency to depict minorities as apelike.*

Not only do stereotypes deny individuals the right to be judged and treated on the basis of their own personal merit, but also, by attributing a particular image to the entire group, they become a justification for discriminatory behavior. Negative stereotypes also serve as important reference points in people's evaluations of what they observe in everyday life. Following is an excellent illustration of how a prejudiced person arbitrarily uses stereotypes to interpret other people's behavior motives and behavior:

> Prejudiced people see the world in ways that are consistent with their prejudice. If Mr. Bigot sees a well-dressed, white, Anglo-Saxon Protestant sitting on a park bench sunning himself at three o'clock on a Wednesday afternoon, he thinks nothing of it. If he sees a well-dressed black man doing the same thing, he is liable to leap to the conclusion that the person is unemployed— and he becomes infuriated, because he assumes that his hard-earned taxes are paying that shiftless good-for-nothing enough in welfare subsidies to keep him in good clothes. If Mr. Bigot passes Mr. Anglo's house and notices

that a trash can is overturned and some garbage is strewn about, he is apt to conclude that a stray dog has been searching for food. If he passes Mr. Garcia's house and notices the same thing, he is inclined to become annoyed, and to assert that "those people live like pigs." Not only does prejudice influence his conclusions, his erroneous conclusions justify and intensify his negative feelings.[32]

Both dominant-group and minority-group members may hold stereotypes about each other. The activation of a stereotype in one's mind can validate negative thoughts about others.[33] Often, people are aware of the stereotypes others may have of them, and they may believe that more individuals hold that view than actually do. Stereotypes can affect both self-image and social interactions, creating social barriers to intergroup understanding and respect. Mass-media portrayals further reinforce stereotypes, giving such thinking a false aura of validity (see the Ethnic Experience box).

## Ethnophaulisms

An **ethnophaulism** is a derogatory word or an expression used to describe a racial or an ethnic group. This is the language of prejudice, the verbal picture of a negative stereotype that reflects the prejudice and bigotry of a society's past and present.

Ethnophaulisms fall into three types: (1) disparaging nicknames (e.g., chink, dago, polack, jungle bunny, honky, or Bruno, from the film of that name to disparage homosexuals); (2) alleged physical characteristics or foods (e.g., darky, skirt, porker, potato eater, frog, spaghetti eater); (3) alleged behaviors (e.g., "jew him down" for trying to get something for a lower price, "luck of the Irish" suggesting undeserved good fortune, "to be in Dutch" meaning to be in trouble, or "welsh" on a bet for failure to honor a debt).[34] The context of words is important. For example, the once derogatory expressions "Dutch treat" and "luck of the Irish" now have a neutral or positive connotation.

Both majority and minority groups coin and use *ethnophaulisms* to degrade groups. The emotional power of such labels has the effect of a less-than-human abstraction.[35] Such usage helps justify discrimination, inequality, and social privilege for the dominant group, and it helps the minority cope with social injustices caused by others. Them-versus-us name-calling is divisive, and the frequency of their usage reveals the degree of group prejudice in a society. In addition, people tend to express these negative terms more often as a function of the size, "foreignness," and appearance of groups.[36]

Sometimes members of a racial- or ethnic-minority group use an ethnophaulism directed against themselves in their conversations with one another. On occasion, they may use the term as a reprimand to one of their own kind for acting out the stereotype, but more often, they mean it as a humorous expression of friendship and endearment. However, when an outsider uses that same term, they resent it because of its prejudicial connotations.

The use of ethnophaulisms has behavioral consequences. For example, in an examination of archival research data spanning a 150-year period of U.S. history, Brian Mullen explored the effects of using ethnophaulisms in the representation of ethnic immigrant groups.[37] He found that the smaller, less familiar, and "more foreign" ethnic immigrant groups were typically portrayed in a simplistic and negative manner, with a corresponding tendency to exclude those groups from the host society. His study illustrates the "them" and "us" divisiveness, mentioned earlier, that results from the use of disparaging terms to refer to others.

## Ethnic Humor

Why do some people find ethnic jokes funny, whereas others find them distasteful? Studies show the response often reflects the listener's attitude toward the group being ridiculed. If you hold favorable or positive attitudes toward the group that is the butt of the joke, then you are less likely to find it funny than if you hold unfavorable or negative views. If you dislike a group about which a joke implies something negative, you will tend to appreciate the joke.[38]

A common minority practice is to use ethnic humor as a strategy for defining one's ethnicity positively. Lois Leveen suggests that, in telling ethnic jokes about one's own group, the speaker challenges stereotypes within the dominant culture.[39] If an ethnic tells the joke to the ethnic ingroup, the phenomenon of laughing together through joke sharing is "an ethnicizing phenomenon" that develops a sense of "we-ness" in laughing with others. If an ethnic tells that joke to outsiders, it can serve as a means to undermine the stereotype by ridiculing it. Ethnic humor can thus serve as a powerful force to facilitate a positive, empowered position for the ethnic individual within the dominant culture. Of course, we must realize that there is also the potential risk that the joke will confirm the stereotype, not undermine it.

## The Influence of Television

Virtually every U.S. household owns at least one television set, and families in the United States watch more than seven hours of TV daily, on average. Does all this viewing make us think or act differently? Does it change our attitudes or shape our feelings and reactions about minority groups? Or is it only entertainment with no appreciable effect on perceptions and behavior? Abundant research evidence indicates television programming distorts reality; promotes stereotypical role models; and significantly shapes and reinforces our attitudes about men, women, and minority groups (see the Reality Check box).

## Reality Check
## The Impact of the Media

As a reflector of society's values, the media have a tremendous impact on the shaping of our personal and group identities. Radio, television, films, newspapers, magazines, and comics can convey the rich textures of a pluralistic society or they can, directly or indirectly (by omission and distortion), alter our perception of other ethnic groups and reinforce our defensiveness and ambivalence about our own cultural backgrounds. As an Italian-American, I've realized this myself when comparing the ethnic invisibility of 50s television with modern shows that concentrate on Mafia hit men and multiple biographies of Mussolini. Having squirmed as I watched some of these portrayals, I can empathize with Arabs who resent being characterized as villainous sheikhs, Jews seen as mendacious moguls or even the current vogue for matching a Russian accent with a kind of oafish villainy. Although such stereotypes may or may not serve political ends, they share the cartoonlike isolation of a few traits that ignore the humanity and variety of a group's members.

What is the impact of ethnic stereotypes on TV and in films on how people feel about themselves and how they perceive other ethnic groups?

Although research in this area is limited, what is available suggests that TV and film's portrayal of ethnics does have a deleterious effect on perceptions of self and others. In my own clinical work, I have found that minority children and adults will often internalize negative stereotypes about their own group. Other studies have shown that ethnic stereotypes on television and in the movies can contribute to prejudice against a particular group—especially when the person is not acquainted with any members of that group. . . .

In studies of youngsters who commit hate acts—desecration of religious institutions, racial and anti-Semitic incidents—many youngsters apprehended reported they got the idea of performing vandalism from news coverage of similar acts (the copy cat syndrome). They saw media coverage as conferring recognition and prestige, temporarily raising their low self-esteem.

Add to TV fiction and news the rash of "truly tasteless" joke books, radio call-in shows that invite bigoted calls from listeners, late-night TV hosts and comedians who denigrate ethnic groups, and the impact on people's perceptions is considerable. While the media cannot be blamed for creating the bigotry, their insensitive reporting and encouragement of inflammatory comments establishes a societal norm that gives license to such attitudes and behavior.

*Source:* Joseph Giordano, "Identity Crisis: Stereotypes Stifle Self-Development." Accessed at http://www.sicilianculture.com/news/2002-idcrisis.htm on December 28, 2010.

## Perpetuation of Stereotypes

Twice in the late 1970s, the U.S. Commission on Civil Rights charged the television industry with perpetuating racial and sexual stereotypes in programming and news.[40] A generation later and a full decade into the

21st century, how much improvement do we see? In programs on some cable stations or small, independent stations, we can now find strong female, ethnic or racial lead characters. However, in news, commercials, and programming, many problems remain.

Studies of regular viewers reveal a strong association of their exposure to local or national newscasts and their racial attitudes and perceptions. They were more likely to think African Americans were poor, intimidating, violent, and/or criminal. They also were more prone to hold racially prejudiced views.[41]

Prime-time commercials still perpetuate traditional stereotypes of women and men.[42] "Distinct racial segregation" occurs in prime-time ads, with mostly Whites appearing in ads for upscale, beauty, or home products (with the notable exceptions of such celebrities as Halle Berry and Beyoncé). People of color, in contrast, appeared in ads for low-cost, low-nutrition products (e.g., fast food and soft drinks) and in athletic and sports equipment ads. Such depictions raise questions about the continuance of racial stereotypes, notably a somewhat one-dimensional view of people of color as key consumers of low-cost products.[43] The niche station, Black Entertainment Television (BET), is more likely to offer some positive Black female representations compared to the network stations, but they too are often portrayed in commercials as sexually desirable and available, continuing the problematic stereotyped representations of gender.[44] Even most major, active characters in commercials aired during children's cartoon programming are male, thus perpetuating stereotyped sex-typed behaviors, despite their decrease in the real world.[45]

Reality television shows such as *COPS, Deal or No Deal, The Contender,* and *The Real World* are edited or directed for desired effects and thus present characters from various races that reinforce stereotypes.[46] Other minorities, such as Asian and Pacific Islander Americans, are underrepresented, stereotyped, and marginalized in prime-time programs.[47] Female characters mostly inhabit interpersonal roles involved with romance, family, and friends, while male characters are more likely to enact work-related roles. Interestingly, shows with women writers or creators are likely to feature both female and male characters in interpersonal roles, whereas programs employing all-male writers and creators are more likely to feature both female and male characters in work roles.[48]

## Influencing of Attitudes

Television influences attitudes toward racial or ethnic groups by the status of the parts it assigns to their members, the kind of behavior they display within these parts, and even the type of products they promote. Television greatly influences children's attitudes in this area. Children watch television during prime time more than any other time of day. Yet prime time remains

*The MTV reality show, "Jersey Shore," followed eight young adults in a New Jersey beach house. Italian-American organizations denounced the show for using the word* guido *and portraying negative Italian-American stereotypes, but its young adult audience typically rejected such criticism, saying the cast only made themselves look bad, not Italian Americans. What explains these different reactions?*

overwhelmingly White, with people of color appearing largely in secondary and guest roles. Whites account for 73 percent of the prime-time population, followed by African Americans (16 percent), Latinos (4 percent), Asian/Pacific Islanders (3 percent), and Native Americans (0.2 percent). However, prime-time diversity dramatically increases as the evening progresses, with the 8 P.M. hour the least racially diverse and the 10 P.M. hour the most racially diverse. Thus, children and youths are more likely to see a much more homogeneous prime-time world than are adults who watch television later in the evening.[49]

*All in the Family*, a popular comedy series in the 1970s and still in syndicated reruns, received an NAACP award for its contribution to race relations but divided critics over the question of whether it reduced or reinforced racial bigotry. Liberal viewers saw the program as satire, with son-in-law Mike effectively rebutting Archie's ignorance and bigotry or minority members besting Archie by the end of the program. In contrast, prejudiced viewers—particularly adolescents—were significantly more likely to admire Archie more than Mike and to perceive Archie as the winner in the end.

Thus, the program probably reinforced prejudice and discrimination as much as it combated it.

Similarly, ethnic humor in such televisions shows as *South Park, The Simpsons,* or *The Family Guy,* along with such films as *Borat* and *Bruno,* has the same dangerous potential. Although these shows and movies can be viewed as humorous, exaggerated exposures of bigotry, they also can ring true to prejudiced individuals (see the Reality Check box). [50]

## The Influence of Advertising and Music

Social scientists are paying increasing attention to the impact of corporate advertising, rap music lyrics, and music videos on attitudes about men and women. Beyond the obviousness of marketing products and entertainment lie their powers of seduction, imagery, and conditioning of attitudes.

### Advertising

The average American watches three years' worth of television ads during the course of a lifetime. What effect do they have on our attitudes? In a content analysis of popular TV commercials designed for specific target audiences, researchers found the characters in them enjoyed more prominence and exercised more authority if they were Whites or males. Images of romantic and domestic fulfillment also differed by race and gender, with women and Whites disproportionately shown in family settings and in cross-sex interactions. In general, the researchers found that these commercials tended to portray White men as powerful, White women as sex objects, Black men as aggressive, and Black women as inconsequential. They suggest that these commercial images help perpetuate subtle prejudice against African Americans by exaggerating cultural differences and denying positive emotions.[51]

Another study of prime-time television ads found Blacks generally portrayed in a more diverse, equitable manner compared to Whites, but Asians, Hispanics, and Native Americans underrepresented and sometimes negatively depicted. Hispanics were often suggestively clad and shown engaging in alluring behaviors and sexual gazing, thus stressing physical appearance and sexuality over intelligence. Asians were most commonly young, passive adults at work in technology ads, thus promoting the stereotype of submissiveness and superior achievements as measures of their self-worth.[52]

Exploitation of women in ads is worse today than ever before, writes Jean Kilbourne, who points out that women—and girls, in particular—need to be mindful of the influential power of advertising. Women's bodies, frequently portrayed as headless torsos, have long been used to sell every-thing from toothbrushes to chain saws. In addition, endless glossy spreads in women's magazines feature beauty products, fashion, and diets to keep women focused on exterior "problems." She doesn't blame ads alone for demonizing fat women or causing binge drinking, teenage pregnancy, and violence against women. The cumulative effect is what appalls her. Taken together, she says, advertising fosters an inescapable, poisonous environment in which sexist stereotypes, cynicism and self-hatred, and the search for quick fixes flourish. Consumers may think they are unaffected, but advertisers successfully create a false consciousness and teach young women that they are appetizing only when "plucked, polished and painted."[53]

## Music

One of the major criticisms of rap music is that it may affect attitudes and behavior regarding the use of violence, especially violence against women. Although some rap artists—such as Arrested Development and Queen Latifah—reflect a concern for humanity and offer inspiration and hope, others—such as Eminem, 2 Live Crew, Apache, N.W.A., and Scarface—routinely endorse violence and homophobia and portray women as punching bags, strippers, or simply sperm receptacles. Such portrayals prompted the National Black Women's Political Caucus to seek legislation to control the access to rap music. In 2005, *Essence*, one of the leading magazines for Black women, launched a one-year "Take Back the Music" campaign against anti-women lyrics in rap music. In 2007, after the firing of radio personality Don Imus (now back on the air) for his racist remarks about the Rutgers University women's basketball team, some Black leaders next went after rap music producers to curtail offensive lyrics.

Pop culture has enormous influence on how young men and women see themselves and each other in terms of sexuality and gender. Powerful sexual imagery in hundreds of music videos, produced mostly by men, objectifies and dehumanizes women, frequently portraying them as existing solely for males' sexual satisfaction. In fact, one study found a strong link between increased exposure to rap music videos and problems with the law, drugs, and sexually transmitted diseases.[54]

## Can Prejudice Be Reduced?

Organized efforts to lessen or eliminate prejudice generally fall into one of three approaches: intergroup contact, education, and workplace diversity programs. No approach has been successful in all instances, probably because the inequalities that encourage prejudicial attitudes still exist.

## Interaction

Contact between people of different racial and ethnic backgrounds does not necessarily lead to friendlier attitudes. In fact, the situation may worsen if such contact is unwelcome, as happened frequently when schools and neighborhoods experienced an influx of people from a different group. However, interaction does reduce prejudice, depending on the frequency and duration of contacts; the relative status of the two parties and their backgrounds; and whether they meet in a political, religious, occupational, residential, or recreational situation.[55]

### Reality Check
### What You Can Do to Fight Prejudice and Racism

**Be honest:** Look at your own prejudices, biases, and values. Discuss your own experiences of being hurt by prejudice as well as the ways you have benefited from discrimination.

**Be secure:** Be proud of your own group identity. Having a sense of your own background will help reduce antagonism and suspicion toward others. Knowing your own strengths also will help you to see strengths in others.

**Be open-minded:** Don't be afraid of diversity and making friends with others. Don't let cultural difference stand in the way of friendship. Working together is one of the best ways to find out about others and undo prejudice.

**Be a role model:** Don't criticize others. Instead help to educate them about issues and about your own experiences. Lead by example.

**Be a friend:** Don't be afraid to offer support to victims of bullying and prejudice. Let them know that not everyone is a bully.

**Be active:** Work to reduce institutional discrimination and prejudice in government, corporations, the media, and other institutions.

**Be a member:** Support/join anti-prejudice and anti-racist organizations.

**Be vocal:** Don't be afraid to speak up against your peers if they are being offensive. It's not easy but you may find others will support your viewpoint if you take a stand.

**Be a listener:** Don't shut out other people's voices and opinions.

**Be a learner:** Remember no one has all the answers. Educate yourself and others. Reading books, seeing movies, and going to hear speakers about the experiences of other groups are some enjoyable ways to improve understanding and empathy.

Especially helpful here is the **contact hypothesis**, which speaks to the importance of contact for intergroup relations to improve. However, certain critical conditions are necessary for any intergroup interaction to have positive consequences. These include the necessity for members of different groups to:

1. Have equal status within the contact situation;
2. Work together cooperatively;
3. Pursue common goals;
4. Have institutional support from administrators;
5. Have time to allow cross-group friendships to develop.[56]

An important element, then, are the commonalities shared by the members of different groups in their joint efforts. If culturally different individuals are in a situation that is competitive, such as being rivals for a promotion, or forced, such as busing students to integrate a school, then increased hostility, not less, is a likely result. Only when the contact is positive does prejudice decrease. As minority group members experience upward mobility through better education and good-paying jobs, their entry into the middle class offers a good example of the contact hypothesis at work. The emerging cross-group friendships and work relationships typically lessen prejudices.

A good example of the significance of the type of contact emerges from the experiments in the **jigsaw classroom** of Elliot Aronson and Neal Osherow.[57] This research team observed that classroom competition for teacher recognition and approval often created a special hardship on minority children less fluent in English or less self-assured about participating in class. The researchers created interdependent learning groups of five or six children, each member charged with learning one portion of the day's lesson in a particular subject. The children learned the complete lesson from one another and then took a test on all the material. Because it creates interdependent groups, this technique is *not* the same as the cooperative learning approach so common in U.S. schools. In fact, Australian researchers compared use of the two approaches among children in grades 4 to 6 and found that the jigsaw classroom produced significant improvements on measures of academic performance, liking of peers, and racial prejudice, in contrast to the effect of the cooperative approach that exacerbated preexisting intergroup tensions.[58]

## Education

Many people have long cherished the hope that education would reduce prejudice. Evaluation research studies show that special programs aimed at promoting intergroup understanding do have a positive effect.[59] Still, these positive results are not necessarily universal among all students nor long-lasting among other students.

*Cooperative learning, where each child tells the others about parts of the lesson, is now a common teaching technique in U.S. elementary schools. Experiments by social scientists show that a variation of this approach, the jigsaw method, is also an effective means of reducing the walls of prejudice and social distance, while simultaneously building self-esteem and motivation in minority youngsters.*

One reason for this failure is that people tend to use **selective perception**; that is, they absorb information that accords with their own beliefs and rationalize away information that does not. Another reason is the almost quantum leap from a detached perspective in the classroom is one thing; dealing with it in everyday life is quite another because emotions, social pressures, and many other factors are involved.

Despite these criticisms, courses in race and ethnic relations certainly have value because they raise the students' level of consciousness about intergroup dynamics. However, a significant reduction or elimination of prejudice is more likely to occur by changing the structural conditions of inequality that promote and maintain prejudicial attitudes. As long as the dominant group does not react with fear and institute a countermovement, the improvement of a minority's social position changes power relations and reduces negative stereotypes. Therefore, continued efforts at public enlightenment and extension of constitutional rights and equal opportunities to all Americans, regardless of race, religion, or national origin, appear to be the most promising means of attaining an unprejudiced society.

One measure of shifting group positions is the expanding inclusiveness of the mainstream U.S. ingroup; previously excluded minority groups, once victims of prejudice, are gaining the social acceptance of structural assimilation. In its founding, the United States has experienced a changing definition of *mainstream "American"*—from only those whose ancestry was English, to the British (English, Welsh, Scots, and Scots Irish), to peoples from Northern and Western Europe, and now to all Europeans. People of color, however, have yet to gain unquestioned entry into this national cultural identity group, and that entry is the challenge before us.[60]

## Diversity Training

A workplace environment that promotes positive intergroup interaction is more efficient, has higher morale, and retains experienced personnel. Conversely, a hostile work environment has lower productivity, disgruntled personnel, and a higher attrition rate. Moreover, if an organization develops a reputation for insensitivity to diversity, it will attract fewer qualified job applicants among women and people of color, and businesses will lose market share by attracting fewer clients from our increasingly diverse society for their goods and services.

With women and non-White males now constituting 75 percent of the people entering the U.S. labor force, and with nearly 36 percent of the nation's enlisted military personnel identifying themselves as a minority, it has become critical for all organizations to take steps to prevent prejudice from creating dysfunctions within their daily operations.[61]

As someone who has conducted numerous diversity training workshops for military leaders and corporate management (including health care), let me give you some insight into these programs. The best ones heighten awareness by providing informational insights into the diversity of cultural value orientations, as well as into the current and future demographics of employees and clients. Most valuable in broadening perceptions is the inclusion of interactive learning sessions such as role-playing demonstrations of wrong and right handlings of situations and the creation of small groups to discuss and offer solutions to hypothetical but realistic problems.

Although programs vary greatly in their length, structure, and content, the most effective ones are comprehensive, actively supported by management as part of the organization's general mission statement, and fully integrated into all aspects of the organization. The latter includes a diversity orientation session for new employees, occasional reinforcement sessions for continuing employees, and all levels of management working together to promote an inclusive, hospitable work climate. Such efforts can make a significant contribution to reducing prejudice in the workplace.

How effective are these programs? The majority of studies conclude that they are effective, but a key variable appears to be selection bias. That is, when participants attend by choice, the positive effects are stronger.[62] Critics, however, say most interventions are not grounded in theory and there is little evidence of program impact. They call for action research to study and improve diversity training to achieve greater prejudice reduction.[63]

## Retrospect

The psychology of prejudice focuses on individuals' subjective states of mind, emphasizing the levels of prejudice held and the factors of self-justification, personality, frustration, and scapegoating. The sociology of prejudice examines the social forces in society behind prejudicial attitudes, such as socialization, economic competition, and social norms.

Stereotyping often reflects prejudice as a sense of group position. Once established, stereotypes are difficult to eradicate and often manifested in ethnophaulisms and ethnic humor. Television has a profound impact in shaping and reinforcing attitudes; unfortunately, it tends to perpetuate racial and sexual stereotypes instead of combating them.

Increased contact between groups and improved information do not necessarily reduce prejudice. The nature of the contact, particularly whether it is competitive or cooperative, is a key determinant. Information can develop heightened awareness as a means of improving relations, but external factors (economic conditions and social pressures) may override rational considerations.

The imagery in advertising, rap and hip hop music lyrics, and music videos can have a cumulative effect in shaping values about men and women. These images and words help perpetuate subtle prejudice and a false consciousness.

Diversity in the workplace, whether corporate or military, has prompted many organizations to create a more positive, inclusive environment through diversity training workshops. The most effective ones are comprehensive, actively supported by management, and fully integrated into all aspects of the organization.

## KEY TERMS

Action-orientation level of prejudice
Authoritarian personality
Cognitive level of prejudice
Contact hypothesis
Displaced aggression
Emotional level of prejudice
Ethnophaulism
Jigsaw classroom
Jim Crow laws

Prejudice
Relative deprivation
Scapegoating
Selective perception
Self-justification
Social norms
Socialization process
Stereotype

## DISCUSSION QUESTIONS

1. This chapter offers various causes of prejudice. Have you ever seen or experienced any examples of any of these causes?

2. What are some of the possible causes of prejudice?

3. What role does television play in combating or reinforcing stereotypes?

4. In what ways can advertising be harmful to minorities?

5. What are the criticisms against some rap music and music videos?

6. How can we reduce prejudice?

## INTERNET ACTIVITIES

1. At http://stop-the-hate.org, you'll find intriguing and inspiring quotations and poetry that also offer insights into how prejudice and hatred undermine the beauty of life.

2. At the Institute for Research on Poverty (www.irp.wisc.edu), you'll be able to access answers to frequently asked questions about poverty and also find relevant recent articles.

# CHAPTER 5

# Discrimination

*"In the end anti-black, anti-female, and all forms
of discrimination are equivalent to the same
thing—anti-humanism."*

—SHIRLEY CHISHOLM

Whereas prejudice is an attitudinal system, **discrimination** is actual behavior, the practice of differential and unequal treatment of other groups of people, usually along racial, religious, or ethnic lines. The Latin word *discriminatus*, from which the English word is derived, means "to divide or distinguish," and its subsequent negative connotation has remained relatively unchanged through the centuries.

## Levels of Discrimination

Actions, like attitudes, have different levels of intensity. As a result, discrimination may be analyzed at five levels. The first level is *verbal expression*, a statement of dislike or the use of a derogatory term. The next level is *avoidance*, in which the prejudiced person takes steps to avoid social interaction with a group. Actions of this type may include choice of residence, organizational membership, activities located in urban centers, and primary relationships in any social setting (see the Reality Check box).

At the third level, *exclusion* from certain jobs, housing, education, or social organizations occurs. In the United States, the practice of **de jure segregation** was once widespread throughout the South. Not only were children specifically assigned to certain schools to maintain racial separation, but segregationist laws kept all public places (theaters, restaurants, restrooms, transportation, etc.) racially separated as well. This exclusion can

# Reality Check
# Minority College Students and Discrimination

How do minority college students respond to encounters with discrimination or perceived discrimination? The answer, of course, depends on the individual and the situation, but several studies of different racial and ethnic groups reveal that strong social bonding is the common element that enables one to deal with such experiences without developing a negative self-image.

In examining the adjustment of Latina/o university students in predominantly White institutions, researchers found that those with strong family relationships and secure peer attachments had a healthy self-worth image. Parental support and encouragement for their children in meeting the demands of college, as well as similar positive back-up from peers, helped Latina/o students overcome that ethnic negativity and instead feel good about themselves. Such healthy self-esteem thus served to mediate any distress experienced by feelings of marginalization and/or discriminatory victimization that other studies often report occurring.

Numerous studies have revealed that African American college students view their campus climate as more negative than White students. A recent study of students of color (African Asian, and Hispanic American) at a small, mostly White university campus reconfirmed their frustration with the lack of awareness that led White students, faculty, and staff to deny the existence of the racism that was part of everyday life for the participants. As a result, they felt the need to connect with other students of color for support in coping with these frustrations, and also felt as if they lived in a separate world due to that lack of awareness.

Another study of Chinese-American college students at an ethnically diverse university in Northern California found that their sense of family obligation had a positive association with their ethnic engagement and ethnic pride. Furthering these self-affirming responses were such community factors as ethnic density and cultural resources. Perceived discrimination, however, both promoted and hindered their strong ethnic identity. Students responded with greater ethnic engagement (interacting more fully with ingroup members) but were also less inclined to feel a sense of ethnic pride, given their perception of discrimination.

Although discrimination might be a widespread societal problem, it is experienced on a personal level. Even so, it appears that one of the best counteractions for one's own mental health is through strong attachment relationships and interactions within one's own group.

*Sources:* Derived from Patton O. Garriott, et al., "Testing an Attachment Model of Latina/o College Students' Psychological Adjustment,"*Hispanic Journal of Behavioral Sciences* 32 (2010): 103–17; Gina Zanolini Morrison, "Two Separate Worlds: Students of Color at a Predominantly White University," *Journal of Black Studies* 40 (2010): 987–1015; Linda P. Juang and Huong H. Nguyen, "Ethnic Identity Among Chinese-American Youth: The Role of Family Obligation and Community Factors on Ethnic Engagement, Clarity, and Pride," *Identity: An International Journal of Theory and Research* 10 (2010): 20–38.

also take the form of **de facto segregation** as residential patterns become embedded in social customs and institutions. Thus, the standard practice of building and maintaining neighborhood schools in racially segregated communities creates and preserves segregated schools.

Another form of exclusion is **redlining**—designating certain neighborhoods as "bad risk" areas for mortgages and home improvement loans. Although this is an illegal practice, it still occurs, creating a self-fulfilling prophecy. With owners unable to secure loans to fix up their properties and potential buyers unable to obtain mortgages for properties in such areas, market values drop, and the neighborhood declines, intensifying the racial segregation in that area. Such mortgage disinvestment is most common in African American neighborhoods.[1]

The fourth level of discrimination is *physical abuse*—violent attacks on members of the disliked group. Unfortunately, this behavior still occurs often in the United States. The Prejudice Institute applies **ethnoviolence** to a range of actions—verbal harassment and threats, vandalism, graffiti, swastika painting, arson, cross burning, physical assault, and murder—committed against people targeted solely because of their race, religion, ethnic background, or sexual orientation.[2] Thousands of incidents of ethnoviolence against members of various minority groups occur each year throughout the United States on college campuses and in both suburban and urban areas.

The most extreme level of discrimination is *extermination*: the massacres, genocide, or pogroms conducted against a people. Such barbarous actions, from the monstrous actions of Stalin in the 1930s and the Nazis in the 1940s, continue to occur in modern times. Among the more recent examples are the killings in Bosnia, Rwanda, and Darfur.

## Relationships between Prejudice and Discrimination

Prejudice can lead to discrimination, and discrimination can lead to prejudice, or neither can lead to the other. There is no simplistic cause-effect relationship. Our attitudes and our overt behavior are closely related, but they are not identical. We may harbor hostile feelings toward certain groups without ever making them known through word or deed. Conversely, our overt behavior may effectively conceal our real attitudes.

Prejudiced people are more likely than others to practice discrimination and so discrimination quite often represents the overt expression of prejudice. It is wrong, however, to assume that discrimination is always the simple acting out of prejudice. Instead it may be the result of a policy decision protecting the interests of the majority group, as happens when legal immigration is curtailed for economic reasons. It may be due to social

| Prejudiced | Discriminates | |
| --- | --- | --- |
| | No | Yes |
| No | All-weather liberal | Fair-weather liberal |
| Yes | Timid bigot | Active bigot |

FIGURE 5.1    **Relationships between Prejudice and Discrimination**

conformity, as when people submit to outside pressures despite their personal views. Sometimes discriminatory behavior may precede prejudicial attitudes as, for example, when organizations insist that all job applicants take aptitude or IQ tests based on middle-class experiences and then form negative judgments of lower-income people who do not score well.

Robert Merton created a model showing how relationships between prejudice and discrimination can vary (Figure 5.1). He illustrated that an unprejudiced person in fact may discriminate and a prejudiced person might not do so. In his four categories, Merton classified people according to how they accept or reject the American Creed: "the right of equitable access to justice, freedom and opportunity, irrespective of race or religion, or ethnic origin."[3]

*The Unprejudiced Nondiscriminator.*    Unprejudiced nondiscriminators, or all-weather liberals, are not prejudiced and do not discriminate. Merton observes, though, that they often are not in direct contact or competition with minority group members. They talk chiefly to others who share their viewpoint, and so they deceive themselves into thinking that they represent the consensus. Furthermore, because their "own spiritual house is in order," they feel no pangs of conscience pressing them to fight discrimination elsewhere. Despite Merton's pessimism, many unprejudiced nondiscriminators are activists and do what they can to reduce prejudice and discrimination in society.

*The Unprejudiced Discriminator.*    Expediency is the byword for these "fair-weather liberals," for their actions often conflict with their personal beliefs. For example, they may be free of racial prejudice, but they will join clubs that exclude racially different people, they will vote for unfair measures if they would benefit materially from these measures, and they will support efforts to keep certain minorities out of their neighborhood for fear of its deterioration. These people frequently feel guilt and shame because they are acting against their beliefs.

*The Prejudiced Nondiscriminator.*   Merton's term *timid bigots* best describes prejudiced nondiscriminators. They believe in many stereotypes about other groups and definitely feel hostility toward these groups. However, they keep silent in the presence of those who are more tolerant; they conform because they must. If there were no law or pressure to avoid bias in certain actions, they would discriminate.

*The Prejudiced Discriminator.*   Prejudiced discriminators are active bigots. They demonstrate no conflict between attitudes and behavior. Not only do they openly express their beliefs, practice discrimination, and defy the law if necessary, but they consider such conduct virtuous.

The unprejudiced discriminator and the prejudiced nondiscriminator are the most sociologically interesting classifications because they demonstrate that social-situational variables often determine whether discriminatory behavior occurs. The pressure of group norms may force individuals to act in a manner inconsistent with their beliefs.

## Social and Institutional Discrimination

Discriminatory practices are encountered frequently in the areas of employment and residence, although such actions often are concealed and denied by those who take them. Another dimension of discrimination, often unrealized, is **social discrimination**—the creation of a "social distance" between groups that we discussed in Chapter 1. Simply stated, in their close, primary relationships, people tend to associate with others of similar ethnic background and socioeconomic level; thus, dominant-group members usually exclude minority-group members from close relations with them. Therefore, we can make a distinction between *active* and *passive* discrimination. In the first, one takes action against someone, while in the second, one's silent acquiescence to others' discriminatory actions is still a form of discrimination, just as theologians speak of sins of omission as well as sins of commission.

Discrimination is more than the biased actions of individuals, however. In their influential book, *Black Power* (1967), Stokely Carmichael and Charles Hamilton called attention to the fact that far greater harm occurs from **institutional discrimination**—the unequal treatment of subordinate groups inherent in the ongoing operations of society's institutions.[4]

Entrenched in customs, laws, and practices, these discriminatory patterns can exist in banking, criminal justice, employment, education, health care, housing, and many other areas in the private and public sectors. Critical to understanding this concept is the fact the practices are so widespread that individuals helping to perpetuate them may be completely unaware of their existence. Examples are:

1. Banks rejecting home mortgage applications of minorities;
2. Sentencing inequities in the criminal justice system;
3. The concentration of minorities in low-paying jobs;
4. The former "separate but equal" educational structure in the South;
5. Segregated housing.

## Residential Segregation

Picking up on the last point, racial residential segregation remains stubbornly rooted in the nation's older cities, where Blacks and Whites always have lived apart (see Figure 5.2). Although Blacks remain the most segregated group, they are less segregated than 10 years ago. Meanwhile, Hispanics increasingly are living in ethnic enclaves where none existed a decade ago; Asian segregation also is increasing in numerous metropolitan areas.[5] Hispanics, however, are more segregated than they were a decade ago.

   This pattern holds true from coast to coast, in cities and suburbs, and in every region of the country. Nationally, fewer than 4 in 10 non-Hispanic Whites live in nearly all-White neighborhoods compared to more than half in 1990. Only in the Midwest do the majority of Blacks live in nearly all-Black neighborhoods. The lowest levels of Black–White segregation are in the high-growth Sunbelt, which attracts both Whites and minorities, thereby generating a growing share of Americans living in areas where the two races mix freely.

   Of the 50 metropolitan areas with the largest Black populations, those with the highest levels of segregation (in descending order) are Detroit, Milwaukee, New York City, Newark, Cleveland, and Cincinnati. Such urban residential segregation limits job opportunities for minorities and prevents them from moving closer to suburban jobs.[6] Suburbia also is becoming more integrated, although its outer rings still are mostly White. Despite the notion advanced by some that middle-class Blacks are almost as segregated from Whites as are poor Blacks, researchers, controlling for numerous socioeconomic characteristics, found that they are not. These suburban Blacks have far more White neighbors than do low-income, inner-city Blacks, although their White neighbors often are less affluent than they are. It would appear that race still powerfully shapes their residential options, even if they are less segregated than poor Blacks.[7]

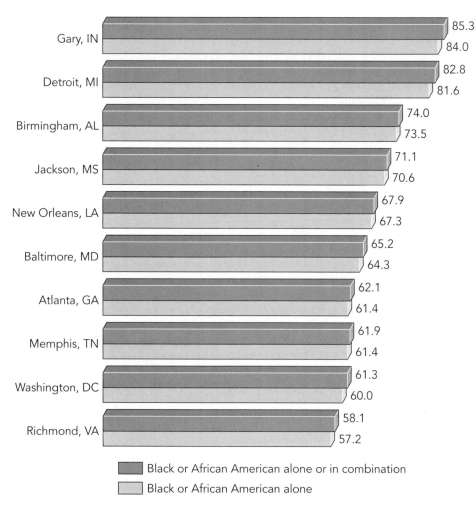

FIGURE 5.2 **Major Cities with Largest Black Populations, by percentage**

## Religion

Another form of institutional discrimination can be found in religious bigotry. Throughout U.S. history, religious minorities have fallen victim to systemic biased actions. Whenever a dominant group feels that its self-interests—such as primacy and the preservation of cherished values—are threatened, reactionary and discriminatory measures usually result Numerous studies have found that the dominant group will not hesitate to act discriminatorily if it thinks that this approach will effectively undercut the minority group as a social or an economic competitor[8] (see the International Scene box).

## The International Scene
## Discrimination in Northern Ireland

The population of Northern Ireland exceeds 1.5 million, of whom about 53 percent are Protestants with loyalties to the overwhelmingly Protestant United Kingdom and about 44 percent are Catholics with a preference for unification with the Catholic-dominated Republic of Ireland. Despite some progress toward reconciliation since the 1998 peace agreement, it remains today a polarized society, its sporadic violence fed by centuries of deep-seated hostility.

Sociologically, Catholics are the minority group, with limited political power. They are more likely than Protestants to be poor, to suffer prolonged unemployment, and to live in substandard housing in segregated communities. Catholics tend to be in low-status, low-skill jobs and Protestants in high-status, high-skill positions. It is difficult, however, to determine whether these employment patterns result from overt job discrimination, from structural factors of community segregation, education, and class, or from both.

Although the degree of actual discrimination employed to maintain their dominance is unclear, Protestants rationalize about the situation through a set of negative beliefs about Catholics. Many Protestants stereotype Catholics as lazy welfare cheats who are dirty, superstitious, and ignorant. They also view them as oversexed (as "proved" by the typically larger size of Catholic families) and brainwashed by priests, whose primary allegiance, they say, is to a foreign entity—the Pope. Moreover, many Protestants suspect that Catholics are intent on undermining the Ulster government to force reunification with the Republic of Ireland. Most Protestants see no discrimination on the basis of religion in jobs, housing, and other social areas. Catholics "get what they deserve" because of their values, attitudes, and disloyalty.

For their part, most Catholics in Northern Ireland strongly believe that they suffer from discrimination as a direct consequence of their religion. They view Protestants as narrow-minded bigots who stubbornly hold onto political power and have no desire to relinquish any part of it. A vicious circle of prejudice and discrimination, despite the peace accord, intensifies Protestant resistance to sharing power and Catholic reluctance to support the government.

Not yet fully implemented, the hard-fought pragmatism and promise of the 1998 peace accord could still fall victim to political opportunism, fickle public opinion, or the evil intent of the radicals on both sides, who have never agreed to forswear the use of bombs and murder to pursue their political ends.

In contrast, Protestants living in the Republic of Ireland, who constitute only 3 percent of that population, live in harmony with their Catholic neighbors. They are fully integrated socioeconomically and do not, for the most part, experience prejudice.

*Critical thinking question:*    What must be done to reduce the prejudice and discrimination that sows the seeds of violence in Northern Ireland?

# The Affirmative-Action Controversy

At what point do efforts to secure justice and equal opportunities in life for one group infringe on the rights of other groups? Is justice a utilitarian concept—the greatest happiness for the greatest number? Or is it a moral concept—a sense of good that all people share? Is the proper role of government to foster a climate in which people have equal opportunity to participate in a competitive system of occupations and rewards, or should government ensure equal results in any competition? These issues have engaged moral and political philosophers for centuries, and they go to the core of the affirmative-action controversy.

## The Concepts of Justice, Liberty, and Equality

More than 2,300 years ago, Plato wrote in the *Republic* that justice must be relative to the needs of the people who are served, not to the desires of those who serve them. For example, physicians must make patients' health their primary concern if they are to be just. In *A Theory of Justice* (2005, 1971), John Rawls interpreted justice as fairness, which maximizes equal liberty for all.[9] To provide the greatest benefit to the least advantaged, society must eliminate social and economic inequalities, by placing minority persons in offices and positions that are open to all under conditions of fair equality of opportunity. Both men saw the ideal society as well ordered and strongly pluralistic: Each component performs a functionally differentiated role in working harmony; society must arrange its practices to make this so.

Americans, though, often have been more concerned with liberty than with equality, identifying liberty with the absence of government interference. When government becomes more powerful, bringing an area of activity under its control or regulation (like health care), to that extent equality (health insurance coverage for all) replaces liberty (freedom to choose coverage) as the dominant ideal and constitutional demand. In contrast, those who insist on constitutional rights for all are not demanding the removal of government restraints but instead are asking for positive government action to provide equal treatment for the less powerful.[10]

The quest for equality thus curtails the liberty of others and has led to some to denounce "big brother" interference with calls to "get the government off our backs." Critics counter that "the greater good" sometimes outweighs individual choice, as it also does in wartime restrictions or the public confiscation of private property for redevelopment ("eminent domain"). Since the 1960s, responsibility for promoting individual rights has increasingly been placed on the federal government.

## Affirmative Action Begins

We can trace the origin of government affirmative-action policy to July 1941, when President Franklin D. Roosevelt issued Executive Order 8802, obligating defense contractors "not to discriminate against any worker because of race, creed, color, or national origin." Subsequent executive orders by virtually all presidents continued or expanded the government's efforts to curb discrimination in employment. President Kennedy's Executive Order 10925 in 1961 was the first to use the term **affirmative action**; it stipulated that government contractors would "take affirmative action that applicants are employed, and that employees are treated during employment, without regard to their race, creed, color, or national origin."

The legal basis for affirmative action appears to rest on two points. Passage of the Thirteenth Amendment, which abolished slavery, also set the precedent for action against any vestiges of slavery manifest through racial discrimination.[11] Both supporters and opponents, however, point to Title VII, Section 703(j), of the 1964 Civil Rights Act as the keystone of their positions on affirmative action.

Title VII seems to address the need for fairness, openness, and color-blind equal opportunity. It specifically bans preference by race, ethnicity, gender, and religion in business and government. Opponents claim that this clear language outlawing preferences makes affirmative action unnecessary and illegal. Supporters contend that President Lyndon Johnson's Executive Order 11246 is linked to Title VII by mandating employer affirmative-action plans to correct existing deficiencies through specific goals and deadlines. This was, supporters say, a logical step from concern about equal rights to concern about actual equal opportunity.[12]

Addressing an expanded list of protected categories (Asians, Blacks, Hispanics, Native Americans, women, the aged, people with disabilities, and homosexuals), an array of state and federal policy guidelines began to regulate many aspects of business, education, and government practices. Legislation in 1972 amended the 1964 Civil Rights Act, giving the courts the power to enforce affirmative-action standards. Preference programs became the rule, through reserved minority quotas in college and graduate school admissions and in job hirings and promotions, as well as through government set-aside work contracts for minority firms.[13]

## Court Challenges and Rulings

The resentment of Whites over "reverse discrimination" crystallized in the 1978 *Regents of the University of California v. Bakke* case, when the U.S. Supreme Court ruled that quotas were not permitted but race could be a factor in university admissions. In a separate opinion, Justice Harry A. Blackmun stated:

> In order to get beyond racism, we must first take account of race. There is no other way. And in order to treat some persons equally, we must treat them differently. We cannot—we dare not—let the Equal Protection Clause perpetuate racial superiority.[14]

For the next 11 years, the Court upheld the principle of affirmative action in a series of rulings (see Table 5.1). Since 1989, however, a more conservative court has shown a growing reluctance to use "race-conscious remedies"—the practice of trying to overcome the effects of past discrimination by helping minorities. This has been true not only in affirmative-action cases involving jobs and contracts but in school desegregation and voting rights as well. The 1995 *Adarand Constructors v. Peña* decision scaled back the federal government's own affirmative-action program, mandating "strict scrutiny and evidence" of alleged past discrimination, not just a "general history of racial discrimination in the nation." In another 1995 decision, the Supreme Court declared that race could no longer be the "predominant factor" in drawing congressional districts—or by implication, any jurisdiction for any government body, from school boards to state legislatures.

In 1995, the California Board of Regents banned affirmative action for graduate and undergraduate admissions. The following year, California voters overwhelmingly passed the California Civil Rights Initiative that dismantled state affirmative-action programs. Also in 1996, a sweeping ruling by the U.S. Circuit Court of Appeals in *Hopwood v. Texas* banned affirmative action in admissions, scholarships, and outreach programs. When Florida ended its affirmative-action program in 1999, three of the four largest states in the nation (New York excluded) and the three with the largest high school and college populations had rescinded affirmative action for the purpose of achieving racial and ethnic diversity.

What was the impact on minority enrollments? By 2005, it was clear that California fared the worst, with its Black freshmen enrollments at major universities down an average of 50 percent. In Texas and Florida, however, special initiatives—that, respectively, guaranteed college admission to the top 10 or 20 percent of high school graduates—lessened the effect somewhat. Buoyed by a growing population, Hispanic enrollments remained fairly constant in California and increased in the other two states. Asians benefited the most, while White enrollment declined slightly, partly reflective of changing societal demographics.[15]

In 2003, a 5–4 Supreme Court decision preserved affirmative action in university admissions at the University of Michigan law school, while at the same time striking down that university's undergraduate admissions

**TABLE 5.1    Affirmative Action: Five Decades of Actions and Decisions**

| | |
|---|---|
| **1964** | The Civil Rights Act of 1964 prohibits discrimination based on race, color, religion, sex, or national origin in public accommodations, transportation, public education, and federally assisted programs. |
| **1972** | Legislation authorizes the courts to enforce affirmative-action standards. |
| **1978** | The Court ruled that racial quotas are illegal but colleges and universities could consider race as one factor in admitting students. |
| **1980** | The Court ruled that a federal public works program that set aside 10 percent of its spending for minority contractors was constitutional. |
| **1981** | The Court ruled that Hartford, Connecticut, could require that 15 percent of all workers on city-financed projects be women or minorities. |
| **1987** | For the first time, the Court upheld an affirmative-action plan for women, ruling that companies can give special preferences to hire and promote female employees to create a more balanced work force. |
| **1989** | The Court threw out a set-aside program in Richmond, Virginia, in which contractors on city building contracts were required to give at least 30 percent of the project to firms at least one-half minority owned. |
| **1990** | The Court upheld federal policies favoring women and minorities in granting broadcasting licenses. |
| **1995** | The Court set a stricter standard on state programs or laws designed to help minorities. Only race-based preferences narrowly tailored to address identifiable past discrimination would be deemed constitutional. |
| **1996** | The Court declined to hear an appeal of a Fifth U.S. Circuit Court of Appeals ruling that "race itself cannot be taken into account" by the University of Texas in admitting students to its law school, which knocked down its affirmative-action admissions plan. |
| **1996** | The Court ordered the Virginia Military Institute to admit women or give up state funding. The decision also affected The Citadel, South Carolina's state-run military school. |
| **1996** | Californians voted to forbid any consideration of race, gender, or national origin in hiring or school admissions. |
| **1997** | The Court declined to hear a challenge to California's Proposition 209, the measure that banned race or gender from being a factor in state hiring or school admission. |
| **1998** | Washington state voters eliminated all preferential treatment based on race or gender in government hiring and school admissions. |
| **2000** | Florida ended the consideration of race in university admissions and state contracts, instead calling for more aid based on financial need. |
| **2003** | The Court upheld an affirmative-action program at the University of Michigan law school but struck down the university's system that awarded extra points to minorities in its points-based admissions policy. |
| **2006** | The Court ruled as unconstitutional the programs in Seattle and Louisville, Kentucky, which tried to maintain diversity in schools by considering race when assigning students to schools. |

*(Continued)*

**TABLE 5.1    Affirmative Action: Five Decades of Actions
and Decisions    (*Continued*)**

| | |
|---|---|
| 2008 | Nebraska voters approved a ban on affirmative action; Colorado voters did not. |
| 2009 | The Court ruled in favor of New Haven firefighters, stating that the city cannot ignore test results for fear of litigation by minority applicants. |

program that used a point system based in part on race. Its endorsement of the role of racial diversity on campus in achieving a more equal society strengthened the solitary view of Justice Lewis Powell at the time of the *Bakke* decision that there was a "compelling state interest" in racial diversity. At the same time, the Court suggested a time limit on such programs, with Justice Sandra Day O'Connor writing in the majority opinion, "We expect that 25 years from now the use of racial preferences will no longer be necessary to further the interest approved today."[16]

*In 2003, as the U.S. Supreme Court justices heard arguments for and against the use of affirmative action in admissions decisions at the University of Michigan, demonstrators outside made their views known. The Court's subsequent 5–4 ruling was a broad one, endorsing continuance of this practice, but under broad guidelines not intended for an indefinite period.*

The Court's 5–4 ruling in 2009 in *Ricci v. DeStefano* in favor of 18 White (including one Hispanic) New Haven firefighters brought another interpretation to the issue of affirmative action. In this case, the justices said promotion test results cannot be tossed out over fear of litigation because they favored Whites.

With so many close decisions and new Supreme Court justices on the bench even as others near retirement, new challenges to a differently constituted court may result in different rulings.

## Has Affirmative Action Worked?

Evidence about the success of affirmative-action programs is as mixed as public debate on the subject. Research on the impact of affirmative action offers "compelling evidence" that it does increase employment, college enrollments, and minority contracts, with opportunities for White males decreasing only slightly. Women appear to have benefited the most, and no significant negative effect on productivity or performance occurred in organizations where such programs existed.[17]

Although some of the motivations behind the challenges to affirmative action may well be racist or sexist, the preservation of White privilege and conservative political ideology appear to be more significant underpinnings. Addressing this point in defense of affirmative action, Tim J. Wise argues that reverse discrimination is a myth fueled by White hysteria, and he insists "affirmative action remains important and necessary because racism remains prevalent and damaging to the life prospects of people of color in the United States."[18]

Still, some minority group spokespersons, conservatives themselves, have also spoken against affirmative action, arguing that it has had a destructive influence on their own communities. Thomas Sowell (Black) and Linda Chavez (Latina) maintain that universities recruit talented minority students away from local colleges where they might do very well and into learning environments where the competition for grades is intense. Opponents also argue that affirmative action is "misplaced condescension" that has poisoned race relations and that the achievements of minorities become tainted by the assumption that they resulted from special favorable treatment rather than being earned on merit.[19]

## Public Opinion

When asked in a 2009 NBC/*Wall Street Journal* nationwide poll about affirmative action, 63 percent said it was still needed and 28 percent said it should be ended. A 2009 AP-GfK national poll found 56 percent in favor of affirmative action programs for racial and ethnic minorities and 63 percent approving such programs for women. In contrast, a 2009 Quinnipiac national poll found Americans evenly divided with 20 percent endorsing affirmative action program to overcome discrimination, another 27 percent in favor to increase diversity, but 47 percent saying we should not have such programs at all.[20] Interestingly, other studies also show a public acceptance of programs to increase diversity but opposition for ones "to overcome past discrimination." Follow-up questions reveal that respondents' thinking that "the past is the past" is not a denial of historic events, but they dismiss their connection to today's racial realities.[21]

Although divided about preferences based on race and gender (Blacks less in opposition than Whites), most Americans seem willing to support affirmative action based on economic class.[22] Under such a provision, for example, the White son of a poor coal miner in West Virginia could be eligible for special help, but the daughter of an affluent African American stockbroker would not.

Even as affirmative action withers in some states, it continues in others. Proposed federal legislation in the Congress would end it everywhere. Supporters of affirmative action argue "mend it, don't end it," whereas opponents urge that it be dismantled completely. The next few years undoubtedly will see a continuing battle and perhaps significant changes in affirmative action as we know it.

## Racial Profiling

Although racial profiling has a long history, only in recent years have the government and public given it so much attention. **Racial profiling** refers to action taken by law enforcement officials on the basis of race or ethnicity instead of an individual's behavior. Such thinking, for instance, has led authorities to routinely stop vehicles driven by Blacks and Latinos in the expectation of finding drugs in their possession. Their experiences led Blacks to use the term "driving while black" or "DWB" to express their outrage about such discriminatory practices.[23]

Some argue that overall discrepancies in crime rates among racial groups justify such profiling in traffic enforcement activities to produce a greater number of arrests for non-traffic offenses (narcotics trafficking, for example). Critics contend that an emphasis on minority-group drug use would naturally result in more minority arrests. In fact, a 2009 Human Rights Watch report covering the last three decades revealed that, even though Blacks and Whites engage in drug offenses—possession and sales—at roughly comparable rates, Blacks are the principal targets of the "war on drugs" and thus are three to six times more likely to be arrested. This occurs because, even though Whites are just as likely to be pulled over in routine traffic actions as are minorities, Blacks and Hispanics are far more likely to have their vehicles searched.[24]

In the 1990s, racial profiling received a great deal of attention through media exposés, special reports, commissions, and legislative initiatives. In 2001, the U.S. government took steps and acted to ban it in federal law enforcement, but the terrorist attacks later that year changed the government view of racial profiling from an undesirable police activity to one of necessity for national security. As a result, airline security, customs officials, and police place Arab and Muslim Americans under special scrutiny, and immigration officials prosecute them for minor violations often ignored for resident aliens of other ethnic backgrounds. In national surveys, more than half of all Americans favor the racial profiling of Arab male airline passengers.[25]

In 2003, the U.S. Department of Justice issued guidelines rejecting racial profiling. It argued that such activity is immoral and perpetuates negative racial stereotypes that are "harmful to our diverse democracy, and materially impair our efforts to maintain a fair and just society." However, in that same statement, it included a broad and largely undefined exception

*Although police officers have an obligation to stop motorists who commit traffic violations, members of the Black community complain that often they get stopped for no other cause than "DWB," or "driving while black." After 9/11, national security concerns extended racial profiling specifically to Arabs and Muslims, an action some see as necessary and others decry as biased.*

when "national security" concerns come into play.[26] At the present time, then, a dichotomy exists between racial profiling attitudes and actions.

Pressure from the media, coupled with changes in police leadership, though, can reduce racial inequality in aggressive enforcement practices. Such was the finding of a study comparing traffic stop data in 2001 and 2005 in Rhode Island.[27] However, a contradictory finding was reported by the American Civil Liberties Union (ACLU) in four reports covering 2005–2006 that detailed how racial minorities in Rhode Island were disproportionately stopped in virtually every municipality and were twice as likely as White drivers to be searched, even though they were *less* likely to be found with contraband.[28]

## Retrospect

Discriminatory behavior operates at five levels of intensity: verbal expression, avoidance, exclusion, physical abuse, and extermination. Discrimination is not necessarily an acting-out of prejudice. Social pressures may oblige unprejudiced individuals to discriminate or may prevent prejudiced people from discriminating. Social and institutional discrimination still exists, particularly in racial residential segregation and in manifestations of religious bigotry.

The debate over affirmative action involves these questions: Is it a democratic government's responsibility to provide a climate for equal opportunity or to ensure equal results? If the latter, at what point do efforts to secure equality for one group infringe on the rights of other groups? After several decades of implementation, affirmative-action programs face dismantling through court decisions, public initiatives, and legislative actions, even as others insist that these programs are necessary.

Racial profiling remains a serious concern, given its mixed interpretation since the 2001 terrorist attacks.

## KEY TERMS

Affirmative action

De facto segregation

De jure segregation

Discrimination

Ethnoviolence

Institutional discrimination

Racial profiling

Redlining

Social discrimination

# DISCUSSION QUESTIONS

1. What is discrimination? What are some of its manifestations?

2. What is the relationship between prejudice and discrimination?

3. Why would institutional discrimination be difficult to eliminate?

4. What is the intent of affirmative action?

5. Some Whites and minority leaders complain about affirmative action as unfair and attaching a stigma to minority achievement. Still other Whites and minority leaders say it is still necessary to create a level playing field. What do you think and why?

6. Is racial profiling always bad? Why or why not?

# INTERNET ACTIVITIES

1. At http://results.about.com/affirmative_action/, you will find pro and con arguments on affirmative action, as well as a wealth of other material on this subject.

2. The U.S. Department of Justice released a Resource Guide on Racial Profiling (www.ncjrs.gov/pdffiles1/bja/184768.pdf), in which you will gain insights into its nature and extent, as well as a profile of several states' experiences in this area.

# CHAPTER 6

# Dominant–Minority Relations

*"We've learned to fly the air like birds, we've learned to swim the seas like fish, and yet we haven't learned to walk the earth as brothers and sisters."*

—MARTIN LUTHER KING, JR.

So far, we have looked at people's behavioral patterns in relating to strangers, the role of culture and social structure in shaping perceptions and interactions, and the complexities of prejudice and discrimination. In this chapter, we examine response patterns that dominant and minority groups follow in their dealings with each other.

The following pages suggest that these patterns occur in varying degrees for most groups, regardless of race, ethnicity, or time period. They are not mutually exclusive categories, and groups do not necessarily follow all these patterns at one time. To some degree, though, each minority or dominant group in any society shares these pattern commonalities. Before we examine these general patterns, two cautionary notes are necessary. First, all groups are not alike, for each has its own unique beliefs, habits, and history. And second, variations *within* a group prevent any group from being a homogeneous entity.

## Minority-Group Responses

Although personality characteristics play a large role in determining how individuals respond to unfavorable situations, behavioral patterns for almost any group are similar to those of other groups in comparable circumstances.

External factors play an important role, but social interpretation is also a critical determinant, as explained in the next section on ethnic- and racial-group identity. Also, the minority group's perception of its power resource significantly influences its response, which may include avoidance, deviance, defiance, acceptance, and negative self-image.[1]

## Ethnic- and Racial-Group Identity

Any group unable to participate fully in the societal mainstream typically develops its own group identity. This is a normal pattern in ingroup–outgroup relationships. In the field of race and ethnic relations, group identity can serve as a basis for positive encounters, a source of comfort and strength, or entry into the mainstream. It can also be a foundation for prejudice and discrimination, negative self-image, a barrier to social acceptance, or a source of conflict.

*Ethnic-group identity* exists when individuals choose to emphasize cultural or national ties as the basis for their primary social interactions and sense of self. Leaving the taken-for-granted world of their homeland, immigrants—as strangers in a strange land—become more self-conscious of their group identity. Even as the acculturation process and ethnogenesis unfold, these group members retain some of the "cultural baggage" they brought with them and see themselves—as does the mainstream society—as possessing distinctiveness because of their ethnicity.

Many factors determine the duration of an ethnic-group identity. A cohesive ethnic community, continually revitalized by the steady influx of newcomers, will maintain a strong resilience. Ethnic-minority media can play a significant role in strengthening that sense of identity. Indeed, minority media can even affect the assimilation process, either by promoting it (as did the New York *Daily Forward* newspaper among Jewish immigrants in the late nineteenth and early twentieth centuries) or by delaying that process by stressing the retention of language, customs, and values.

Socialization into one's own ethnic group also promotes this identity. Part of the growing-up process for minorities often involves the existence of a dual identity: one in the larger society and another within one's own group. This multiple reality affects one's roles, behavior, and sense of self, depending on the social setting.

Ethnic-group identity can be especially protracted on the basis of religion. Some good examples are persistent subcultures such as the Amish, Hutterites, and Hasidic Jews mentioned in Chapter 2. Although a group identity usually remains among the adherents of any faith, its existence along other ethnic lines depends on racial and assimilation considerations. For example, Catholic immigrants in the nineteenth century and other Catholic and Jewish immigrants in the early twentieth century once stood apart not only for their religion but also for their other subcultural traits.

Although traces of anti-Catholicism and anti-Semitism remain today in the United States, most members of these religious groups hold a mainstream-group identity alongside their religious-group identity, which was not the case a few generations ago. More recent arrivals—such as Buddhists, Hindus, Muslims, and Sikhs—are not only religiously distinct from the long-standing three main U.S. religions but also are culturally distinct in other ways and often racially distinct as well. Currently, their ethnic-group identities embody all these aspects (religion, race, culture), and only time will tell what evolution in group identity will occur among them.

For most White ethnics, everyday ethnicity eventually yields to assimilation throughout the generations, and ethnic-group identity declines. That change is possible because gradually the group identifies more and more with mainstream society and its subcultural "marks" (clothing, language, customs, behavior, residential clustering) disappear, making the group less noticeable to the rest of society as its members become absorbed into the dominant White culture.

Because of the social definition of race, this metamorphosis is difficult for non-Whites in a color-conscious society. Physical identification through skin color, facial features, and/or hair texture thus maintains differences between the mainstream racial group and others. With their race an inescapable feature affecting their social acceptance and interaction patterns, non-White ethnics typically develop a *racial-group identity*. This ingroup bonding satisfies the human need for a sense of belonging while simultaneously serving as a basis for racial and cultural pride. Such an arrangement can foster a healthier, more positive self-identity than would otherwise develop among racial minorities relegated to secondary social status.

People of color—whether Black, brown, yellow, or red—typically affirm their identity and heritage in a variety of ways. These include combating their stereotypes, teaching the younger generation about their racial history and achievements, adopting slogans (e.g., "Black is beautiful") or special names (e.g., "La Raza" [the race]), and using a dual identity (e.g., African American, Mexican American, Korean American, Native American) as a positive designator of their dual reality. The more militant racial group members often use ethnophaulisms against their own members whom they criticize for "thinking or acting white" and call them, depending on the racial group, "oreos," "coconuts," "bananas," or "apples"—that is, one color on the outside, but White on the inside.

Ethnic- or racial-group identity, then, can have positive and negative consequences. Examining it in both a social and historical context will lead to a more complete understanding of this social phenomenon.

## Avoidance

One way of dealing with discriminatory practices is through **avoidance**, if this avenue is available. Throughout history, minority groups—from the ancient Hebrews to the Pilgrims to Sudanese Christians in recent years—have attempted to solve their problems by leaving them behind. One motive for migrating, then, is to avoid discrimination. If leaving is not possible, minorities may turn inward to their own group for all or most of their social and economic activities. This approach insulates the minority group from antagonistic actions by the dominant group, but also it promotes charges of "clannishness" and "nonassimilation." Lacking adequate economic, legal, or political power, however, the minority group may find avoidance the only choice open to it.

By clustering together in small subcommunities, minority peoples not only create a miniature version of their familiar world in a strange land but also establish a safe place in which they can live, relax, and interact with others like themselves, who understand their needs and interests. For some minority groups, seeking shelter from prejudice probably is a secondary motivation, following a primary desire to live among their own kind.

Asian immigrants, for example, have followed this pattern. When the Chinese first came to the United States, they worked in many occupations in which workers were needed, frequently clustering together in neighborhoods close to their jobs. Prejudicial attitudes commonly had existed against the Chinese, but in the post–Civil War period, they became even more the targets of bitter hatred and discrimination for economic and other reasons. Evicted from their jobs as a result of race-baiting union strikes and limited in their choice of residence by restrictive housing covenants, many had no choice but to live in insular Chinatowns within the larger cities. They entered businesses that did not compete with those of Whites (curio shops, laundries, restaurants, etc.) and followed their old-country tradition of settling disputes among themselves rather than appealing to government authorities for adjudication.

## Deviance

When a group continually experiences rejection and discrimination, some of its members are unable to identify with the dominant society or accept its norms. People at the bottom of the socioeconomic ladder, particularly members of victimized racial and ethnic groups, may respond to the pressures of everyday life in ways they consider reasonable but that others view as **deviance**. This situation occurs in particular when laws serve to impose the moral standards of the dominant group on the behavior of other groups.

Many minority groups in the United States—Irish, Germans, Chinese, Italians, African Americans, Native Americans, and Hispanics—have at one time or another been arrested and punished in disproportionate numbers for so-called crimes of personal disorganization. Among the offenses to the dominant group's morality have been public drunkenness, drug abuse, gambling, and sexual "misconduct." It is unclear whether this disproportion reflects the frequency of misconduct or a pattern of selective arrests.

Moreover, some types of conduct are deviant only from the perspective of the majority group, such as cockfighting or female genital cutting, whereas other types, such as wife beating, also may be considered deviant by the minority community itself.

Part of the problem with law enforcement is its subjective nature and the discretionary handling of violations. Many people criticize the U.S. criminal justice system for its failure to accord fair and equal treatment to the poor and to minority-group members as compared with people from the middle and upper classes.[2] Criticisms include the:

1. Tendency of police to arrest suspects from minority groups at substantially higher rates than those from the majority group in situations where discretionary judgment is possible;
2. Overrepresentation of nonminority groups on juries;
3. Difficulty the poor encounter in affording bail;
4. Poor quality of free legal defense;
5. Disparities in sentencing for members of dominant and minority groups.

Because social background constitutes one of the factors that the police and courts consider, individuals who belong to a racial or ethnic group with a negative stereotype find themselves at a severe disadvantage.

When some racial or ethnic group members commit a noticeable number of deviant offenses, such as delinquency, crime, drunkenness, or some public-nuisance problem, the public often extends a negative image to all members of that group even if it applies to only a few. Some common associations, for example, are Italians and gangsters, Irish and heavy drinking and fighting, Chinese and opium, African Americans and such street crimes as mugging and purse snatching, Puerto Ricans and knife fighting. A number of factors—including values, behavior patterns, and structural conditions in both the native and adopted lands—help explain the various kinds of so-called deviance among different minority groups. The appropriate means of stopping that deviance is itself subject to debate between proponents of corrective versus preventive measures.

Deviant behavior among minority groups occurs not because of race or ethnicity, as prejudiced people think, but usually because of poverty and lack of opportunity. A classic study of juvenile delinquency in Chicago in the 1940s documented this pattern.[3] The highest rates of juvenile delinquency occurred in areas with poor housing; few job opportunities; and widespread prostitution, gambling, and drug use. The delinquency rate was consistently high over a 30-year period, even though five different ethnic groups moved in and out of those areas during that period. *Nationality was unimportant; the unchanged conditions brought unchanged results.* Subsequent studies still demonstrate a correlation between higher rates of juvenile or adult crime and income level and place of residence.[4]

Because many minority groups are heavily represented among low-income populations, studies emphasizing social-class variables provide insight into the minority experience. The most common finding is that a lack of opportunities encourages delinquency among lower-class males.[5] Social aspirations may be similar in all levels of society, but opportunities are not. Belonging to a gang may give a youth a sense of power and help overcome feelings of inadequacy; hoodlumism becomes a conduit for expressing resentment against a society whose approved norms seem impossible to follow.[6] Notwithstanding the economic and environmental difficulties they face, the large majority of racial-group and ethnic-group members do not join gangs or engage in criminally deviant behavior. But because some minority groups are represented disproportionately in such activities, the public image of the group as a whole suffers.

Some social factors, particularly parental attitudes about education, appear to be related to delinquency rates. Generally, parental emphasis on academic achievement and extensive involvement in their children's schooling leads to more educationally committed adolescents. The greater their commitment is, the lower the rates of delinquency, and vice versa. Sometimes though, a high-quality school environment can offset a lack of parental involvement.[7]

## Defiance

If a minority group is sufficiently cohesive and conscious of its growing economic or political power, its members may act openly to challenge and eliminate discriminatory practices—through **defiance**. In previous years, some activists may have been pioneers with court challenges or other individual actions, but at this stage, the group takes a strong stand in defying the discrimination it is experiencing.

Sometimes the defiance is violent and seems spontaneous, although it usually grows out of long-standing conditions. One example is the Irish draft riot in New York in 1863 during the Civil War. When its volunteer armies proved insufficient, the Union used a military draft to secure needed troops. In those days, well-to-do males of draft age could legally avoid conscription by buying the military services of a substitute. Meanwhile, because the Irish were mostly poor and concentrated in urban areas, many of them had no recourse when drafted. Their defiance at what they considered an unfair practice blossomed into a riot in which Blacks became the scapegoats, with lives lost and property destroyed or damaged. Similarly, the 1969 Stonewall riots (a series of violent demonstrations by the New York Greenwich Village homosexual community against a police raid on their club) and the 1992 Los Angeles riot (following the acquittal of police officers videotaped beating Rodney King, a Black man) may both have been spontaneous reactions, but only within the larger context of smoldering, deep-seated, long-standing resentments.

A militant action, such as the takeover of a symbolic site, is a moderately aggressive act of defiance. The late 1960s witnessed many building takeovers by African Americans and other disaffected, angry, alienated students on college campuses. In many instances, the purpose of the action was to call public attention to what the group considered administrative indifference toward or discrimination against their people. Similar actions occurred in this period to protest the war in Vietnam. A small group of Native Americans took this approach in the 1970s to protest their living conditions; at different times, they seized Alcatraz Island in California, the Bureau of Indian Affairs in Washington, D.C., and the village of Wounded Knee in South Dakota. Media attention helped validate and spread the idea of using militant actions to promote a group's agenda.

Any peaceful action that challenges the status quo, though less aggressive, is defiant nonetheless; parades, marches, picket lines, mass meetings, boycotts, and demonstrations are examples. Another form of peaceful protest consists of civil disobedience: deliberately breaking discriminatory

*In recent years on May 1, tens of thousands march for immigrant rights in cities across the country, including New York, Chicago, Milwaukee, and Los Angeles (shown here). Calling for the legalization of the undocumented, an end to raids and deportation, and maintaining family unity, their actions echo past minority attempts to gain fair treatment.*

laws and then challenging their constitutionality, or breaking a discrimina-tory tradition. The civil-rights actions of the 1960s—sit-ins, lie-ins, and free-dom rides—challenged decades-old Jim Crow laws that restricted access by Blacks to public establishments in the South. Shop-ins at stores that catered to an exclusively White clientele represented deliberate efforts to break tra-ditional store practices by attempting to make purchases.

## Acceptance

Many minority people, to the frequent consternation of their leaders and sympathizers, accept the situation in which they find themselves. Some do so stoically, justifying their decision by subtle rationalizations. Others are re-sentful but accept the situation for reasons of personal security or economic necessity. Still others accept it through false consciousness, a consequence of the dominant group's control over sources of information. Although **acceptance** maintains the superior position in society of the dominant group and the subordinate position of the minority group, it does diminish the open tensions and conflicts between the two groups.

In some instances, conforming to prevailing patterns of interaction be-tween dominant and minority groups occurs subconsciously, the end result of social conditioning. Just as socialization can instill prejudice, so too can it cause minority-group members to disregard or be unaware of alternative status possibilities. How much acceptance of lower status takes this form and how much is characterized by resentful submission and mental rejec-tion is difficult to determine.

African Americans, Mexican Americans, and Native Americans have experienced a subordinate position in the United States for multiple genera-tions. Until the 1960s, a combination of structural discrimination, racial stratification, powerlessness, and a sense of the futility of trying to change things caused many to submit to the situation imposed on them. Similarly, Japanese Americans had little choice when, following the bombing of Pearl Harbor and the subsequent rise in anti-Japanese sentiment, the U.S. govern-ment in 1942 dispossessed and imprisoned 110,000 of them in "temporary relocation centers."[8]

Acceptance as a minority response is less common in the United States than it once was. More aware of the alternative ways of living presented in the media, today's minorities are more hopeful about sharing in them. No longer do they passively accept the status quo, which denies them the com-fortable life and leisure pursuits others enjoy. Simultaneously, through court decisions, legislation, new social services, and other efforts, society has cre-ated a more favorable climate for improving the status of minority groups. Televised news features and behavioral-science courses may have height-ened the public's social awareness as well.

# Consequences of Minority-Group Status

Among the possible outcomes faced by minority groups experiencing sustained inequality are negative self-image, a vicious circle of continued discrimination, marginality, and status as middleman minorities.

## Negative Self-Image

The apathy that militant leaders sometimes find among their own people may result from a **negative self-image**, a common consequence of prejudice and discrimination. **Labeling theory**, originally conceived by Howard Becker, helps us to understand this process. Using racial or ethnic stereotypes, the mainstream group may stigmatize a minority group and thereafter identify and treat its members as having those negative attributes. If the labeling process is pervasive and powerful enough, group members may come to accept the definition society forces on them and have lowered self-esteem.[9]

Continual treatment as an inferior encourages a loss of self-confidence. If everything about a person's position and experiences—jobs with low pay, substandard housing, the hostility of others, and the need for assistance from government agencies—works to destroy pride and hope, the person may become apathetic. To remain optimistic and determined in the face of constant negative experiences from all directions is extremely difficult.

The pervasiveness of dominant-group values and attitudes, which include negative stereotypes of the minority group, may cause the minority-group member to develop a negative self-image.[10] A person's self-image includes race, religion, and nationality; thus, individuals may feel embarrassed, even inferior, if they see that one or more of the attributes they possess are despised within the society. In effect, minority-group members may begin to perceive themselves as negatively as the dominant group originally did.

Negative self-image, or self-hatred, manifests itself in many ways. People may try to "pass" as members of the dominant group and deny membership in a disparaged group. They may adopt the dominant group's prejudices and accept their devalued status. They may engage in ego defense by blaming others within the group for the low esteem in which society holds them:

> Some Jews refer to other Jews as "kikes"—blaming them exclusively for the anti-Semitism from which all alike suffer. Class distinctions within groups are often a result of trying to free oneself from responsibility for the handicap from which the group as a whole suffers. "Lace curtain" Irish look down on "shanty" Irish. Wealthy Spanish and Portuguese Jews have long regarded themselves as the top of the pyramid of Hebraic peoples. But Jews of German

origin, having a rich culture, view themselves as the aristocrats, often looking down on Austrian, Hungarian, and Balkan Jews, and regarding Polish and Russian Jews at the very bottom.[11]

Negative self-image, then, can cause people to accept their fate passively. It also can encourage personal shame for possessing undesired qualities or antipathy toward other members of the group for possessing them. Minority-group members may attempt to overcome their negative self-image by changing their name or religion, having cosmetic surgery, or moving to a locale where the stereotype is less prevalent.

We must not assume, however, that negative self-image is a fairly general tendency among minority-group members. For example, members of tightly cohesive religious groups may draw emotional support from their faith and from one another. The insulation of living in an ethnic community, having strong ingroup loyalty, and/or having a determination to maintain a cultural heritage may prevent minority-group members from developing a negative self-image.

Studies have shown that people who are stigmatized can protect their self-esteem by attributing the negative feedback they receive to prejudice. Ethnic identity pride can serve as a buffer against the effects of dominant-group prejudice.[12] A positive group image enhances personal self-esteem, and high personal self-esteem enhances one's ability to cope more successfully with ethnic and racial discrimination.[13]

## The Vicious Circle

Sometimes the relationship between prejudice and discrimination is circular. Gunnar Myrdal referred to this pattern as **cumulative causation**—a **vicious circle phenomenon** in which prejudice and discrimination perpetuate each other.[14] For example, a discriminatory action in filling jobs leads to a minority reaction, poverty, which in turn reinforces the dominant-group attitude that the minority group is inferior, leading to more discrimination and so on.

In addition, the pattern of expectation and reaction may produce desirable or undesirable results. To illustrate, if the dominant group makes the newcomers welcome, they in turn are likely to react in a positive manner, which reinforces their friendly reception. If the new group is ignored or made to feel unwelcome, the members may react negatively, which again reaffirms original attitudes and actions. As Gordon Allport says, "If we foresee evil in our fellow man, we tend to provoke it; if good, we elicit it."[15] In other words, negative expectations lead to negative reactions, broadening the social distance between the groups and causing the vicious circle to continue.

When Jews were denied access to many U.S. vacation resorts during the nineteenth century, their reactions served to reinforce their negative stereotype in the minds of some, reinforcing the discriminatory behavior. Some Jews demanded equal access, which the resort operators took as proof that Jews were "pushy." When Jews responded to this discriminatory policy by establishing and patronizing their own resorts in the Catskill Mountains of New York, the majority group labeled them "clannish." Similarly, the Irish encountered severe job discrimination in the mid-nineteenth century; the resulting poverty forced many of them to live in urban slums, where they often had trouble with the law. Given this evidence of their "inferiority" and "undesirability," majority-group employers curtailed Irish job opportunities further. In the same way, discrimination by Whites against Blacks, based partly on the low standard of living endured by many of the latter, worsen even more the problems of poverty, fueling even more the antipathy of some Whites toward Blacks.

## Marginality

Minority-group members sometimes find themselves caught in a conflict between their own identity and values and the necessity to behave in a certain way to gain acceptance by the dominant group. This situation—**marginality**—usually arises when a member of a minority group is passing through a transitional period. In attempting to enter the mainstream of society, the marginal person internalizes the dominant group's cultural patterns without having gained full acceptance. Such individuals occupy an ill-defined position, no longer at ease within their own group but not yet fully a part of the *reference group*, the one by whose standards they evaluate themselves and their behavior.

Some sociologists, such as Robert E. Park, who gave this social phenomenon its name, have believed that it caused the individual a great deal of strain and difficulty. A marginal person, he observed, is one "whom fate has condemned to live in two societies and in two not merely different but antagonistic cultures."[16] The marginal person—whether an adult or a child—may suffer anxiety because of a conflict of values and loyalties. Adults leave the security of their cultural group and thereby risk being labeled renegades by their own people. They seek sustained social contacts with members of the dominant group, which may view them as outsiders. No longer comfortable with the old ways but nonetheless influenced by them and identified with them, marginal adults often experience feelings of frustration, hypersensitivity, and self-consciousness.

Children of immigrants likewise find themselves caught between two worlds. At home, their parents attempt to raise them in their social heritage, according to the established ways of the old country. Meanwhile, through school and other outside experiences, the children are exposed to the U.S. culture and want to be like other children in the society. Moreover, they may learn that the dominant group views their parents' ways as inferior and that they too are socially rejected because of their background. Consequently, many young people in transition develop emotional problems and are embarrassed to bring classmates home.

Not all sociologists share this view of marginality as an example of cultural conflict caused primarily by the clash of values within the individual. Instead, they believe that the reaction to marginal status depends largely on whether the individual receives reassurances of self-worth from the surrounding community. Thus, successfully defining the situation and adjusting to it are contingent on the individual's sense of security, solidarity, and support within the community.[17] What exists, they say, is a transitional phase involving stable individuals in a marginal culture rather than marginal persons in a dominant culture. Individuals in a marginal culture share their cultural duality with many others in primary-group relationships, in institutional activities, and in their interaction with members of the dominant society without encountering any contradiction between their desires and actuality.[18]

Whether this phase of the assimilation process represents an emotionally stressful experience or a comfortably protected one, minority-group members nonetheless pass through a transitional period during which they are not fully a part of either world. An immigrant group may move into the mainstream of U.S. society within the lifetimes of the first-generation members, it may choose not to do so, or it may not be permitted to do so. Usually, marginality is a one- or two-generation phenomenon. After that, members of the minority group either have assimilated or have formed a distinctive subculture. Whichever route they take, they are no longer caught between two cultural worlds.

## Middleman Minorities

Building on theories of marginality, Hubert Blalock suggested the model of **middleman minorities**.[19] This model identifies certain minorities in middle-income positions, typically in trade and commerce, where they play the role of middleman between producer and consumer and between the elite and the masses.[20] Historically, minorities commonly were trading peoples whose history of persecution (Jews, Greeks, and Armenians) or sojourner orientation (Chinese, Japanese, and Koreans) obliged them to perform risky or marginal tasks that permitted easy liquidation of their assets when necessary.[21]

Middleman groups often serve as buffers and hence experience hostility and conflict from above and below. Jews in Nazi Germany in the 1930s and Asians in Uganda in the early 1970s, for instance, became scapegoats for the economic turmoil in those societies. Their susceptibility to such antagonism

*German, Irish, Italian, and Jewish merchants and small businesses once served as middleman minorities to other ethnic groups. Today some Africans, Asians, and Hispanics repeat the pattern, such as in this Black neighborhood pizzeria where a Hispanic cook sells slices and whole pies, along with other foods and drinks.*

and their nonassimilation into the host society promoted high ingroup solidarity.

Systematic discrimination can prolong the duration of a group's middleman-minority status, as in the case of European Jews throughout the medieval period. Sometimes the entrepreneurial skills developed in trade and commerce provide middleman minorities with adaptive capabilities and competitive advantages, enabling them to achieve upward mobility and to assimilate more easily, such as with earlier Jewish immigrants and more recent Korean and Asian Indian immigrants. In other cases, a group may emerge as a middleman minority because of changing residential patterns. One example is Jewish store owners in city neighborhoods where they once served their own people. When their original neighbors moved away and they found themselves unable to follow them, these urban merchants served new urban minority groups who were situated lower on the socioeconomic ladder.

# Dominant-Group Responses

Members of a dominant group may react to minority peoples with hostility, indifference, welcoming tolerance, or condescension. The more favorable responses usually occur when the minority is numerically small, not perceived as a threat, or both. As the minority group's population increases, threatening the natives' monopoly on jobs and other claims to privileged cultural resources, the dominant group's attitude is likely to become suspicious or fearful. If the fear becomes great enough, the dominant group may take action against the minority group.

Dominant groups often use religion in varying aggressive ways against minority groups. Besides religious persecution (a push factor in many migrations throughout world history), they often use missionaries to convert minorities. Dominant groups do not necessarily conduct these sometimes forced conversions with the intent of assimilating a minority group. For example, teaching Christianity to slaves enabled southern Whites to create a false consciousness among the Africans in accepting their fate but working hard to please their masters. In the case of Native Americans, the federal government gave reservation land to several Protestant religions in an effort to convert the "heathens" and remake them in the White man's image, while maintaining their isolated, segregated confinement.

# Legislative Controls

If the influx of racial and ethnic groups appears to the dominant group to be too great for a country to absorb, or if prejudicial fears prevail, the nation may enact measures to regulate and restrict their entry. Australia, Canada, and the United States—the three greatest receiving countries in international migration—once had discriminatory immigration laws that either excluded or curtailed the number of immigrants from countries other than those of northern and western Europe. Through similar patterns of policy change, Canada (in 1962), the United States (in 1965), and Australia (in 1973) began to permit entry from all parts of the world.

To maintain a paternalistic social system, the dominant group frequently restricts the subordinate group's educational and voting opportunities. This denial assures the dominant group of maintaining its system of control, whether over internal minorities, such as Blacks in the Old South and various ethnic minorities in the former Soviet Union, or over colonized peoples, such as Africans and Asians once ruled by the Belgians, British, Dutch, French, Japanese, and Portuguese. Most colonial powers committed themselves to stability, trade, and tapping the natural resources of a country rather than to developing its infrastructure and preparing it for self-governance. As a result, native populations under colonial rule largely experienced ceremonial leadership from figureheads installed and approved by the colonial authority (and who lacked real power in important matters), limited educational opportunities, and restricted political participation. Other means of denying political power have included disenfranchising voters through high property qualifications (British West Indies), high income qualifications (Trinidad), and poll taxes (United States), although none of these practices exist today in these areas. The most conspicuous recent example of rigid social control was in South Africa, where a legislated apartheid society denied Blacks not only equal education and the ballot but almost every other privilege as well.

## Segregation

Through a policy of containment—avoiding social interaction with members of a minority group as much as possible and keeping them "in their place"—the dominant group can effectively create both spatial and social segregation.

**Spatial segregation** is the physical separation of a minority people from the rest of society. This most commonly occurs in residential patterns, but it also takes place in education, in the use of public facilities, and in occupations. The majority group may institutionalize this form of segregation by law (*de jure* segregation) or establish it informally through pervasive practice (*de facto* segregation).

Spatial segregation of minorities has a long history. Since the days of the preindustrial city, with its heterogeneous populations, the dominant group has relegated racial and ethnic minorities to special sections of the city, often the least desirable areas.[22] In Europe, this medieval ecological pattern resulted in minority groups being situated on the city outskirts nearest the encircling wall. Because this pattern remains in much of Europe today, Europeans, unlike people in the United States, consider it a sign of high prestige to live near the center of the city (see the International Scene box).[23]

The dominant group may use hidden or obvious means to achieve spatial segregation of a minority group. Examples of hidden actions include restrictive covenants, "gentlemen's agreements," and collusion between the community and real estate agents to steer "undesirable" minorities into certain neighborhoods.[24] Obvious actions include restrictive zoning, segregation laws, and intimidation. Since the 1954 *Brown v. Board of Education* desegregation ruling, U.S. courts continually have declared both methods of segregation unlawful.

An important dimension of spatial segregation is that the dominant group can achieve it through avoidance or residential mobility. Usually referred to as the *invasion-succession* ecological pattern, this common process has involved different religions and nationalities as well as different races. The most widely recognized example in the United States is

## The International Scene
## Segregation and Defiance in France

In late 2005, three weeks of riots and violent clashes broke out in Paris and spread to other French cities, eventually engulfing all 15 of the country's largest urban areas. By the time the riots ended, the counts were one dead, approximately 2,900 arrested, and thousands of vehicles and numerous public buildings burned, including a Roman Catholic Church.

The spiraling events began with the accidental electrocution of two teenagers—one the son of West African immigrants and the other the son of Tunisian immigrants—who ran from police (conducting one of their frequent identity checks of minorities) and hid in a power substation. A third teenager, the son of Turkish Kurdish immigrants, was injured and hospitalized. The three victims thus represented the primary minority groups in France—Arab, Black, and Muslim—and became the catalyst to ignite the preexisting tensions.

In November 2007 and July 2009, other riots occurred also sparked by the deaths of minority teens or young adults. In 2007, more than 70 cars and buildings (including a library, two schools, a police station, and several shops) were burned and 130 policemen injured. In 2009, 317 cars were burned and 13 police officers injured. Hundreds were arrested in each instance.

For decades, French government policy had concentrated immigrants and their families in well-defined districts of poorly maintained public housing projects on the edges of cities. Isolated from the city center, these *de facto* ethnic ghettos have little activity at night or on Sundays, and there is limited public transportation to the center. In addition, much higher unemployment for the foreign-born compared to the native-born—even worse among college graduates—contributed extensively to the mounting frustration and desperation.

Amid charges of job discrimination and police harassment, the common use by the media and general population of the expression "second generation of immigrants," even for those born in France, suggested a cultural mindset that differentiated who was "really" French. (At age 18, immigrant children born in France may go through a bureaucratic application process to be citizens; their birth there does not automatically bestow citizenship on them as in the United States.)

Experts cite the racial and social discrimination against persons with dark skin or Arabic- and/or African-sounding names as a major cause of unhappiness in the riot-torn areas. Although such discrimination is illegal, children of immigrants claim that they frequently encounter economic segregation, problems getting a job or renting an apartment, or even getting into a nightclub, just because of their name or the color of their skin. Since the riots, little has changed, and thus the potential for still other violent outbreaks remains.

*Critical thinking questions:*   How similar or dissimilar are the experiences of U.S. minorities today? Does the difference in French and U.S. citizenship laws have any impact on the acceptance and integration of minorities into society? How so?

previously all-White neighborhoods becoming Black, but any study of old urban neighborhoods would reveal the same pattern, as successive waves of immigrants arrived throughout the years. Residents of a neighborhood initially may resist the influx of a minority group but, eventually, they abandon the area when their efforts are not successful. This pattern results in neighborhoods with a concentration of a new racial or ethnic group—a new segregated area.

**Social segregation** involves confining participation in social, service, political, and other types of activities to members of the ingroup and thereby excluding the outgroup from any involvement. Organizations may use screening procedures to keep out unwanted types, and informal groups may act to preserve the composition of their membership.

Segregation, whether spatial or social, may be voluntary or involuntary. Minority-group members may choose to live by themselves rather than among the dominant group; this is an avoidance response, discussed previously. In contrast, minority-group members may have no choice about where they live because of economic or residential discrimination.

Whether by choice or against their will, minority groups form ethnic subcommunities, whose existence in turn promotes and maintains the social distance between them and the rest of society. Not only do minority-group members physically congregate in one area and thus find themselves spatially segregated, but they also do not engage in much social interaction with others outside their own group.

Under the right conditions, frequent interaction reduces prejudice, but when interaction is limited severely, the acculturation process slows considerably. Meanwhile, values regarding what is normal or different are reinforced, paving the way for stereotyping, social comparisons, and prestige ranking.

## Expulsion

When other methods of dealing with a minority group fail—and sometimes not even as a last resort—an intolerant dominant group may persecute the minority group or eject it from the territory where it resides—**expulsion**. Henry VIII banished the Gypsies from England in the sixteenth century, Spanish rulers drove out the Moors in the early seventeenth century, and the British expelled the French Acadians from Nova Scotia in the mid-eighteenth century. More recent examples include Idi Amin, who decreed in 1972 that all Asians must leave Uganda; Muammar al-Qaddafi, who expelled Libya's ethnic Italian community in 1970; and Serbs, who forced ethnic Albanians out of Kosovo in 1999.

The United States also has its examples of mass expulsion. In colonial times, the Puritans forced Roger Williams and his followers out of Massachusetts for their nonconformity, and the group resettled in what became Rhode Island. The forcible removal of the Cherokee from fertile Georgia land and the subsequent "Trail of Tears," during which 4,000 perished along the 1,000-mile forced march to Oklahoma Territory, is another illustration.

Mass expulsion is an effort to drive out a group that is seen as a social problem rather than attempting to resolve the problem cooperatively. This policy often arises after other methods, such as assimilation or extermination, have failed. Whether a dominant group chooses to remove a minority group by extermination or by expulsion depends in part on how sensitive the country is to world opinion, which in turn may be related to the country's economic dependence on other nations.

## Xenophobia

If the dominant group's suspicions and fears of the minority group become serious enough, they may produce volatile, irrational feelings and actions. This overreaction is known as **xenophobia**—the undue fear of or contempt for strangers or foreigners. This almost hysterical response—reflected in print, speeches, sermons, legislation, and violent actions—begins with ethnocentric views. Ethnocentrism encourages the creation of negative stereotypes, which in turn invites prejudice and discrimination and can escalate through some catalyst into a highly emotional reaction.

Many examples of xenophobia exist in U.S. history. In 1798, the Federalists, fearful of "wild Irishmen" and "French radicals" and anxious to eliminate what they saw as a foreign threat to the country's stability, passed the Alien and Sedition Acts to arrest, even deport, "undesirables." When a bomb exploded at an anarchist gathering at Chicago's Haymarket Square in 1886, many Americans thereafter linked foreigners with radicals. The Bolshevik Revolution in 1917 led to the Palmer raids, in which foreign-born U.S. residents were rounded up illegally and incarcerated for their alleged Communist Party affiliation; some were even deported. In 1942, 110,000 Japanese Americans, many of them second- and third-generation U.S. citizens, were interned in concentration camps as a result of irrational suspicions that they would prove less loyal during the ongoing World War II than German Americans and Italian Americans, although the United States was fighting all three countries. The U.S. English movement's current efforts to pass official English laws reflect a xenophobic fear that foreigners won't learn English.

## Annihilation

The Nazi extermination of more than 6 million Jews brought the term *genocide* into the English language, but the practice of **annihilation**—killing all the men, women, and children of a particular group—goes back to ancient times. In warfare among the ancient Assyrians, Babylonians, Egyptians, Hebrews, and others, the usual practice was for the victor to slay every member of an enemy civilization, partly to prevent their children from

*Xenophobia is not limited to any one country. In 2008 in Johannesburg, marchers protested attacks against foreigners that killed about 50 people, seriously injured hundreds, and displaced about 15,000 African immigrants, mostly refugees from Zimbabwe, who poor South Africans blamed for taking their scarce job opportunities.*

seeking revenge. For example, preserved in Deuteronomy are these words of Moses:

> Then Sihon came out against us, he and all his people, to fight at Jahaz. And the LORD our God delivered him before us; and we smote him, and his sons, and all his people. And we took all his cities at that time, and utterly destroyed the men, and the women, and the little ones, of every city, we left none to remain: Only the cattle we took for a prey unto ourselves, and the spoil of the cities which we took.
>
> Then we turned, and went up the way to Bashan: and Og the king of Bashan came out against us, he and all his people, to battle at Edrei. . . . So the LORD our God delivered into our hands Og also, the king of Bashan, and all his people: and we smote him until none was left to him remaining. And we took all his cities at that time, there was not a city which we took not from them, threescore cities, all the region of Argob, the kingdom of Og in Bashan. . . . And we utterly destroyed them, as we did unto Sihon king of Heshbon, utterly destroying the men, women, and children, of every city. But all the cattle, and the spoil of the cities, we took for a prey to ourselves.[25]

In modern times, various countries have used extermination as a means of solving a so-called race problem. The British, through extermination and close confinement of survivors, annihilated the entire aboriginal population of Tasmania between 1803 and 1876.[26] The Dutch considered South African San (Bushmen) to be less than human and attempted to obliterate them.[27] In the 1890s and again in 1915, the Turkish government systematically massacred hundreds of thousands of Armenians, events still solemnly remembered each year by Armenian Americans. One of the largest genocides in U.S. history occurred at Wounded Knee in 1890, when the U.S. Seventh Cavalry killed about 200 Native American men, women, and children. Even in the past 50 years, campaigns of genocide have occurred around the globe in such countries as Bangladesh, Bosnia, Burundi, Cambodia, Indonesia, Iraq, Kosovo, Nigeria, Rwanda, and Sudan.

Lynchings are not a form of annihilation because the intent is not to exterminate an entire group but to set an example through selective, drastic punishment. Nonetheless, the victims usually are minority-group members. Although lynchings occurred in the United States throughout its history, only since 1882 do we have reasonably reliable statistics on their frequency (Figure 6.1). Archived data at the *Chicago Tribune* and the Tuskegee Institute reveal that at least 5,000 lynchings have occurred since 1882. They happened in almost every state, with southern states (especially Mississippi, Georgia, and Texas) claiming the most victims. In fact, 90 percent of all lynchings during this period have occurred in the southern states, with Blacks accounting for 80 percent of the victims. The statistics, however, do not cover lynchings during the nation's first 100 years, including those in the western frontier, when many Mexican and Native Americans also met this fate.[28]

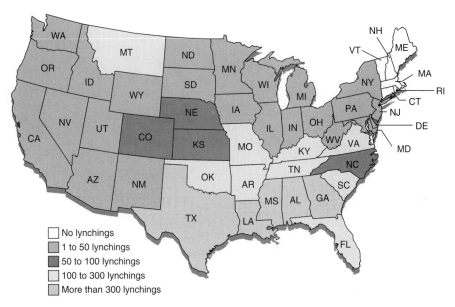

**FIGURE 6.1    Lynchings in the United States Since 1882**

*Source:* Based on data from the Tuskegee Institute.

Annihilation sometimes occurs unintentionally, as when Whites inadvertently spread Old World sicknesses to Native Americans in the United States and Canada, to Inuit (Eskimos), and to Polynesians. With no prior exposure to such ailments as measles, mumps, chicken pox, and smallpox, the native populations had little physiological resistance to them, and thus succumbed to these contagious diseases in unusually high numbers. Other forms of annihilation, usually intentional, occur during times of mob violence, overzealous police actions, and the calculated actions of small private groups.[29]

## Hate Groups

Like most nations, the United States has had its share of hate groups and hate crimes. Most prominent among hate groups of the past were the Know-Nothings of the mid-nineteenth century and the Ku Klux Klan in the late nineteenth and early twentieth centuries. In fact, bias crimes against Europeans, Native Americans, Asians, and numerous religious groups occurred frequently in the nineteenth and twentieth centuries. Deplorably, this ugly pattern remains a brutal force in U.S. society in the twenty-first century.

The Intelligence Project of the Southern Poverty Law Center—the nation's preeminent monitor and analyst of American extremism—reported that the number of hate groups operating in the United States increased by 55 percent since 2000, driven in large measure by immigration and economic issues (Figure 6.2).[30] Of the 932 organized, active hate groups in 2009, the

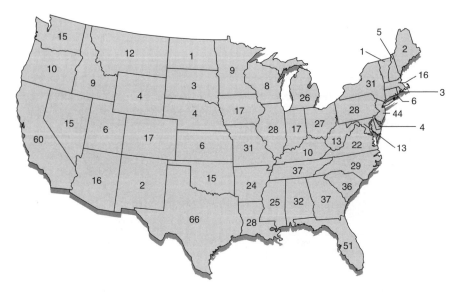

**FIGURE 6.2    Hate Groups in the United States: 2009**

*Source:* Southern Poverty Law Center Intelligence Project.

largest types were nativist extremists, anti-government Patriot groups, neo-Nazi organizations, the Ku Klux Klan, White nationalists, neo-confederates, Black separatist groups, anti-gay groups, racist skinheads, and Christian Identity groups, which identify Whites as God's chosen people and Jews as satanic. Texas contained the largest number of active hate groups (66), followed by California (60), Florida (51), New Jersey (44), Georgia and Tennessee (37), South Carolina (36), Alabama (32), Missouri and New York (31), North Carolina (29), Illinois, Louisiana, and Pennsylvania (28). One or more hate groups existed in all 50 states.

## Hate Crimes

Reported hate crimes—only some of which are committed by members of organized hate groups—numbered 6,604 in 2009 and claimed 8,336 victims. Racial bias motivated 52 percent of the incidents, religious bias another 9 percent, sexual-orientation bias 22 percent, and ethnicity/national origin bias 15 percent (Table 6.1). Crimes against persons accounted for 83 percent of hate crime offenses, while damage/destruction/vandalism of property (sometimes in conjunction with crimes against persons) constituted 23 percent.[31]

To combat hate crimes—commonly defined as any criminal offense against a person or property that is motivated in whole or part by the offender's bias against a race, religion, ethnic/national origin, group, or sexual orientation—states have passed laws mandating severe punishments for persons convicted of these crimes. Federal law (18 U.S.C. 245) also permits federal prosecution of a hate crime as a civil-rights violation if the assailant intended to prevent the victim from exercising a "federally protected right" such as voting or attending school. Despite such sanctions, however, the numbers of hate groups and hate crimes continue to rise (see the Reality Check box).

## Exploitation

The **exploitation** of minority groups has been a common occurrence in virtually all countries. Sometimes the perpetrators of this abuse are members of the same group—the operators of Asian sweatshops in U.S. cities, for instance, and the *padroni* of earlier Italian immigrant communities, both of whom often benefited at the expense of their own people. Most often, however, members of dominant groups exploit minority groups.

Middle-range conflict theories are often helpful in understanding specific forms of exploitation, such as the internal-colonialism theory discussed in Chapter 3. Another analytical explanation came from Edna Bonacich, who introduced the concept of a **split-labor-market theory** as a means of

TABLE 6.1   Bias Motivation of Hate Crime Incidents in 2009

| | Percentage of Category | Percentage of Total |
|---|---|---|
| **Race** | | 52.1 |
| Anti-Black | 66.6 | |
| Anti-White | 23.5 | |
| Anti-Asian/Pacific Islander | 3.3 | |
| Anti-multiracial group | 4.1 | |
| Anti-Native American | 2.7 | |
| **Religion** | | 9.4 |
| Anti-Jewish | 60.2 | |
| Anti-Islamic | 16.2 | |
| Anti-Protestant | 2.9 | |
| Anti-Catholic | 4.3 | |
| Anti-multireligious group | 6.5 | |
| Other | 9.9 | |
| **Ethnicity/National Origin** | | 15.0 |
| Anti-Hispanic | 69.5 | |
| Other | 30.5 | |
| **Sexual Orientation** | | 22.4 |
| Anti-male homosexual | 58.6 | |
| Anti-female homosexual | 14.1 | |
| Anti-homosexual | 25.0 | |
| Anti-heterosexual | 1.0 | |
| Anti-bisexual | 1.2 | |
| **Disability** | | 1.0 |
| Anti-physical | 39.1 | |
| Anti-mental | 60.9 | |

*Source:* Federal Bureau of Investigation, "2009 Hate Crime Statistics," adapted from Table 1. Accessed at www2.fbi.gov/ucr/hc2009/data/table_01.html [December 28, 2010].

understanding the ethnic antagonism in the workplace.[32] This model refers to two fields of employment, the *primary labor market* where workers enjoy decent wages, pay payroll taxes, and receive health insurance and other benefits, compared to the *secondary labor market*, in which minorities, mostly, work in unregulated low-paying jobs, usually on a cash basis with no payroll tax deductions, health insurance, or other benefits.

Part of the secondary labor market also is known as the **underground economy**, where employers pay workers in cash "under the table." Neither employers nor workers report these hidden services and earnings to the government. As a result, employers—such as those in lawn and landscaping services, home construction and remodeling, and in food service industries—do

## Reality Check
## College Campuses and Hate Crimes

Many people assume that those who commit hate crimes typically are ignorant, poorly educated individuals with little to no respect for those unlike themselves. If that were true, then we would expect that bias incidents would be few and far between on college campuses. After all, these are learning environments of diversity, intellectual curiosity, and courses promoting intergroup relations. Open-mindedness should be the norm and narrow-minded bigotry the rare exception. Colleges in many ways, however, are microcosms of the larger society, and the reality is that hatred exists on campuses too.

The Southern Poverty Law Center (SPLC), after a two-year study, found campuses across the country—from north to south, from east to west—struggling with the problem of bias incidents and hate crimes. In fact, the statistics are disturbing. The SPLC reported in 2009 that every single year, more than a half million college students are targets of bias-driven slurs or physical assaults.

Such a large number may be hard to put in perspective. Perhaps this statistic will make the problem clearer. Every day at least one hate crime occurs on a U.S. college campus. Some experts argue that this figure is too low, because it only covers reported crimes, and that the actual number may be three to five hate crimes every day.

More common than hate crimes are bias incidents: name-calling, threatening emails and telephone calls, insulting signs and symbols, and other forms of verbal aggression or intimidation.

Every minute, a U.S. college student somewhere sees or hears racist sexist, homophobic, or otherwise biased words or images. The Prejudice Institute estimates that as many as 1 million college students are targets of ethnoviolence in any given year on the nation's college campuses.

*Critical thinking question:*   What can you do to make a difference in promoting mutual respect and tolerance at your college? Think it through first on your own, then go to the Internet Activities section at the end of this chapter for a link to some answers.

---

not pay into employee health or pension plans, Medicare, or Social Security, and those savings enable them to be more competitive in getting work and in maximizing profits. The workers—many of them immigrants familiar only with a cash economy in their homeland—do not pay any payroll or income taxes but also have no health insurance coverage and will not qualify for Social Security in their old age.

> To understand how a split labor market works, we must first realize that, even though higher-price workers are quick to blame minorities for undercutting their wages, the reality is that the vulnerability of both groups to economic

pressures enables businesses to control the situation.[33] Ethnic antagonism subsequently results from a combination of economic exploitation by employers and economic competition between two or more groups of laborers, which produces a wage differential for labor. Much ethnic antagonism thus is based not on ethnicity and race but on the conflict between higher-paid and lower-paid labor. The lower-paid group—its wages nonetheless higher than its members can find back home—threatens the higher-paid labor group with possible displacement through such wage undercutting.

When a labor market splits along ethnic lines, racial and ethnic stereotyping becomes a key factor in the labor conflict, and prejudice, ethnic antagonism, and racism become overt. The conflict may not be due to religious differences or even depend on which group was first to move into the area because examples of ethnic antagonism can be found in which these variables were controlled. Bonacich argues that the one characteristic shared by all societies where ethnic antagonism is acute is an indigenous working class that earns higher wages than do immigrant workers.

This common characteristic fuels anti-immigration sentiments, intensified even more these days by the concern over the millions of undocumented

*Today, sweatshops remain a form of economic exploitation just as they did three generations ago. Asian and Hispanic newcomers—many undocumented—work long hours for low pay. Fewer workers are seen in this Massachusetts garment factory two weeks after officials raided and rounded up 361 workers, arresting the owner and three top managers.*

immigrants in the country. The generations-old complaint that "they're taking jobs away from Americans" has at its core the fear of higher-priced American labor displaced by cheaper immigrant labor.

Employers are seldom passive observers of this clash between higher-priced and cheaper labor along racial and ethnic lines. They are the ones, after all, who control the lower wages offered to the minority workers. Moreover, employers will often actively manipulate the situation to keep the groups divided. For example, they could practice *majority paternalism* (promoting a racial hierarchy to cultivate majority-group loyalty) or *minority paternalism* (cultivating minority-group loyalty through jobs, home loans, or funds for community projects to encourage company unionism). A more militant approach would be a divide-and-rule strategy either by hiring minorities as strikebreakers or by encouraging state intervention to demobilize a possible coalition of workers.[34]

Today, employers are less likely to assign workers to inferior jobs on the basis of race and sex than to create nonstandard work arrangements with immigrants lacking U.S. citizenship. Employers can more easily persuade a group to work for a lower price if that group's initial standard of living— either in the United States or in the homeland left behind—is low; they can less easily tempt another group coming from a more favorable economic resource position. Although this labor market segmentation has increased substantially since the 1970s, recent studies also show that most workers who begin their careers in these secondary (bad) jobs eventually do move on to better jobs.[35]

# Retrospect

Ethnic- and racial-group identity is a normal pattern in ingroup–outgroup relationships. It can have positive and negative results depending on the social context in which it exists. A group identity based on immigrant status is normally of shorter duration than one based on religion or race. Minorities typically experience a dual identity, one in the larger society and another within their own group.

Minority-group responses to prejudice and discrimination include avoidance, deviance, defiance, and acceptance depending in large measure on the group's perception of its power to change the status quo. After prolonged treatment as an inferior, a person may develop a negative self-image. Continued inequality intensifies through a vicious circle or cumulative causation.

Marginality is a social phenomenon that occurs during the transitional period of assimilation; it may be either a stressful or a sheltered experience depending on the support system of the ethnic community. Some groups become middleman minorities because of their historical background or sojourner orientation. They may remain indefinitely in that intermediate place in the social hierarchy, a potential scapegoat for those above and below them, or they may achieve upward mobility and assimilation.

Dominant-group actions toward the minority group may take various forms, including favorable, indifferent, or hostile responses. When the reaction is negative, the group in power may place restraints on the minority group (e.g., legislative controls and segregation). If the reaction becomes more emotional or even xenophobic, expulsion or annihilation may occur. Sensitivity to world opinion and economic dependence on other nations may restrain such actions. Another dominant response is exploitation as illustrated by the internal-colonialism theory, discussed in Chapter 3, or by the split-labor-market theory, in which differential wage levels can spark ethnic antagonism.

## KEY TERMS

| | |
|---|---|
| Acceptance | Marginality |
| Annihilation | Middleman minorities |
| Avoidance | Negative self-image |
| Cumulative causation | Social segregation |
| Defiance | Spatial segregation |
| Deviance | Split-labor-market theory |
| Exploitation | Underground economy |
| Expulsion | Vicious circle |
| Labeling theory | Xenophobia |

## DISCUSSION QUESTIONS

1. What are some common minority-group responses to prejudice and discrimination?

2. What is marginality? Why it may be a stressful experience in some cases but not in others?

3. Have you or anyone you know personally experienced marginality, or being caught in two worlds?

4. Can you give specific local examples of a middleman minority enterprise where members of one minority group provide services to members of different minority groups?

5. What are some common majority-group responses to minorities?

6. Can you give a specific example of residential (and thus school) segregation in any nearby communities?

# INTERNET ACTIVITIES

1. Want to make a difference now? The Rutgers University Office of Social Justice suggests "10 Ways to Fight Hate" at http://socialjustice.rutgers.edu/fightinghate.html.

2. Go to the Hate Groups Map at the Southern Poverty Law Center (www.splcenter.org/intel/map/hate.jsp). Take a look at what hate groups are in your state and nearby ones by moving your cursor to that state, left clicking your mouse, and scrolling down. Were you surprised?

3. Read one of the articles in the Intelligence Report of the Southern Poverty Law Center, called "Hate Groups Find a Home on the Net" (www.splcenter.org/intel/intelreport/article.jsp?aid=455). What is your reaction?

4. "The Lynching Calendar" (http://www.autopsis.org/foot/lynch.html) gives the dates, places, and names of the more than 6,000 African Americans who died in racial violence in the United States.

# CHAPTER 7

# Immigration Patterns and Issues

*"Ultimately, America's answer to the intolerant
man is diversity, the very diversity which our
heritage of religious freedom has inspired."*

—ROBERT F. KENNEDY

As a nation of immigrants, the United States has seen many different groups of strangers arrive and interact with its people. The strangers perceived a different world that the native population took for granted, and their reactions ranged from wonder to bewilderment to dismay, from fulfilled expectations to culture shock. Because their language, appearance, and cultural background often made them conspicuous, the newcomers were categorically identified and judged as a group rather than as individuals. Native-born U.S. residents' responses ranged from receptive to impatient and intolerant, while their actions ranged from indifferent to helpful to exploitative.

Throughout the nation's history, varied patterns of majority–minority relations existed. Ethnocentric values prompted the natural development of ingroup loyalty and outgroup hostility among both indigenous and migrant groups. Competition for scarce resources, colonialism, and political dominance by the Anglo-Saxon core groups also provided a basis for conflict. However, the resulting prejudicial attitudes and discriminatory actions varied greatly in intensity. In addition, changes in attitudes and social and economic conditions in this country throughout the years affected the newcomers' experiences.

Not all groups came for the same reasons or from the same backgrounds. Because of variations in social class, education, and occupational skills, not all immigrants began at the bottom of the socioeconomic ladder. Some came as sojourners, intending to stay only long enough to earn enough money for a better life back in their homeland. Some came with the desire to become U.S. citizens in every sense of the word; others insisted on retaining their own culture.

Dominant attitudes about immigration, minority adaptation, pluralism, and assimilation greatly influence dominant–minority relations. For example, if assimilation is held to be the "proper" goal, then evidence of pluralism will probably draw negative reactions, even though pluralism is a normal manifestation among first- and second-generation Americans. In recent years, the growing presence in U.S. cities and suburbs of Spanish-speaking peoples and of people of color from non-Western cultures has led many other U.S. residents to question the country's immigration policies. Although race and economics undoubtedly are influencing factors, genuine concerns about widespread pluralism overwhelming the "melting-pot" capabilities of the United States is another important influence.

Stir in words such as *affirmative action*, *illegal aliens*, and *multiculturalism*, and the debate reaches "white heat" temperatures (the double meaning of that adjective is deliberate). These aspects of intergroup relations suggest that the majority group and the dominant culture may feel seriously threatened. In some parts of the country, the level of intolerance for any manifestation of pluralism has risen to alarming proportions.

How important is ethnicity today? Are immigration and assimilation concerns justified? What is the future of race and ethnicity in the United States? In this chapter, we attempt to answer these questions as we examine concepts of ethnic consciousness; evolutionary changes in ethnicity; and issues of legal and illegal immigration, bilingual education, and multiculturalism.

## Ethnic Consciousness

What factors encourage or discourage ethnic self-awareness or culture preservation? If succeeding generations supposedly identify less with their country of origin, how do we explain the resurgence of ethnicity among White ethnics in recent years? Are there ethnic differences in social mobility, social change, and behavior patterns even among third-generation U.S. citizens?

### Country of Origin as a Factor

Immigrants arrive with cultural baggage as well as with their packed belongings. In adjusting to a new life in a new land, those distinguishing aspects of their ethnic identity (customs, language, values, and practices) are the everyday underpinnings of their ethnic consciousness. Once interacting with similar others in the old country, they quickly develop an awareness of how different they now are from the mainstream group and so they find comfort in interacting with fellow ethnics. The continuing vibrancy of that ethnicity depends partly on conditions in the receiving country, such as size of the ethnic community, the arrival of new immigrants, and the assimilation process.

Another powerful element in the maintenance of ethnic consciousness is homeland influence. For some, the memories and emotional ties to one's native land are too strong, and homesickness and yearnings prompt a permanent return. For others, frequent contact with family and friends back home, events occurring there that make the news, and/or an ongoing inflow in fellow nationals migrating, all ease the transition to a new life while also keeping strong one's ethnic identity. In contrast, a lessening of migration and interaction gradually will reduce ethnic consciousness.

To illustrate this fact, in the early twentieth century, the United States experienced such an enormous influx of immigrants that ethnicity was the norm in our cities, with first- and second-generation Americans often outnumbering native-born Americans of other backgrounds. Immigration restrictions in the 1920s sharply curtailed the number of new immigrants. The physical distance and limited contact by mail created a barrier that gradually reduced ethnic identification and aided the assimilation process, as fewer newcomers arrived to reinforce the language and customs of the old country.

In today's world, however, an immigrant group can maintain instant and continuous contact with the country of origin through telecommunications, rapid transportation, and the continued arrival of newcomers. Mexican and Caribbean immigrant communities, for example, benefit from geographical proximity. With instant communications, the homeland can exert more influence over its emigrants than in years past, and where greater social contact occurs, cultural transmission is greater also.

Such contact with one's country of origin also affects politics. In an analysis of the political activities of Asian Americans, three general and overlapping phases of acculturation were found in their political activities. These were: (1) the *alien phase,* when the political locus remains with the country of origin; (2) the *reactionary phase,* when immigrants create political organizations to protect their interests and fight discrimination; and (3) the *acceptance phase,* when they display a greater degree of cultural and structural discrimination.[1] In other words, the homeland influence among Asian Americans initially affected their U.S. political noninvolvement until the acculturation process firmly took root.

Similarly, the political activities of immigrants from the Dominican Republic, Haiti, and El Salvador also manifest that first phase. Their involvement varies though, depending on the government structure and political

*Immigrants leave their native lands and put down roots in their adopted country, but the homeland connection remains strong, especially in times of political unrest and disasters affecting friends and families back there. The 2010 earthquake that struck the Haitian capital, Port-au-Prince, touched all hearts but none more than the Haitian Americans.*

parties in the country of origin. Affecting the immigrants' political orientation to the homeland is the home country's need for a steady flow of remittances, ethnic organizations in the host country, and competitive politics in democratic regimes.[2]

An immigrant community whose country of origin has a stable or gradually changing culture is more likely to promote retention of that ethnic culture. If that culture holds pro-education values—such as Armenians, Chinese, Greeks, Japanese, and Vietnamese—then ethnic retention is a reliable predictor of higher academic achievement.[3] In turn, educational achievement appears to influence both ethnic identity and assimilation. A longitudinal study of the children of Latin American and Caribbean immigrants found that educated adults identify both with the United States and with their country of origin.[4]

In contrast, an immigrant community whose country of origin has experienced drastic changes in a short period of time may either change as well or, if the changes are unwelcome, seek to preserve the old traditions and a fantasy of the homeland. The former can be illustrated by the Chaldean immigrants from Iraq who settled in Detroit both before and after

World War II when Iraq evolved from a colonial land of different tribes into a modern nation-state. More recent immigrants, with more education and experience with urban settings and bureaucracies, were more likely to interact with members of other groups, making them a more assimilable group than the earlier arrivals.[5] Examples of communities ignoring change and constructing an imagined ethnic reality unlike the homeland would be some of today's German and Iranian enclaves.[6]

## The Three-Generation Hypothesis

Pulitzer Prize–winner and historian Marcus Hansen conceptualized a normal pattern of ethnic revival in what he called the "Law of the Return of the Third Generation."[7] The third generation, more secure in its U.S. identity and socioeconomic status, becomes interested in the ethnic heritage that the second generation neglected in its efforts to overcome discrimination and marginality. Simply stated, "What the child wishes to forget, the grandchild wishes to remember." Hansen, who based his conclusions mainly on Midwestern Swedish Americans, reaffirmed his position several years later:

> Whenever any immigrant group reaches the third-generation stage in its development a spontaneous and almost irresistible impulse arises which forces the thoughts of many people of different professions, different positions in life and different points of view to interest themselves in that one factor which they have in common: heritage—the heritage of blood.[8]

Hansen suggested a pattern in the fall and rise of ethnic identity in succeeding generations of Americans. His hypothesis generated extensive discussion in the academic community, resulting in studies and commentaries that both supported and criticized his views.

**Hansen's law** assumes that the second generation perceives its ethnicity as a disadvantage in being accepted in U.S. society. However, not all second-generation Americans respond that way. Hansen's law may be flawed as a precise predictor of generational differences within specific ethnic groups, but his basic insight remains valid. Assimilation is not simply a linear progression but instead is a process that moves back and forth across generations. Moreover, assimilation is not irreversible. Subsequent generations, even those who are the product of intermarriages, may emphasize their ethnic identity and learn the language of their cultural heritage.[9]

Just as earlier research found lower levels of attitudinal ethnicity throughout several generations of Europeans, newer studies of more recently arrived groups also find a similar decline in ethnicity among second-generation Asian and Hispanic Americans as they seek to assimilate.

Among Hispanic college students, a negative relationship appears to exist between cultural assimilation and Hispanic identity; the acculturation process functioned as a trade-off between traditional Latino tendencies and mainstream Anglo-American practices.[10] Similarly, immigrant children from south Florida and southern California who adopted the "Hispanic" label are the least well assimilated; these children had poorer English skills, lower self-esteem, and higher rates of poverty than those who identified themselves as Americans or as hyphenated Americans.[11]

Among Asian Americans, one study found that second-generation Chinese, Japanese, and Korean Americans developed a sense of a shared Asian American culture in their socialization into the Asian values of education, family, hard work, and respect for elders. In this instance, the "backlash" in the construction of a common cultural background was an attempt to distinguish it from the homogeneously conceived White mainstream culture.[12] The experience of Japanese Americans, among whom many are third-, fourth-, and even fifth-generation Americans, may offer further insight into Hansen's law. With above-average educational, occupational, and income levels, as well as high intermarriage rates, they are arguably the most assimilated of all Asian Americans. Still, they retain symbolic vestiges of their heritage and cling to the aforementioned values as part of their sense of self and group identity.[13] Perhaps a similar future awaits our newest groups, although undoubtedly their racial experiences will mediate their identity formation.

Another dimension in examining both intergenerational assimilation and mobility lies in a fairly new social science concept of the **1.5 generation**, which refers to immigrants who arrive under the age of ten.[14] The term recognizes that their socialization began in the home country inculcating them with certain cultural characteristics, but their socialization continues in the host country, resulting in a blended cultural identity of the old and new. Although many factors will affect their sense of group identity, generally their bilingualism and biculturalism serve as a bridge for their parents in their own acculturation.

Further refining the ethnic dimensions of family is the concept of the **2.5 generation**, which deals with those who have a U.S.-born parent and a foreign-born parent. Presently, approximately one in three Asian and Hispanic Americans born to immigrant parents belongs to the 2.5 generation. For Australian and Canadian Americans, it is four in five, whereas for European Americans more than half fit this category, as do slightly less than half of Middle Eastern Americans. In total numbers, the 2.5 generation is only slightly less than those identified as part of the 2.0 generation. Among the many considerations about ethnicity and adaptation is how a native-born parent may offer the 2.5 generation advantages over the 2.0 generation.[15]

## The Changing Face of Ethnicity

We can gain helpful insights into the complex, varied experiences and adjustments of different racial and ethnic groups by considering two other important concepts: transnationalism and naturalization.

### Transnationalism

Past immigration of even a generation ago typically resulted in a sharp, total, and rather permanent change in focus and orientation as the new ways replaced the old ways. Today, the ease of email and telephone communication, the Internet, and relatively inexpensive air travel have changed that. Even as immigrants put down roots and establish new relationships, they easily can maintain connections back home, keeping business, political, and social networks strong, and also sending money home to support those left behind. Their culture and community no longer confined to one locale; many immigrants live in both worlds simultaneously. Whereas past immigrants found themselves caught between two worlds and not fully part of either, many of today's immigrants—thanks to a shrinking world created by technology and a globalized economy—have plural identities, even dual citizenships, with one foot planted in the old country and one in the new.[16]

We have long recognized the fact that immigrants, even when intent on blending into the societal mainstream of the host country, nevertheless retain much of their "cultural baggage" that affects not only their adjustment to their new land but also serves as a stabilizing link to their homeland and sense of self.[17] Despite that "old world" influence, the traditional view of social scientists was that the political and social behavior of the newcomers occurred within the cultural/structural framework of the host society. However, the new realities just described have led scholars in recent years to revise traditional migration theory in recognition of a changed interaction pattern between immigrants and the host society.[18]

This new orientation recognizes that recent global transformations have led to the creation of social ties and support networks no longer restricted by national boundaries. **Transnationalism** thus refers to sustained ties of persons, networks, and organizations across national borders that result from the current international migration patterns and refugee flows. The easy flow of people and their ideas back and forth between two countries has given many people the ability to maintain dual identities, with strong cultural ties and the capacity to make contributions to both places.

Instant transactions and communications have compressed time and space, allowing populations to be culturally and socially anchored at multiple sites. Instead of a permanent move from one country to another, today's immigrant retains more intense, interconnected, even legitimized links (cultural, economic, familial, and political) than ever before. Some scholars therefore argue that transnationalism makes obsolete the traditional terms of assimilation, integration, or segregation, in which states have dealt with immigration.[19]

## Naturalization

After five years of continuous legal residence in the United States, immigrants are eligible to become naturalized citizens, provided they are of good moral character and demonstrate a command of English and knowledge of U.S. history and government. We can reasonably assume that those who become U.S. citizens are demonstrating a desire to join fully in U.S. society through this formal process.

As Figure 7.1 shows, the longer the residence in the United States, the higher the percentage of naturalized citizens. Those who arrived in the 1970s, for example, have a greater proportion of naturalized citizens than those who arrived in the 1980s, who in turn exceed those who arrived in the 1990s, who surpass those arriving in the 2000s. Moreover, Asian immigrants lead all other groups in all time periods in the percentage of those who became U.S. citizens. How much of a role transnationalism or segmented assimilation plays in the level of naturalization among groups is a matter of great interest to social scientists.

We must be careful in analyzing the citizenship data. At first glance, the smaller proportion of newer arrivals compared to earlier immigrants in becoming naturalized citizens would seem to support the argument that newcomers are less likely to "become Americans." However, the correlation between length of U.S. residence and the proportion of those becoming citizens has been fairly constant for a great many decades. For example, although 8 in 10 of all immigrants who arrived in the 1970s are citizens now, less than half of them were citizens in the early 1990s.

In recent years, the number of naturalized citizens has grown steadily, increasing from 463,000 in 2003 to more than 743,000 in 2009. The leading countries of birth of new citizens were Mexico (111,630), India (52,889), the Philippines (38,934), the People's Republic of China (37,130), Vietnam (31,168), and Cuba (24,891).[20]

## Ethnicity as a Social Process

Ethnicity is a creation of a pluralistic U.S. society. Usually, culture shock and an emerging self-consciousness lead immigrant groups to think of themselves in terms of an ethnic identity and to become part of an ethnic community to gain the social and emotional support they need to begin a new life in their adopted country. That community is revitalized with a continual influx of new arrivals.

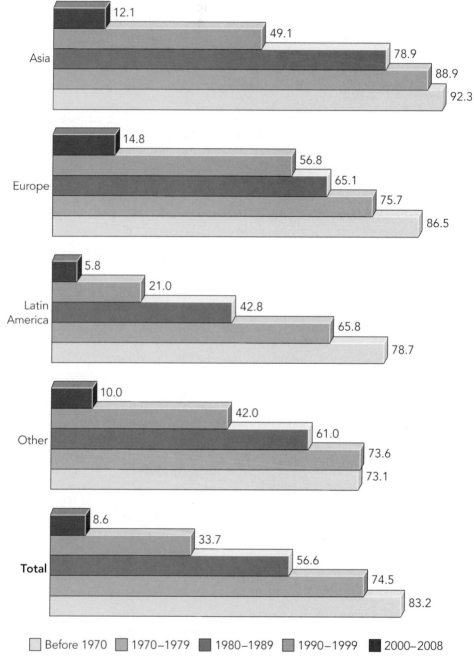

**FIGURE 7.1** **Percentage of Naturalized Citizens by Period of Entry, 2008**

*Source:* U.S. Census Bureau.

Some sociologists argue that ethnicity should be regarded not as an ascribed attribute, with only the two discrete categories of assimilation and pluralism, but as a continuous variable. Conditioning ethnic behavior is occupation, residence, and institutional affiliation—in other words, the structural situations in which groups have found themselves.[21] Earlier immigrants, migrating before the Industrial Revolution, had a more dispersed residential pattern than did later immigrants, who bunched together because of concentrated large-scale urban employment and the need for low-cost housing near their place of employment. Furthermore, these immigrants were drawn to areas of economic expansion, and the migration chains—the subsequent arrival of relatives and friends—continued their concentrated settlement pattern.

> The Germans and Irish, who were earlier immigrants, concentrated in the older cities such as Philadelphia and St. Louis. By contrast, the new immigrants from Poland, Italy and Russia concentrated in Buffalo, Cleveland, Detroit and Milwaukee, as well as in some of the older cities with expanding opportunities. Different migration patterns occurred for immigrants with and without skills. . . . Rewards for skilled occupations were greater, and the skilled immigrant went to the cities where there were opportunities to practice his trade. Less highly skilled workers went to the cities with expanding opportunities. Thus, the Italian concentration in construction and the Polish in steel were related to the expansion of these industries as these groups arrived. The Jewish concentration in the garment industry may have been a function of their previous experience as tailors, but it was also dependent upon the emergence of the mass production of clothing in the late nineteenth century.[22]

Group consciousness arises and crystallizes within work relationships, common residential areas, interests, and lifestyles in working-class conditions. Moreover, normal communication and participation in ethnic organizations on a cosmopolitan level can reinforce ethnic identity even among residentially dispersed groups.

## Migration Patterns

The longer a group is in the United States, the less geographically concentrated it is. Although this is hardly a surprising finding, ethnicity still plays a role in the changing spatial patterns. Distinctive geographic ethnic concentrations remain in the nation because groups differ in their inclination to enter or leave an area according to the existing ethnic compositions of those areas. At least for the present, ethnic linkage to certain regions remains strong.[23]

A numerically small group, if highly concentrated in a small number of localities, possesses greater political and social influence than one dispersed more uniformly. Thus, the linkage between demographic size and location influences visibility, occupational patterns, interaction patterns, intermarriage, and assimilation.

In 2008, 63 percent of the 1.1 million immigrants who came to the United States entered through just six states.[24] At the same time, three of these gateway states—California, New York, and Texas—had considerable net outmigration of their foreign-born populations to other states. As the leading destination for migrants from abroad, California and New York were also the leaders in this internal migration, sending 295,000 and 181,000, respectively, to other states in 2007.[25]

Just as chain migration is an important factor in migration from abroad, so too does it appear to play an important role in this population re-distribution of the foreign-born to other states. As a result, the ethnic dimension in internal migration patterns that Lieberson and Waters found 20 years earlier is still significant. By far, the greatest numbers of interstate movers have been Asians, followed by Mexicans and other Latin Americans. States where this internal migration had the most dramatic impact on population composition were Nevada, North Carolina, Georgia, Arkansas, Minnesota, Nebraska, and Indiana.[26]

Focusing on ethnic and racial settlement patterns is helpful in under-standing part of the assimilation process. In his influential ecological model of Chicago's growth and development, Robert Park noted the linkage between social and spatial mobility. Where one lives is as valid an indicator of upward mobility as income, education, and occupation.[27]

Housing markets are segmented along class and racial lines, and because the most desirable neighborhoods tend to be inhabited by non-Hispanic Whites, the relocation by minority members typically involves a process of in-tegration. Because such spatial mobility implies greater access to cultural, eco-nomic, physical, and social resources and is indicative of social and economic assimilation, the term **spatial assimilation** is often used to identify this process. What we are witnessing is the reduction in differences in the residential pat-terns across groups, although its extent and pace among immigrants is affected by their race and ethnicity. Higher-educated immigrants, for example, tend to be less segregated than less-educated ones, who also are likely to be poorer.[28]

## Symbolic Ethnicity

Among first-generation U.S. immigrants, ethnicity is an everyday reality that everyone takes for granted. For most immigrants living within an eth-nic community, shared communal interactions make ethnic identity a major factor in daily life. Not yet structurally assimilated, these immigrants find that their ethnicity provides the link to virtually everything they say or do, what they join, and whom they befriend or marry.

What happens to the ethnicity of subsequent generations depends on the immediate environment. As one would expect, the presence of ethnic neighborhoods or organizations in the vicinity helps sustain a strong sense of ethnic identity.[29] For most Whites of European origin, living away from visible ethnic links and becoming part of the societal mainstream reduce the importance of their ethnic identity compared to their occupational and social identity. At this point, European ethnicity rests on acknowledging ancestry through attachment to a few ethnic symbols not pertinent to everyday life.

Sociologist Richard D. Alba spoke about a "twilight" stage among White ethnics, an ebbing of those visible ethnic markings of language, parallel social institutions, and residential clusters.[30] Aside from assimilation resulting in a lessening of ethnicity, high ethnic intermarriage rates also have reduced the intergenerational transmission of distinctive cultural traits and diversified the ethnic ancestry of third- and fourth-generation European Americans. A coalesced new ethnic group, European Americans, has emerged. Its ethnicity is muted and symbolic, a personal and voluntary identity that finds occasional expression in observing ethnic traditions during festivals, holidays, or other special times connected to one's heritage. It also includes supporting a political cause associated with the country of origin, such as statehood for Palestine or the return of democracy to Cuba.

Although socially assimilated and integrated into middle-class society, third- and fourth-generation European Americans maintain this quiet link to their origins. It can find form in small details, such as objects in the home with an ethnic meaning, occasional participation in an old-country ritual, a fondness for ethnic cuisine, even the use of religious symbols without regular participation in a religious culture or organization.[31] Individuals may remain interested in the immigrant experience, participate in ethnic political and social activities, or even visit the ancestral homeland. All these private, leisure-time activities help preserve ethnicity in symbolic ways, giving people a special sense of self in the homogenized world of White U.S. culture.

African Americans express symbolic ethnicity through such elements as musical styles, fashion and dress styles (Afros, braids, dreadlocks, tribal symbols cut into the hair, bandanna headbands, Kufi hats, harem pants, African beads), cuisine (soul food), and festivals (such as Kwanzaa, a weeklong festival honoring African American heritage that is celebrated primarily in the United States). Sometimes called *manifestations of cultural nationalism*—a movement toward African American solidarity based on encouraging African culture and values—these activities resemble those of the descendants of other ethnic groups proudly recalling their heritage.

## Current Ethnic Issues

Two highly controversial issues punctuate race and ethnic relations in the United States: immigration and bilingual education. Today's arguments against both repeat objections that were hotly asserted in the late nineteenth and early twentieth centuries. Nativist fears of being overrun by too many "non-American types" and losing societal cohesion as a result of their cultural pluralism are quite similar to concerns raised by dominant-group members of past generations. Closely related to these two issues is a third one: multiculturalism, which causes ongoing debates between its advocates and those insisting on assimilation.

## Immigration Fears

The ebb and flow of immigrant waves have an impact on the host nation in many ways. Their cultural impact can enrich the society—in architecture, art, foods, and music, to name just a few—but some fear language retention and non-assimilation will undermine societal cohesion. Immigrant labor can be a boon to the economy, but critics express concern about the lowering of wages and loss of jobs for native workers. Because most immigrants now are people of color and have a higher birth rate than native-born Americans, some worry about the changing racial demographics. Moreover, with developing countries now the primary sending areas, the interests of the newly naturalized citizens—and, in turn, U.S. foreign policy—become increasingly involved in developments in those parts of the world (see Table 7.1).

Many immigrants still come from European countries, but they now account for approximately 13 percent annually of the total number, due to the large increase in Asian and Hispanic immigrants. Given the ongoing processes of chain migration and family reunification—and contrasting birth rates in Europe as compared to Asia and Latin America—we can safely assume the continued dominance of developing countries in sending additional immigrants.

Approximately 9.8 million legal immigrants (including undocumented immigrants who were subsequently granted amnesty) came to the United States in the 1990s, exceeding the previous record set in 1901–1910, when 8.8 million arrived. With a total of 10.3 million newcomers arriving between

**TABLE 7.1   Major Sources of Newcomers to the United States: 2009**

| 1 | Mexico | 164,067 | 9 | Korea | 25,582 |
|---|--------|---------|----|-------|--------|
| 2 | China, People's Republic | 60,896 | 10 | Haiti | 23,994 |
| 3 | Philippines | 58,107 | 11 | Canada | 22,508 |
| 4 | India | 54,360 | 12 | Jamaica | 21,494 |
| 5 | Dominican Republic | 49,381 | 13 | El Salvador | 19,342 |
| 6 | Cuba | 38,111 | 14 | United Kingdom | 17,417 |
| 7 | Vietnam | 28,397 | 15 | Peru | 16,706 |
| 8 | Colombia | 27,221 | 16 | Brazil | 14,428 |

*Source:* U.S. Department of Homeland Security, *Yearbook of Immigration Statistics: 2009*, Table 2.

2000 and 2009, the first decade of the twenty-first century has set an even higher record number of legal immigrants. Add in the millions of undocumented immigrants, now thought to exceed 12 million, and the issue of immigration becomes a fiercely debated one.

Some opposition to current immigration results from concern about the ability of the United States to absorb so many immigrants. Echoing xenophobic fears of earlier generations, today's immigration opponents worry that U.S. citizens will lose control of the country to foreigners. This time, instead of fears about the religiously different Catholics and Jews or the physically different Mediterranean Whites who were dark-complexioned, the new anti-immigration groups fear the significantly growing presence of religiously and physically different immigrants of color.

Visible differences, together with the prevalence of languages other than English, constantly remind native-born Americans about the strangers in their midst, whom some perceive as a threat to U.S. society as they know it. This is especially true for Arab and Muslim Americans, whom anti-immigration advocates point to as illustrating the problem of too liberal an immigration policy that allowed terrorists in our midst. The reality that virtually all Arab and Muslim Americans denounce terrorism does little to reduce public fears.

It not only is the increasing visibility of so many "strangers" in neighborhoods, schools, and workplaces that encourages this backlash. The nation's stable birthrate means that immigrants account for a larger share of population growth than in previous years. According to the Population Reference Bureau, immigration contributed at least a third to the total population increase between 1990 and 2000.[32] Consequently, the Census Bureau projects that the U.S. racial composition will change dramatically in the next two generations, a prospect that displeases some people.

Another concern about immigration is economic. The public worries that immigrants take away jobs, drive down wages, and use too many government services at taxpayers' expense while not contributing significantly to that cost. How real are these fears?

**Jobs.**    Do immigrants take jobs away from Americans?, In a 2008 Gallup Poll, 15 percent of respondents nationwide thought so, but 79 percent thought that they mostly took jobs Americans don't want.[33] On the one hand, immigrants create many new jobs by starting new businesses (approximately 18 percent of the total). The explosion of lawn-care businesses and nail salons are only two examples. Or, consider that immigrants from Russia, Taiwan, and India founded Google, Yahoo!, and Sun Microsystems, respectively. Furthermore, immigrants increase the demand for goods and services that still others fill through these new jobs.

At the same time, the decline in native-born employment is most pronounced in states with heavier immigrant concentrations where the

*Although undocumented immigrants are an important part of the underground economy, and are seeking amnesty to become citizens, a large segment of the public wants the nation to regain control of its borders and even evict those who did not enter legally. This rally in Los Angeles is one of many such organized protests to occur in recent years.*

foreign-born increased their share of workers the most. Immigration has its biggest impact on the lower part of the labor market—particularly building maintenance, construction, and food services—where native-born unemployment numbers closely match the increase in immigrant employment numbers. In other labor sectors, there appears to be far less impact.[34]

*Wages.* The debate over immigrants lowering wages typically does not deal with skilled workers, as near-unanimous agreement exists that they give a big lift to the U.S. economy. Instead, the debate centers on the continuing arrival of millions of unskilled laborers, who some fear take away jobs and lower wages. One study of Mexican immigration concluded that it reduced the wages of high school dropouts by 7 percent between 1980 and 2000.[35] However, even the most pessimistic economists think such downward pressure on wages affects no more than 10 percent of the labor force or that the drop has been more than 5 percent during the past 20 years.

Immigration has not lowered for U.S. workers because not only has the percentage of native-born high school dropouts fallen sharply in the past few decades, but also immigrants and low-skilled U.S. workers fill rather different roles in the economy. To give only two examples of many, 54 percent of tailors in the United States are foreign-born, compared with less than

1 percent of crane operators, and 44 percent of plaster-stucco masons are immigrants, whereas less than 1 percent of sewer-pipe cleaners are foreign-born. With different skills, inclinations, and ideas, most immigrants do not seek the same jobs as U.S. workers.[36]

*Costs and Contributions.*   At the local and state levels, immigrants typically use more in services than they pay in local taxes. Those with low levels of education and job skills cost the most, particularly in health care and use of schools. In some states with large concentrations of immigrants, such as California, the newcomers consume far more in government benefits (education, health care, and social services) than they contribute in taxes (an average cost of $1,178 per native-born household in the 1990s). However, in most states, the cost per native-born household is $100 or $200 per year, but this is offset in their contributions to the states' economies in consumer spending and sales and property taxes paid.[37]

A helpful insight comes to us from North Carolina, which has one of the fastest-growing foreign-born populations in the country. Throughout the past decade, while filling one-third of the state's new jobs, their consumer spending totaled $9.2 billion. Add in the $1.9 billion they placed in savings, and North Carolina experienced a total growth dividend of $11 billion, which far exceeded the $61 million that the newcomers cost the state (or $102 per native-born taxpayer) in the difference between taxes paid and services required.[38]

On a national level, immigrants contributed about $15 billion to the U.S. gross domestic product (GDP) in 2010.[39] Applied against their costs in education, health, and social services, economists are in general agreement that the net gain to the United States from immigration is approximately $7 billion annually.[40]

Immigrant labor allows many goods and services to be produced more cheaply and provides the work force for some businesses that otherwise could not exist. These include U.S. textile and agricultural industries, as well as restaurants and domestic household services. In addition, economists say, immigrants and their children bring long-term benefits for most U.S. taxpayers because—like most U.S. residents—they and their descendants will add more to government coffers than they receive over their lifetimes.

*Public Opinion Polls.*   Statistics notwithstanding, Americans have mixed opinions about immigration. For example, in a 2009 Gallup Poll, 58 percent of respondents nationwide said they felt that, on the whole, immigration was good for the country, whereas 36 percent thought it was a bad thing. Yet, in a December 2007 NBC News/*Wall Street Journal* national poll, 52 percent said immigration hurts more than it helps the United States, and 39 percent said the opposite.[41]

These and other differing poll findings are likely reflecting the public blurring of legal and illegal immigration, as the various national polls consistently find two-thirds or more Americans think that illegal immigrants weaken the U.S. economy. When specifically asked in a CBS News/*New York Times* poll how serious a problem they thought illegal immigration was, 61 percent viewed it as "very serious," and another 30 percent said it was "somewhat serious." Moreover, when Arizona passed an anti-illegal immigrant law in 2010 that was challenged by the federal government as usurping its own authority, polls showed that the majority of Americans supported Arizona's action.[42]

In Chapter 2, we discussed how the linguistic relativity of language may connote intended or unintended meanings. A good example is use of the term *illegal immigrants* versus *unauthorized immigrants*. Although both mean the same thing, the first expression is more value-laden but used in public opinion polls. In this book, we hereafter will use the second or value-neutral term.

## Unauthorized Immigrants

In the aftermath of the terrorist attacks on September 11, 2001, amid concerns about insufficient screening of aliens coming to the United States and the growing presence of unauthorized immigrants, the government reorganized in 2003. Services once provided by the much-criticized Immigration and Naturalization Service now occur within the Department of Homeland Security under the U.S. Citizenship and Immigration Services (USCIS). With 18,000 federal employees working in 250 offices around the world, this office adjudicates immigrant visa petitions, naturalization petitions, and asylum and refugee applications.[43]

What fuels public debate about immigration is the rising number of unauthorized foreign-born people in the United States, now estimated to be approximately 12 million. This population grew rapidly from 1990 to 2006, but since has stabilized. Current estimates place unauthorized immigrants as 4 percent of the total population and 5.4 percent of the workforce in 2008. Their children, an estimated 3.2 million with nearly three-fourths of them U.S.-born, constitute 6.8 percent of the nation's elementary and secondary schools.[44]

Mexicans comprise the largest segment of unauthorized immigrants, an estimated 59 percent of the total, a proportion that has remained steady for a decade. Another 11 percent are from Central America, 7 percent from South America, 4 percent from the Caribbean, and another 4 percent from Europe and Canada. South and East Asia is another large source, sending approximately 11 percent, while the Middle East accounts for less than 2 percent.[45] A large number of people from foreign lands continue to slip across U.S. borders, but others (approximately 165,000 annually) first arrive legally as visitors (tourists, students, or businesspeople) but do not leave—and so then become visa violators.

Entering the country easily and then disappearing within it, these unauthorized immigrants usually escape detection by the Department of Homeland Security, which spends millions to patrol the borders of the United States. In the Southwest, the problem draws the greatest amount of public attention and generates the most apprehensions of undocumented aliens occurs (approximately 792,000 in 2008). Mexicans dominated the list of those apprehended, at 88 percent of the total. Other major source countries of those apprehended were, in descending order, Honduras, Guatemala, El Salvador, Cuba, Brazil, Ecuador, the Dominican Republic, Nicaragua, China, Colombia, and Haiti.[46]

In 2006–2007, public pressure mounted about doing something about better border control and dealing with unauthorized immigrants already here. Political debates, opposing legislative proposals for amnesty or a crackdown on "illegals," calls for a 700-mile wall along the Mexican border, Congressional hearings and mass demonstrations in many U.S. cities all illustrated the fundamental disagreements about how to deal with the situation. Since then, however, a divided Congress has been unable to pass any immigration reform bill as of this writing. Calls for reform come at a time when parts of the U.S. economy are dependent on the labor of undocumented migrants. Mostly Latinos, these unskilled workers have spread to a wide range of industries (see Figure 7.2). Moreover, approximately 10 percent of the labor force of Mexico—as well as several other Central American and Caribbean countries—now are working in the United States, and their sending monies to their families back home is a major source of financial support there.[47]

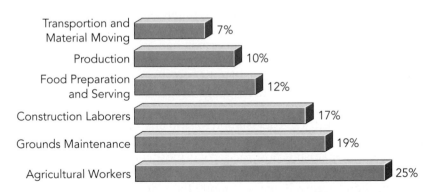

Transportion and Material Moving — 7%
Production — 10%
Food Preparation and Serving — 12%
Construction Laborers — 17%
Grounds Maintenance — 19%
Agricultural Workers — 25%

**FIGURE 7.2    Percent of Undocumented Migrants in U.S. Labor Force: 2005**

*Source:* Jeffrey Passel and D'Vera Cohn, "A Portrait of Unauthorized Immigrants in the United States," Pew Hispanic Center Research Report (April 19, 2009).

## Language Retention

One of the most divisive issues involving immigration is language retention. For many native-born Americans, the presence of groups not speaking English goes to the heart of their assumptions that the newcomers aren't even trying to assimilate. The large-scale presence of an immigrant group—whether on a national level such as the Hispanics or in a local area such as the Vietnamese in California—intensifies this perception. On a personal level, witnessing foreign-born parents speaking in public to their children in the language of their homeland, or seeing signs or television programs in languages other than English, also deepens an individual's concern about societal cohesion.

However, if we examine language retention concerns about past immigrants, we find similar patterns. For example, when colonial Pennsylvania was one-third German, Benjamin Franklin asked,

> Why [should] the Pennsylvanians . . . allow the Palatine Germans to swarm into our settlements, and by herding together to establish their language and Manners to the exclusion of ours? Why should Pennsylvania, founded by the English, become a colony of Aliens, who will shortly be so numerous as to Germanize us instead of our Anglifying them?[48]

Concerned about their meager command of English and need for interpreters, Franklin also remarked, "I suppose in a few years they will also be necessary in the Assembly, to tell one-half of our legislators what the other half say."[49] A century later, so many hundreds of thousands of Germans lived within the area bounded by Cincinnati, Milwaukee, and St. Louis, that the area became known as the "German triangle." Here, everyday speaking in German was so commonplace that several states in the region passed legislation permitting the use of German in public schools for all classroom instruction.[50] Needless to say, many Americans were aghast at what they thought was the encouragement of German non-assimilation.

Similarly, as millions of Italian immigrants in the first two decades of the twentieth century settled in what became the Little Italys of many U.S. cities, the prevalence of Italian language usage, signs, newspapers, and radio programs led many Americans to denounce these "inassimilable" Italians and to seek restrictive legislation to stop any more from coming here. Sound familiar?

Although Spanish is now the second-most common language spoken at home (approximately 31 million do so), other languages also have been increasing significantly. Foremost among these are Chinese, Russian, Tagalog (Philippines), and Vietnamese. In 1990, French was the third-most common language spoken; today it is Chinese (see Figure 7.3).

With a million or more immigrants entering the United States each year, the extensive use of other languages alarms many nativists. The U.S.

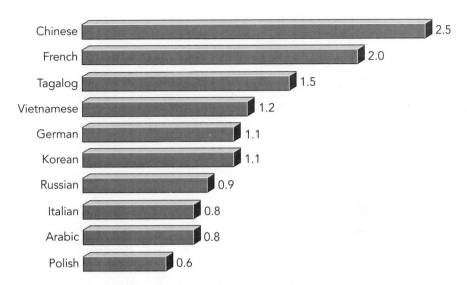

**FIGURE 7.3  Ten Languages Most Frequently Spoken at Home Other Than English and Spanish, Age 5 Years and Older, in Millions: 2008**

*Source:* U.S. Census Bureau, *2008 American Community Survey.*

Census Bureau estimates that nearly one in five Americans does not speak English at home. In fact, more than 10.5 million said they speak little or no English, up from 6.5 million in 1990. According to experts, some of the rise is due to the fast growth of the new-immigrant population, which included millions of people who came here illegally. The share of people who speak little English is highest among those in their working years, ages 18 to 64.[51]

## Bilingual Education

Offering **bilingual education**—teaching subjects in both English and the student's native language—can take the form of a transitional program (gradually phasing in English completely over several years) or a maintenance program (continued native-language teaching to sustain the students' heritage with a simultaneous but relatively limited emphasis on English proficiency).

For the many U.S. residents who assume that English-speaking schools provide the heat for the melting pot, the popularity of bilingual education—particularly maintenance programs—is a sore point. Some see such efforts as reducing assimilation in, and the cohesiveness of, U.S. society, while simultaneously isolating ethnic groups from one another. Advocates of bilingual

*Bilingual education continues to stir controversy over cost, effectiveness, and its alleged "threat" to societal cohesiveness, provoking some demands for its elimination. Several recent studies indicate that immersion programs have success rates comparable to bilingual programs, but contradictory findings in other studies keep the issue in dispute.*

programs emphasize that they are developing **bilingualism**—fluency in both English and the students' native tongue—and that many youngsters are illiterate in both when they begin school.

Public funding for bilingual education began in 1968 with the Bilingual Education Act, designed for low-income families only. Two years later, the Department of Health, Education, and Welfare specified that school districts in which any national-origin group constitutes more than 5 percent of the student population had a legal obligation to provide bilingual programs for low-income families.

The 1974 Bilingual Act eliminated the low-income requirement and urged that children receive various courses that provided appreciation of their cultural heritage. The 1974 Equal Opportunity Act identified failure to take "appropriate action" to overcome language barriers impeding equal participation in school as a form of illegal denial of equal educational opportunity. Since then, **English as a Second Language (ESL) programs** have expanded to function in approximately 125 languages, including 20 Native American languages.

Nearly 11 million immigrant children who speak a language other than English at home presently are enrolled in the public schools, both urban and suburban. Schools therefore must overcome cultural, language, and literacy barriers to provide for their education. Between 1979 and 2008, the number of school-age children (ages 5–17) who spoke a language other than English at home increased from 9 to 21 percent (from 3.8 to 10.9 million).[52]

Because 95 percent of all immigrant children attend urban schools, this challenge falls primarily to these urban areas. This especially is the case in the six states where immigrants are most concentrated (California, New York, Florida, Texas, New Jersey, and Illinois). For example, nearly half of all school-age children in California are children of immigrants. However, new immigrant patterns are doubling, even tripling the enrollment of immigrant children in such states as Nevada, North Carolina, Georgia, and Nebraska.[53]

Nearly half of all U.S. public schools have limited-English-proficient (LEP) students, with certain states having high proportions, such as Arizona (87 percent), California (90 percent), and Hawaii (96 percent). Approximately three-fourths of all limited-English-proficient (LEP) students receive English as a Second Language instruction, and only one-fourth have this instruction paired with native-language academic instruction, more commonly known as bilingual programs. Together, the programs enable educators to teach 11 million school-age students in the United States whose first language is not English, as well as 2.7 million other students whose English proficiency is limited.[54]

The practical value of ESL programs over native-language instruction is readily apparent since it practically is impossible to offer native-tongue classes in so many languages. As it is, urban and suburban schools struggle for funds, space, and qualified teachers for their various bilingual programs.

Older naturalized U.S. citizens often cite difficulty with the English language while they were students as one of the most difficult aspects of adjusting to the United States and gaining acceptance. Bilingual proponents argue that their programs ease that adjustment and accelerate the learning process. Since the 1970s, the National Education Association has supported an **English-plus program** to promote the integration of language minority students into the U.S. mainstream and to develop foreign language competence in native-born U.S. students to function in a global economy.[55]

How effective is bilingual education in helping children learn English? Despite the many studies comparing transitional bilingual education programs to structured English immersion programs, the findings are mixed. On the one hand, numerous studies, including those utilizing a *meta-analysis* (including as many other studies as possible), conclude that bilingual programs are effective, or even superior, in promoting academic achievement compared to all-English approaches.[56] Other studies have found no significant difference in academic performance, that neither bilingual education nor English immersion is superior to the other.[57] Still other studies conclude that instructional programs that teach in English are more effective than programs that provide more instruction in the students' native language.[58]

Perhaps these contradictory findings result from bilingual programs varying so widely in approach and quality. It may be reasonable to assume that students who are given enough assistance and time in any well-taught program will gain English proficiency better than those in overcrowded classrooms do or ones with limited attention given to helping students. In other words, the focus on individually helping students learn English may be a more significant factor than which type of program is used in doing so.

## The Official English Movement

Opponents of bilingual education argue that the program encourages "ethnic tribalism," fostering separation instead of a cohesive society. Their objections come in response to Hispanic leaders in such groups as the National Council of La Raza and the League of United Latin American Citizens (LULAC), who claimed that "language rights" entitled Hispanic people to have their language and culture maintained at public expense, both in the schools and in the workplace. The oldest Hispanic civil-rights group still in existence, LULAC was founded in 1929. Ironically, it began as an assimilationist organization, accepting only U.S. citizens as members, conducting its official proceedings in English, and declaring as one of its goals "to foster the acquisition and facile use of the official language of our country."[59]

In reaction to increasing immigration and foreign-language usage, the nativists have pressed to make English the official language for all public business. The largest national lobbying group, U.S. English, was cofounded by Japanese immigrant S. I. Hayakawa, a former U.S. senator from California and former president of and linguistics professor at San Francisco State University. Its president since 1993 has been Mauro E. Mujica, an immigrant from Chile.

By 2010, the group claimed more than 1.8 million members, and its success prompted critics to attack it as being anti-immigrant, racist, divisive, and dangerous. The group counters that its goal is for official government business at all levels to be conducted solely in English. This includes all public documents, records, legislation, regulations, hearings, official ceremonies, and public meetings. It is not opposed to other languages used in everyday private lives or taught. The organization argues that the ability to speak English is the single greatest empowering tool that immigrants must have to succeed, as it will expand their opportunities greatly.[60]

By 2010, 30 states had passed official English laws. Public opinion polls strongly support making English the official language. A 2009 Rasmussen Reports poll, for example, found 84 percent of Americans saying so.[61] Since 1981, more than 50 bills have been introduced in Congress to make English the nation's official language. Six of these bills passed in one chamber but not in the other; the U.S. Senate passed such legislation in 2006 and 2007. Undaunted, proponents in both houses continue to lobby for passage.

Although proponents of official English legislation claim that such action is essential to preserve a common language and provide a necessary bridge across a widening language barrier within the country, numerous polls and studies demonstrate that this action is unnecessary. For more than 25 years, public opinion polls have consistently shown that the large majority of foreign-born Americans believe learning English is important to become a part of U.S. society and to find a job. For example, a 2009 national poll of immigrants revealed that 45 percent did not know English at all and 31 percent knew only a little when they arrived; 70 percent took English classes; and 84 percent said it is hard to get a good job or do well in this country without learning English.[62]

That attitude manifests itself in action. Today, first- and second-generation Americans are becoming fluent in English at a faster pace than did past immigrants (see the Reality Check box and Figure 7.4). A four-year national study by the Pew Hispanic Center revealed that, while only 23 percent of Latino immigrants speak English very well, 88 percent of their adult children do so, and that figure increases to 94 percent in the next generation.[63]

In the largest longitudinal study of second-generation Americans (5,200 immigrant children in Miami and San Diego), researchers found that 99 percent spoke fluent English and less than one-third maintained fluency in their parents' tongues by age 17.[64] Similarly, another study revealed the

## Reality Check
## Language Acquisition: Newcomers Learning English

Critics fear the end of the historical pattern of immigrant languages dying out and yielding way to English-language-dominance across the generations because the Spanish language is so prevalent today. However, recent research shows this pattern still continues, even in Southern California, with more than 50 years of continuous Mexican immigration. As Figure 7.5 below reveals, native language usage drops significantly, even in the home, with each succeeding generation. Even among Mexicans, by the third generation, 96 percent prefer to speak English.

These results come from analysis of 5,703 young adults in their 20s living in Los Angeles and San Diego. Although the usage of Spanish in the home may last a bit longer, the survival curves for Mexican and other Latin American groups look quite similar to those for Asians and white Europeans. In this study, the 1.0 generation arrived as adult immigrants and the 1.5 generation arrived in the United States as children before age 10. The 2.0 generation was born in the United States of two foreign-born parents, whereas members of the 2.5 generation were born in the United States of one foreign-born parent and one U.S.-born parent.

*(Continued)*

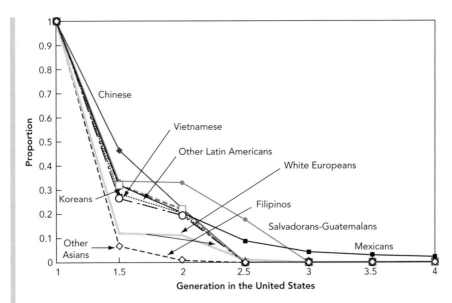

**FIGURE 7.4    Proportion of Immigrant Group Members Who Speak Mother Tongue at Home by Generation**

The U.S.-born 3.0 generation has two U.S.-born parents and three or four foreign-born grandparents, whereas the 3.5 cohort has only one or two foreign-born grandparents.

*Source:* Adapted from Rubén G. Rumbaut, Douglas Massey, and Frank D. Bean, "Linguistic Life Expectancies: Immigrant Language Retention in Southern California," Population and Development Review, 32 (2006): 447–60.

preference by 73 percent of second-generation immigrants in Southern California with two foreign-born parents to speak English at home instead of their native tongue. By the third generation, more than 97 percent of these immigrants—Chinese Filipino, Guatemalan, Korean, Mexican, Salvadoran, and Vietnamese—preferred to speak only English at home.[65]

On a broader scale, the Census Bureau reports that, of those U.S. residents aged 18 to 64 who spoke a language other than English at home in 2000, 55 percent (25.6 million) reported that they spoke English "very well." When combined with those who spoke only English at home, 92 percent of the population aged 5 and older had no difficulty speaking English.[66] Often, those who do not yet speak English well or at all are disproportionately the elderly (especially those in dense ethnic enclaves, such as among the Cubans in Miami), the most recently arrived, the undocumented, and the least educated.[67]

## Multiculturalism

In its early phase, during the 1970s, **multiculturalism** meant including material in the school curriculum that related the contributions of non-European peoples to U.S. history. Next followed efforts to change all areas of the curriculum in elementary and secondary schools and colleges to reflect the diversity of U.S. society and to develop students' awareness of, and appreciation for, the impact of non-European civilizations on U.S. culture. The intent of this movement was to promote an expanded U.S. identity that recognized previously excluded groups as integral components, both in heritage and in actuality.

Some multiculturalists subsequently moved away from an assimilationist or integrative approach, rejecting a common bond of identity among the distinct minority groups. These multiculturalists advocate "minority nationalism" and "separatist pluralism," with a goal not a collective national identity but of specific, separate group identities.[68] To create a positive group identity, these multiculturalists go beyond advocacy for teaching and maintaining a group's own cultural customs, history, values, and festivals. They also deny the validity of the dominant culture's customs, history, values, and festivals. Two examples are Native Americans who object to Columbus Day parades and Afrocentrists who assert that Western culture was merely derived from Afro-Egyptian culture.

Another striking example is the argument that only groups with power can be racist. This view holds that because Whites have power, they are intrinsically racist, whereas people of color lack power and so cannot be racist.[69] The counterargument is that any racial group that blames, criticizes, stereotypes, or acts against another entire racial group is guilty of racist thinking or action. Furthermore, opponents of multiculturalism argue that it undermines the assimilation ethic and that the weaker our assimilation efforts, the fewer immigrants we can accept if we are to remain a cohesive society (see the International Scene box).

Another battleground for multiculturalists involves offering or eliminating courses in Western civilization. Some institutions, such as Providence College in Rhode Island, expanded such course requirements and made them interdisciplinary; other institutions, such as Stanford University, questioned their inclusion at all. At many institutions, the proposals for curriculum change ranged from making all students take non-Western and women's studies courses as part of their degree requirements to excluding all Western history and culture courses from such requirements.

Regardless of their orientation, most multiculturalists are pluralists waging war with assimilationists. Neither side will vanquish the other, though, for both forces remain integral parts of U.S. society. The United States continues to offer a beacon of hope to immigrants everywhere, keeping the rich tradition of pluralism alive and well. And yet, as has been consistently demonstrated for

## The International Scene
## Italy and Spain Struggle with Illegal Immigration

Italy and Spain own islands near the African coast that have become popular staging areas for migrants fleeing the poverty of their homelands. As a result, both countries are overwhelmed with the tens of thousands of illegal arrivals each year.

Italy's long coastline and close proximity to other countries make it especially vulnerable. The most popular clandestine sea route for Africans is from Libya or Tunisia to the Italian island of Lampedusa or to Sicily. The Spanish Canary Islands attract boatloads from Morocco and Mauritania. Despite the dangers of their rickety boats capsizing (hundreds have drowned), the overcrowded boats keep coming. Many are intercepted, but under cover of darkness, others get through.

Italy is also the destination by a second route: a 60-mile speedboat ride by smugglers from Albania across the Adriatic Sea. Albanians, Afghans, Kurds, Turks, and Chinese are the most frequent arrivals this way. A third route brings in eastern Europeans by truck over the Slovenian border into Milan.

The Organization for Economic Cooperation and Development (OECD) reports that, in 2007, Italy's foreign-born population totaled 3,4 million, or 5.8 percent of the total population. Spain had 13.4 million foreign-born, 11.6 percent of its total population. With no border checks among European Union member nations, an illegal migrant reaching either country has essentially reached Europe as well, and so EU officials are attempting to persuade African nations to crack down on these illegal boatloads.

Italy and Spain enacted amnesty programs to cope with the great numbers not fully participating in their economic systems. These amnesties, however, did not solve the problem and instead tended more to attract new illegal migration than to drain the basin of illegality.

Africans and Asians are visible everywhere, selling cheap merchandise on the streets, trying to clean windshields at intersections, or pumping gas. The arrival of so many physically and culturally distinct newcomers in so short a period created an anti-immigrant backlash, transforming relatively open countries into closed ones. Racial incidents, including firebombings, became commonplace and the growing backlash resulted in increased popularity for anti-immigration political parties, forcing the ruling political parties to become more aggressive in their deportation efforts.

*Critical thinking question:* What patterns of similarity do you see between the United States and European experiences with undocumented migrants? What dissimilarities?

---

centuries, assimilationist forces will remain strong, particularly for immigrant children and their descendants (see the Reality Check box). Multiculturalism will no more weaken that process than did the many past manifestations of ethnic ingroup solidarity.

Some analysts recommend the need for a common-ground position that replaces the assimilationist and pluralist models with a cosmopolitan model. Exaggerating and tolerating cultural differences leaves minorities outside the mainstream and does not promote a unified national identity.[70] Insisting on cultural uniformity ignores the reality that we are all members of a culture. Instead, we might consider a "postethnic" perspective that emphasizes a shared civic nationalism that overcomes the politics of race and the politics of identity, and instead recognizes the reality of multiple identities.[71]

## Diversity in the Future

The U.S. Census Bureau—working from current demographic patterns and making certain assumptions about future births, deaths, and international migration—projects a dramatic change in the composition of U.S. society by the mid-twenty-first century. It reports that the cumulative effects of immigration will be more important than births to people already living in the United States. By the mid-twenty-first century, it said, 82 percent of the population increase will be due to immigrants arriving from 2005 to 2050 and their U.S.-born descendants.[72]

The rapid growth of the Hispanic population, says the Census Bureau, enabled Hispanics of all races to surpass the African American population in 2000, when there were 35.3 million Hispanics and 34.7 million African Americans in the United States. By 2050, Hispanics will number approximately 132.8 million, or 30 percent of the total population. The Census Bureau projects that African Americans then will number approximately 65.7 million, or 15 percent (see Figure 7.5). All data reflect midrange projections, not high or low estimates.

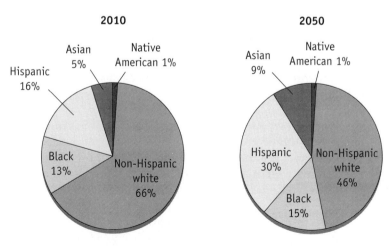

**FIGURE 7.5    America's Growing Diversity**

*Source:* U.S. Census Bureau middle-range projections.

The nation's Asian population will grow to approximately 40.6 million, or 9.2 percent, by 2050. Native Americans will increase to approximately 8.6 million by then, approximately 2 percent of the total. The number of non-Hispanic Whites will be 203.3 million by 2050, or 46 percent of the population.[73]

Some observers have reacted to these projections with alarm, using them to argue for immigration restrictions. Others relish the thought of U.S. society becoming more diverse. These projections, however, have some limitations, not the least of which is their assumption that current trends continue and that conditions worldwide will remain constant several decades into the future. Immigration is the most unstable demographic variable because it is affected by unforeseeable economic, political, and social forces. Certainly, four decades ago, no one would have predicted the current birth, death, and migration patterns that currently affect the United States. A forecast about the year 2050, then, is anything but certain.

Even more significant is the high probability that these Census Bureau projections will fall victim to the **Dillingham Flaw**. Who is to say that today's group categories will have the same meaning in the mid-twenty-first century? Two generations ago, Italian, Polish, and Slavic Americans still were members of distinct minority groups that lacked economic, political, and social power. They displayed all the classic characteristics of minority groups: ascribed status, endogamy, unequal treatment, and visibility. Today, they are mostly in the mainstream, displaying traits of civic, marital, and structural assimilation. Like European Americans who intermarried earlier, those whose ancestry is Italian, Polish, and Slavic are now mostly a blend of other nationalities. Two generations from now, the same may be true of other groups, such as Hispanics. Two generations from now, Americans will likely view one another very differently from how we do now.

## Social Indicators of Change

Although the demographic patterns of fertility, mortality, and migration are helpful in making projections, other patterns give reason for caution in predicting the future.

*Interethnic Marriages.* Our expectation that Hispanic Americans will marry outside their ethnic group, as have European Americans, finds support in the process that is already under way. In 2008, more than 2.2 million Hispanic Americans were married to someone of non-Hispanic origin, up 250 percent from 891,000 in 1980. That is approximately 26 percent of all married Hispanic American couples, and the proportion is growing steadily.[74] The children born from these exogamous marriages are obviously of mixed ethnic heritage, and if this trend continues, one day "Hispanic American" may be no more a distinctly visible ethnic category but rather one similar to today's Italian, Polish, or Slavic identities, a marker of one's heritage, not one's everyday reality.

*Interracial Marriages.*   For generations, we have failed to eliminate the racial barrier, so by mid-century, that barrier may still exist. However, one present-day trend suggests that our current simplistic racial categories are already obsolete. In 2008, approximately 4 percent of all marriages in the continental United States were interracial, compared to 1.3 percent in 1980. By 2008, interracially married couples numbered more than 2.3 million, one-fifth of them (481,000) Black–White couples—seven times more than the 65,000 in 1970. Whites married to a non-White spouse of a race other than Black (most often, Asian) grew from 450,000 in 1980 to 1.74 million. Couples consisting of Blacks married to a non-Black spouse of a race other than White increased from 34,000 to 122,000.[75]

When it comes to interracial dating and romances, the younger generation is more open to this choice than are previous generations. However, studies show that adolescents who interracially date face greater risks of difficulties with their peers than intraracially dating youth. Informal sanctions against them are strongest when the romances involve Black students.[76]

Interracial relationships more often are cohabiting unions than marital unions, but in either case, among Whites and Blacks (including immigrant and native Blacks), they are more likely to be of a Black man and a White woman. Native-born African Americans are more likely than ethnic Blacks to marry Whites. Ethnic Blacks and non-White Puerto Ricans are more likely to marry African Americans than to marry Whites.[77]

Interracial marriages of all combinations (Asian, Black, Hispanic, White) are no more likely to end in divorce than intraracial marriages when compared with other high-risk groups.[78] However, interracial adult couples, particularly Black-White couples, often encounter negative societal reactions, much like the adolescents mentioned earlier. One study found that Whites married to Blacks encounter more racism directly than Whites married to other non-Black minorities. White women encountered more racial incidents with their Black husbands (e.g., inferior service, racial profiling, and racism against their children) and more hostilities from families and others they encounter than did other interracial pairings.[79] Despite the challenges, another study found that partners in interracial relationships reported significantly higher relationship satisfaction compared to those in intraracial relationships.[80]

Racial and interracial marriage patterns vary if we control for ethnicity. For example, West Indian men of any generation have lower exogamy rates than African American men, while exogamy rates are higher among West Indian women who arrived as children or were born in the United States than among African American women.[81] What this tells us is that both gender and racial differences in interracial marriages can exist because of ethnicity.

Interracial romantic relationships are a useful barometer of race relations and structural assimilation in U.S. society. Their increasing prevalence
is an indicator of the decline in social distance between groups. Similar
demographic and social factors among African, Asian, European, and Hispanic Americans help predict outdating across racial groups. Men are more
likely to date interracially than women, particularly if they attend interracial
schools. Neither religious preference nor geographic region is a significant
factor, and neither apparently is status chasing. One study found no evidence of a pattern of majority-group members using interracial dating relationships to "trade up" by dating racial minorities with higher economic
and educational attainment.[82] It would appear that, as also suggested by my
social distance study discussed in Chapter 1, the racial barrier is lowering
when it comes to intimate social relations.

*Racial Identity.*    In 2008, more than 7 million Americans were of mixed
racial ancestry, 2.3 percent of the total population of 304 million.[83] The number of biracial and multiracial Americans continues to grow, so does the matter of racial identity formation. As we discussed in Chapter 1, our responses
to race are within a socially constructed reality, as illustrated by President
Obama, a biracial man with a White mother and a Black father, but whom a
great many people simply classify as an African American. Even the questions raised during his candidacy about whether he was "too black" or "not
black enough" revealed how fixated many were on the old racial categories.[84]

How do biracial or multiracial Americans categorize themselves? Self-
identification also appears to depend on the relationship between physical
appearance and a sense of belonging and exclusion.[85] Although more
Americans than ever identify themselves as biracial or multiracial, many
other biracial or multiracial Americans self-identify as monoracial. This
especially is true among Black biracials who tend to identify as monoracial
Blacks.[86] Many multiracial people growing up in Black neighborhoods tend
to identify themselves as Black as there is great pressure from society to
choose one race.[87]

Slavery reinforced in the American mind a rigid racial classification system that has long outlived slavery itself. Once a social construct that reflected
both that exploitative system and the decades of Jim Crow laws that followed,
and continuing into and past the Civil Rights Movement, it no longer is
an accurate means to describe demographic realities. Instead, say advocates,
an increasingly multiracial America requires us to create a new social construct. We must deconstruct race as an "either-or" mindset and relegate racial
identity to a much less important place in our dealings with one another, perhaps like Mexico, where its census does not even ask about race.[88]

That deconstruction is underway as America's foreign-born population
is challenging traditional views of race. Many are more likely to give their
national origin when identifying their race or ethnicity. For example, the U.S.

*President Barack Obama is a splendid example of the multiple narratives becoming so common in American family life. The son of a White American mother and Black African father, his extended family expands into Africa, Canada, Indonesia, Malaysia, China and slave-period America, and has Christian, Muslim, and Jewish roots. Here, he hugs his half-sister, Maya Soetoro-Ng, at her 2003 wedding to Konrad Ng, third from right, in Hawaii. From left are his daughters, Sasha and Malia; his grandmother Madelyn Dunham, seated; Konrad's parents, Joan and Howard Ng, and brother Perry Ng; and Michelle Obama.*

Census Bureau found that 87 percent of those born in Cuba and 53 percent of those born in Mexico identified themselves as White, but a majority of the more recently arrived Dominicans and Salvadorans would not describe themselves as either Black or White. Both immigration and the higher birth rates among the foreign born have driven the changing perception of race in Census 2010.[89]

***Religion and Migration.***    Earlier immigration waves transformed the United States from an almost exclusively Protestant country into a land of three major faiths: Catholic, Jewish, and Protestant. Because religion often is closely intertwined with ethnicity, current migration patterns offer clues about the religious preferences of future Americans if current trends continue.

Hispanic and Filipino migration may increase the Catholic population from the current 25 percent to perhaps 28 percent by 2050. Migration from Africa, Asia, and the Middle East may increase the Muslim population from 1 percent of the total to 3 percent. Given current patterns, the Jewish population may decline from 2 percent to 1 percent and the Protestant population from 51 percent to 46 percent; the populations of other religions—including Buddhism, Hinduism, and Sikhism—may slightly increase from 2 percent to 3 percent. Those declaring "no religion" may grow from 15 to 18 percent. Even if these predictions turn out to be somewhat inaccurate, the future will show even greater religious diversity than the present does.

Caution is needed in accepting these predictions, of course, because the Dillingham Flaw of oversimplified generalizations and the imposition of present-day sensibilities may lead to a misreading of the eventual reality. Religious intermarriage now is increasing among followers of all faiths, and since the nonreligious segment of society also is growing, we may find a very different future with respect to religion than we accurately can project.

## Beyond Tomorrow

*Diversity* is the word that best describes the past, present, and future of the United States. United by a core culture and shared beliefs in certain ideals, the nation's peoples have not always understood their common bond or openly accepted one another as equals. As the dual realities of assimilation and pluralism continue to pull people seemingly in two directions at once, few people recognize that they are witnessing a recurring set of historical patterns. Instead, some voices cry out again against immigration, brand the newcomers as "unassimilable," and express fear for the character and cohesiveness of society. Yet immigrants always have been important to the growth of U.S. society, and their presence has continually strengthened the country.

Despite some progress, the United States has never fully resolved its race relations problems. As it becomes a more multiracial society than ever before, it may see a worsening of race relations. We've seen some indicators in the late twentieth century: Black–Asian and Black–Latino conflicts in addition to Black–White conflicts. Perhaps, though, the situation will improve with deconstruction of the rigid racial categories that still promote an "us" and "them" mentality and with more sharing of power through the increased presence of people of color in elective offices and other policymaking positions. Perhaps, also, the unity of diverse peoples that occurred after the 2001 terrorist attacks will be a source of inspiration for improved race relations in the years to come. Gender equality—as well as inclusiveness and protection of rights for the aged, disabled, and homosexuals—are other areas in which some gains have occurred but in which additional concerted efforts are necessary for all to achieve their fullest potential.

As we approach the future, we do so with the educational attainment of all Americans rising. If knowledge is power, perhaps that reality will lead us to greater appreciation and tolerance for one another. This book has been an attempt to enhance that understanding. We need to comprehend the larger context and patterns within which the dynamics of intergroup relations exist. We need to realize that pluralism has always been part of the U.S. experience and does not threaten either the assimilation process or the cohesiveness of society. We need to recognize that race and ethnicity are simply other people's humanity. When we reach that level of understanding, we will be able to acknowledge that diversity is the nation's strength, not its weakness; and when that happens, our society will be even stronger.

## KEY TERMS

1.5 generation
2.5 generation
Bilingual education
Bilingualism
Dillingham Flaw
English as a Second Language (ESL)
  programs

English-plus programs
Hansen's law
Multiculturalism
Segmented assimilation
Social capital
Spatial assimilation
Transnationalism

## DISCUSSION QUESTIONS

1. If you are the descendant of immigrants, how realistic or unrealistic is the three-generation hypothesis in your family? If you are an immigrant or the child of immigrant parents, how realistic or unrealistic is transnationalism in your family? If you are the descendant of migrants from the rural South to the urban North, do you find any relevance to these concepts in your family?

2. What in this chapter particularly struck your interest? Why?

3. What do current immigration patterns indicate? Is immigration a problem for native-born U.S. residents? Explain.

4. What are the pros and cons of bilingual education?

5. Describe the varying viewpoints about multiculturalism.

6. Do you have any thoughts on the projections for the future given in this chapter, or on the Dillingham Flaw warning?

## INTERNET ACTIVITIES

1. Check out this YouTube music video at http://www.youtube.com/watch?v=sEJfS1v-fU0. It's an example of what many Americans think about English as the country's language. It's very appropriate to this chapter's discussion. What do you think?

2. U.S. English (http://www.us-english.org/), as mentioned in this chapter, is dedicated to preserving English as the common language and has its own home page. Go to it and read some of their arguments for their cause. What is your reaction?

3. The League of United Latin American Citizens (LULAC) is another advocacy group, but one in favor of immigration. At its website (www.lulac.org/programs/immigration/), you will find many informative links about immigration.

4. Public Agenda is a nonpartisan opinion research and civic engagement organization. At its website (www.publicagenda.org/pages/immigrants), you will find extensive views on immigration, including from immigrants themselves.

# NOTES

## Chapter 1

1. Aristotle, *The Rhetoric* (New York: Appleton, 1932), Book I, Chapter 11.
2. See, for example, R. Matthew Montory, Robert S. Horton, and Jeffrey Kircher, "Is Actual Similarity Necessary for Attraction? A Meta-Analysis of Actual and Perceived Similarity," *Journal of Social & Personal Relationships* 25 (2008): 889–922.
3. See, for example, Ramadhar Singh, Li Jen Ho, Hui Lynn Tan, and Paul A. Bell, "Attitudes, Personal Evaluations, Cognitive Evaluation, and Interpersonal *Attraction*: On the Direct, Indirect, and Reverse-Causal Effects," *British Journal of Social Psychology* 46 (2007): 19–42.
4. Emory S. Bogardus, "Comparing Racial Distances in Ethiopia, South Africa, and the United States," *Sociology and Social Research* 52 (1968): 149–56.
5. See Tom W. Smith and Glenn R. Dempsey, "The Polls: Ethnic Social Distance and Prejudice," *Public Opinion Quarterly* 47 (1983): 584–600.
6. Milton Kleg and Kaoru Yamamoto, "As the World Turns: Ethno-Racial Distances after 70 Years," *Social Science Journal* 35 (April 1998): 183–90.
7. Vincent N. Parrillo and Christopher Donoghue, "Updating the Bogardus Social Distance Studies: A New National Survey," *Social Science Journal*, 42:2 (2005): 257–71.
8. Lyn H. Lofland, *A World of Strangers*, reprint ed. (Long Grove, Ill., 1985), p. 16.
9. Georg Simmel, "The Stranger," in Kurt H. Wolff, (ed.), *The Sociology of Georg Simmel* (New York: Free Press, 1950).
10. Alfred Schutz, "The Stranger," *American Sociological Review* 69 (May 1944): 449–507.
11. Ta-Nehisi Paul Coates, "Is Obama Black Enough?" *Time* (February 1, 2007). Accessed at http://www.time.com/time/nation/article/0,8599,1584736,00.html [December 29, 2010]; and Richard Carter, "Once Again, Is Obama Really Black Enough for Black Voters?" *New York Amsterdam News* (May 3, 2007), pp. 10, 41.
12. See Albert Szymanski, "Racial Discrimination and White Gain," *American Sociological Review* 41 (1976): 403–14; Sidney M. Willhelm, "Can Marxism Explain America's Racism?" *Social Problems* 28 (1980): 98–112.
13. Erving Goffman, *The Presentation of Self in Everyday Life* (Garden City, N.Y.: Doubleday, 1959).
14. Barbara Ballis Lal, "Symbolic Interaction Theories," *American Behavioral Scientist* 38 (1995): 421–41.
15. Peter L. Berger and Thomas Luckmann, *The Social Construction of Reality* (Garden City, N.Y.: Doubleday, 1963).
16. Donald Young, *American Minority Peoples* (New York: Harper, 1932), p. viii.
17. Louis Wirth, "The Problem of Minority Groups," in Ralph Linton (ed.), *The Science of Man in the World Crisis* (New York: Columbia University Press, 1945), pp. 347–72.

18. Richard Schermerhorn, *Comparative Ethnic Relations* (New York: Random House, 1970), p. 8.
19. Tamotsu Shibutani and Kian M. Kwan, *Ethnic Stratification* (New York: Macmillan, 1965).
20. Charles Wagley and Marvin Harris, *Minorities in the New World* (New York: Columbia University Press, 1964).
21. See Ashley Montagu, *Man's Most Dangerous Myth: The Fallacy of Race*, reprint ed. (New York: Whitley Press, 2007).
22. Michael J. Bamshad and Steve E. Olson, "Does Race Exist?" *Scientific American* 289 (December 2003): 78–85.
23. See Hiroshi Fukurai and Darryl Davies, "Races People Play: Social *Deconstruction of Race, Racial Identity, Statutory Passing, and Views on Resource Allocations and Legal Protections.*" Paper presented at the annual meeting of the American Sociological Association, San Francisco, August 1998; and Maria P. P. Root (ed.), *Racially Mixed People in America* (Newbury Park, CA: Sage, 1992).
24. See, for example, "Race and 'Reason,'" *Intelligence Report*, Southern Poverty Law Center, 1999. Accessed at http://www.splcenter.org/intel/intelreport/article.jsp?pid=623 [December 29, 2010].
25. Arab American Institute, "Arab Americans: Demographics." Accessed at http:// www.aaiusa.org/arab-americans/22/demographics [December 29, 2010].
26. Brewton Berry and Henry L. Tischler, *Race and Ethnic Relations*, 4th ed. (Boston: Houghton Mifflin, 1978), pp. 30–32.
27. Milton Gordon, *Assimilation in American Life* (New York: Oxford University Press, 1964), p. 27; Shibutani and Kwan, *Ethnic Stratification*, p. 47; Jerry D. Rose, *Peoples: The Ethnic Dimension in Human Relations* (Chicago: Rand McNally, 1976), pp. 8–12.
28. William Graham Sumner, *Folkways* (New York: Cosimo Books, 2007), p. 13. Originally published in 1906.
29. See Richard Jenkins, *Social Identity*, 3d ed. (New York: Routledge, 2008).
30. See David L. Rousseau and Rocio Garcia-Retamero, "Identity, Power, and Threat Perception," *Journal of Conflict Resolution* 51 (2007): 744–71.
31. Brewton Berry, *Race and Ethnic Relations*, 3d ed. (Boston: Houghton Mifflin, 1965), p. 55.
32. See Molefi Kete Asante, *The Afrocentric Idea*, rev ed. (Philadelphia: Temple University Press, 1998).
33. Martin E. Spencer, "Multiculturalism, 'Political Correctness,' and the Politics of Identity," *Sociological Forum* 9 (1994): 547–67.
34. Vincent N. Parrillo, "Diversity in America: A Sociohistorical Analysis," *Sociological Form* 9 (1994): 523–35.
35. Vincent N. Parrillo, *Diversity in America*, 3d ed. (Thousand Oaks, Calif.: Pine Forge Press, 2009), pp. 13–14.
36. C. Wright Mills, *The Sociological Imagination* (New York: Oxford University Press, 1959), p. 8.
37. Ibid., p. 9.
38. Ibid., p. 146.

## Chapter 2

1. See, for example, Lee Cronk, *The Complex Whole: Culture and the Evolution of Human Behavior* (Boulder, Colo.: Westview Press, 1999).
2. The importance of symbols to social interaction has drawn much attention in sociology. See Benjamin Lee Whorf, *Language, Thought and Reality* (New York: Wiley, 1956); Gertrude Jaeger and Philip Selznick, "A Normative Theory of Culture," *American Sociological Review* 29 (1964): 653–59; Herbert Blumer, *Symbolic Interaction: Perspective and Method* (Englewood Cliffs, N.J.: Prentice Hall, 1969).
3. Institute for Diversity and Ethics in Sport, *2010 Racial and Gender Report Card*. Accessed at http://www.tidesport.org/racialgenderreportcard.html [December 29, 2010].

4. The images show a bear climbing a tree as seen from other side; A giraffe going past a second-story window; a hot dog on a hamburger roll; four elephants at a watering trough.

5. This connection between Lippmann's comments, the Droodles, and human response to definitions of stimuli was originally made by Harry C. Bredemeier and Richard M. Stephenson, *The Analysis of Social Systems*, pp. 2–3.

6. Edward O. Wilson, *Sociobiology: The Abridged Edition* (Cambridge, MA: Belknap Press, 2004), p. 280.

7. See Melissa Wagner and Nancy Armstrong, *Field Guide to Gestures: How to Identify and Interpret Virtually Every Gesture Known to Man* (Philadelphia: Quirk Books, 2003).

8. William I. Thomas, "The Relation of Research to the Social Process," in *Essays on Research in the Social Sciences* (Washington, D.C.: Brookings Institution, 1931), p. 189.

9. Gregory Razran, "Ethnic Dislike and Stereotypes: A Laboratory Study," *Journal of Abnormal and Social Psychology* 45 (1950): 7–27.

10. Making sandals from tires is common now among certain Africans, Indians, Mexicans, and Vietnamese, and also promoted on eco-friendly websites. See, for example, http://www.hollowtop.com/sandals.htm or http://makezine.com/10/heirloom/.

11. Stanley Lieberson, "A Societal Theory of Race and Ethnic Relations," *American Sociological Review* 26 (December 1961): 902–10.

12. See Andrew M. Greeley, *The American Catholic: A Social Portrait* (New York: Basic Books, 1977), Chapter 1; see also Richard D. Alba, *Italian Americans: Into the Twilight of Ethnicity* (Englewood Cliffs, N.J.: Prentice Hall, 1985), pp. 9–12.

13. William M. Newman, *American Pluralism* (New York: Harper & Row, 1973), p. 53.

14. Barbara Solomon, *Ancestors and Immigrants*, reprint ed. (Boston: Northeastern University Press, 1989), pp. 59–61.

15. John Higham, *Strangers in the Land* (New Brunswick, N.J.: Rutgers University Press, 2002), p. 248.

16. Milton Gordon, *Assimilation in American Life* (New York: Oxford University Press, 1964), pp. 70–71.

17. Ibid., p. 81.

18. See Brian Gratton, Myron P. Guttman, and Emily Skop, "Immigrants, Their Children, and Theories of Assimilation: Family Structure in the United States, 1880–1970," *The History of the Family* 12 (2007): 203–33.

19. See Scott J. South, Kyle Crowder, and Jeremy Pais, "Inter-Neighborhood Migration and Spatial Assimilation in a Multi-Ethnic World: Comparing Latinos, Blacks, and Anglos," *Social Forces* 87 (2008): 415–43; and Susan K. Brown, "Structural Assimilation Revisited: Mexican-Origin Nativity and Cross-Ethnic Primary Ties," *Social Forces* 85 (2006): 75–92.

20. Alejandro Portes and Min Zhou, "The New Second Generation: Segmented Assimilation and Its Variants," *The Annals of the American Academy of Political and Social Science* 530 (1993): 74–96.

21. Newman, *American Pluralism*, p. 63.

22. J. Hector St. John de Crèvecoeur, *Letters from an American Farmer* (New York: Albert & Charles Boni, 1925), pp. 54–55. Reprinted from the original edition, London, 1782.

23. Frederick Jackson Turner, *The Frontier in American History* (New York: Henry Holt, 1920), p. 351.

24. Israel Zangwill, *The Melting-Pot: Drama in Four Acts* (New York: Macmillan, 1921), p. 33.

25. Actually, any student of Western civilizations would point out that centuries of invasions, conquests, boundary changes, and so on often resulted in crossbreeding and that truly distinct or pure ethnic types were virtually nonexistent long before the eighteenth century.

26. Samuel P. Huntington, *Who Are We: The Challenges to America's National Identity* (New York: Simon & Schuster, 2005); and "How Anglo Is America?" *Economist* 373 (2004): 39.

27. See Hyoung-jin Shin, "Intermarriage Patterns of New Immigrants: Understanding the Social Boundaries of Hispanic and Asian Americans," *Dissertation Abstracts International, A: The*

*Humanities and Social Sciences* 68 (2008): 4492. Gordon, *Assimilation in American Life*, pp. 109–10.

28. Henry Pratt Fairchild, *Immigration: A World Movement and Its Significance* (Ann Arbor: University of Michigan Library, 2006), p. 396. Originally published in 1925.

29. Will Herberg, *Protestant-Catholic-Jew* (Chicago: University of Chicago Press, 1983), p. 21.

30. Newman, *American Pluralism*, p. 67.

31. Horace M. Kallen, "Democracy Versus the Melting Pot," *The Nation* (February 18, 1915), pp. 190–94; (February 25, 1915), pp. 217–20.

32. Gordon, *Assimilation in American Life*, p. 135.

33. Richard D. Alba, "Assimilation's Quiet Tide," *Public Interest* (Spring 1995): 3–4.

34. Jeff Hitchcock, *Lifting the White Veil: An Explanation of White Culture in a Multiracial Context* (Roselle, NJ: Crandall, Dostie, and Douglass Books, 2003), pp. 115–16.

# Chapter 3

1. See, for example, Francis Leo Collins, "Connecting 'Home' with 'Here': Personal Homepages in Everyday Transnational Life,"*Journal of Ethnic & Migration Studies* 35 (2009): 839–59; Vivian Louie, "Growing Up Ethnic in Transnational Worlds: Identities among Second-Generation Chinese and Dominicans," *Identities: Global Studies in Culture and Power* 13 (2006): 363–94.

2. W. Lloyd Warner and Paul S. Lunt, *The Social Life of a Modern Community*, Yankee City Series, Vol. 1 (New Haven, Conn.: Yale University Press, 1941).

3. Stephan Thernstrom, "Yankee City Revisited: The Perils of Historical Naiveté," *American Sociological Review* 30 (1965): 234–42.

4. W. Lloyd Warner and Leo Srole, *The Social System of American Ethnic Groups*, Yankee City Series, Vol. 3 (New Haven, Conn.: Yale University Press, 1945).

5. Matthew Weeks and Michael B. Lupfer, "Complicating Race: The Relationship between Prejudice, Race, and Social Class Categorizations,"*Personality and Social Psychology Bulletin* 30 (2004): 972–84.

6. Stephen Steinberg, *The Ethnic Myth: Race, Ethnicity, and Class in America*, 3d ed. (Boston: Beacon Press, 2001).

7. Thomas Sowell, *Ethnic America: A History* (New York: Basic Books, 1983).

8. Milton M. Gordon, *Assimilation in American Life* (New York: Oxford University Press, 1964).

9. Ibid., p. 47.

10. See Patricia L. McCall and Karen F. Parker, "A Dynamic Model of Racial Competition, Racial Inequality, and Interracial Violence,"*Sociological Inquiry* 75 (2005): 273–93; Leo Kuper, *Race, Class, and Power: Ideology and Revolutionary Change* (Los Angeles: Aldine Transaction, 2005); Claire J. Kim, "Imagining Race and Nation in Multiculturalist America," *Ethnic and Racial Studies* 27:6 (2004): 987–1005.

11. See Cicely R. Hardaway and Vonnie C. MacLoyd, "Escaping Poverty and Securing Middle-Class Status: How Race and Socioeconomic Status Shape Mobility Prospects for African Americans during the Transition to Adulthood," *Journal of Youth and Adolescence* 38 (2009): 242–56; and Colleen F. Heflin and Mary Pattillo, "Poverty in the Family: Race, Siblings, and Socioeconomic Heterogeneity,"*Social Science Research* 25 (2006): 804–22.

12. E. Franklin Frazier, *The Negro Family in Chicago* (Chicago: University of Chicago Press, 1932); see also *The Negro Family in the United States*, rev. ed. (Chicago: University of Chicago Press, 1932).

13. Daniel P. Moynihan, *The Negro Family: The Case for National Action* (Washington, D.C.: U.S. Department of Labor, 1965).

14. Ibid., p. 5.

15. Ibid., p. 6.

16. Ibid., pp. 30, 47.

17. Daniel P. Moynihan, "Families Falling Apart," *Society* (July–August 1990): 21–22.

18. Originally in Daniel Patrick Moynihan, "A Family Policy for the Nation," *America* 113 (September 18, 1965): 280–83. See also Moynihan, "Families Falling Apart," p. 21; David Gergen, "A Few Candles in the Darkness," *U.S. News & World Report* (May 25, 1992), p. 44.

19. Oscar Lewis, *The Children of Sanchez* (New York: Random House, 1961); *La Vida*, (New York: Vintage, 1966), pp. xlii–lii.

20. Ibid., p. xlv.

21. See David L. Harvey and Michael H. Reed, "The Culture of Poverty: An Ideological Analysis," *Sociological Perspectives* 39 (Winter 1996): 465–95.

22. Edward C. Banfield, *The Unheavenly City: The Nature and Future of Our Urban Crisis* (Boston: Little, Brown, 1970), pp. 210–11.

23. See, for example, William F. Spriggs, "Poverty in America: The Poor *Are* Getting Poorer," *Crisis* 113 (2006): 14–19.

24. William Ryan, *Blaming the Victim*, rev. ed. (New York: Vintage, 1976).

25. Charles A. Valentine, *Culture and Poverty* (Chicago: University of Chicago Press, 1968), p. 129.

26. Harvey and Reed, "The Culture of Poverty."

27. Michael Harrington, *The Other America: Poverty in the United States* (Baltimore: Penguin, 1963).

28. Ibid., p. 21.

29. Lola M. Irelan, Oliver C. Moles, and Robert M. O'Shea, "Ethnicity, Poverty, and Selected Attitudes: A Test of the 'Culture of Poverty' Hypothesis," *Social Forces* 47 (1969): 405–13.

30. Eliot Liebow, *Tally's Corner: A Study of Negro Streetcorner Men*, 2d ed. (Lanham, Md.: Rowman & Littlefield, 2003), pp. 222–23. See also Ulf Hannerz, *Soulside: Inquiries into Ghetto Culture and Community* (Chicago: University of Chicago Press, 2004).

31. See Jemima Pierre, "Black Immigrants in the United States and the 'Cultural Narratives' of Ethnicity," *Identities: Global Studies in Culture and Power* 11 (2004): 141–70; David Steigerwald, "Our New Cultural Determinism," *Society* 42 (2005): 71–5; Richard G. Bagnall, "Lifelong Learning and the Limitations of Economic Determinism," *International Journal of Lifelong Education* 19 (2000): 20–35.

32. See H. D. Forbes, *Ethnic Conflict: Commerce, Culture, and the Contact Hypothesis* (New Haven, CT: Yale University Press, 1997).

33. Michael A. Zarate, Berenice Garcia, and Azenett A. Garza, "Cultural Threat and Perceived Realistic Group Conflict as Dual Predictors of Prejudice," *Journal of Experimental Social Psychology* 40 (2004): 99–105.

34. Peter Burns and James G. Gimpel, "Economic Insecurity, Prejudicial Stereotypes, and Public Opinion on Immigration Policy," *Political Science Quarterly* 115 (2000): 201–25.

35. Thomas F. Pettigrew et al., "Relative Deprivation and Intergroup Prejudice," *Journal of Social Issues* 64 (2008): 385–401.

36. Ashley W. Doane, Jr., "Dominant Group Ethnic Identity in the United States: The Role of 'Hidden' Ethnicity in Intergroup Relations," *The Sociological Quarterly* 38 (Summer 1997), 375–97.

37. Stanley Lieberson, "A Societal Theory of Race and Ethnic Relations," *American Sociological Review* 26 (1961): 902–10.

38. William J. Wilson, *Power, Racism, and Privilege* (New York: Free Press, 1973), pp. 47–65.

39. Robert Blauner, "Internal Colonialism and Ghetto Revolt," *Social Problems* 16 (Spring 1969): 393–406.

40. Ibid., p. 397.

41. Donald L. Noel, "A Theory of the Origin of Ethnic Stratification," *Social Problems* 16 (Fall 1968): 157–72.

42. See, for example, Fred L. Pincus and Natalie J. Sokoloff, "Does 'Classism' Help Us to Understand Class Oppression?" *Race, Gender, & Class* 15 (2008): 9–23.

43. See Hubert M. Blalock, Jr., *Toward a Theory of Minority-Group Relations* (New York: Wiley, 1967), pp. 199–203.

44. See, for example, Cajetan Ngozika Ihewulezi, *The History of Poverty in a Rich & Blessed America* (Bloomington, Ind.: Author-House, 2008).
45. See William J. Wilson, *When Work Disappears: The World of the New Urban Poor* (New York: Vintage, 1997);
46. See Humnath Bhandari and Kumi Yasunobu, "What Is Social Capital? A Comprehensive Review of the Concept," *Asian Journal of Social Science* 37 (2009): 480–510.
47. See Pauline Hope Cheong, Rosalind Edwards, Harry Goulbourne, and John Solomos, "Immigration, Social Cohesion, and Social Capital: A Critical Review," *Critical Social Policy* 27 (2007): 24–49.
48. Min Zhou and Susan S. Kim, "Community Forces, Social Capital, and Educational Achievement: The Case of Supplementary Education in the Chinese and Korean Immigrant Communities," *Harvard Educational Review* 76 (2006): 1–29.
49. Alejandro Portés and Min Zhou, "The New Second Generation: Segmented Assimilation and Its Variants," *Annals of the American Political and Social Sciences* 530 (1993): 74–96.
50. Roger Waldinger and Cynthia Feliciano, "Will the New Second Generation Experience 'Downward Assimilation'? Segmented Assimilation Re-Assessed," *Ethnic & Racial Studies* 27 (2004): 376–402.
51. Charles Herschman, "The Educational Enrollment of Immigrant Youth: A Test of the Segmented-Assimilation Hypothesis," *Demography* 38 (2001): 317–36.
52. Reynolds Farley and Richard Alba, "The New Second Generation in the United States," *International Migration Review* 36 (2002): 669–90.
53. Herschman, "The Educational Enrollment of Immigrant Youth."
54. Min Zhou and Carl L. Bankston, "The Social Adjustment of Vietnamese American Adolescents: Evidence of a Segmented-Assimilation Approach," *Social Science Quarterly* 78 (1997): 508–13.
55. Mary C. Waters, *Black Identities: West Indian Immigrant Dreams and American Realities* (Cambridge, MA: Harvard University Press, 1999).
56. U.S. Department of Homeland Security, *Yearbook of Immigration Statistics*, Table 32.
57. Ibid.

# Chapter 4

1. See Gordon W. Allport, *The Nature of Prejudice*, 25th anniversary ed. (New York: Basic Books, 1979), p. 6.
2. Louis Wirth, "Race and Public Policy," *Scientific Monthly* 58 (1944): 303.
3. Ralph L. Rosnow, "Poultry and Prejudice," *Psychology Today* (March 1972): 53.
4. Gordon W. Allport, "Prejudice: Is It Societal or Personal?" *Journal of Social Issues* 18 (1962): 129–30.
5. Todd D. Nelson, *Handbook of Prejudice, Stereotyping, and Discrimination* (New York: Psychology Press, 2009), pp. 54, 300.
6. L. Perry Curtis, Jr., *Apes and Angels: The Irishman in Victorian Caricature*, rev. ed. (Washington, D.C.: Smithsonian Press, 1997).
7. T. W. Adorno, Else Frankel-Brunswik, Daniel J. Levinson, and R. Nevitt Sanford, *The Authoritarian Personality* (New York: Harper & Row, 1950).
8. See, for example, Thomas F. Pettigrew, "Intergroup Contact Theory," *Annual Review of Psychology* 49 (1998): 65–85.
9. See Adam D. Galinsky and Gillian Ku, "The Effects of Perspective-Taking on Prejudice: The Moderating Role of Self-Evaluation," *Personality and Social Psychology Bulletin* 30 (May 2004): 594–604.
10. Brenda Major, Cheryl R. Kaiser, and Shannon K. McCoy, "It's Not My Fault: When and Why Attributions to Prejudice Protect Self-Esteem," *Personality and Social Psychology Bulletin* 29 (June 2003): 772–81.

11. See Russell G. Geen, *Human Aggression*, 2d ed. (Berkshire, England: Open University Press, 2001).
12. Leviticus 16:5–22.
13. Allport, *The Nature of Prejudice*, p. 244.
14. E. M. Beck and Stewart E. Tolnay, "The Killing Fields of the Deep South: The Market for Cotton and the Lynching of Blacks, 1800–1920," *American Sociological Review* 55 (1990): 526–39.
15. See Leonard Berkowitz, "Frustration-Aggression Hypothesis: Examination and Reformulation," *Psychological Bulletin* 106 (1989): 59–73.
16. Talcott Parsons, "Certain Primary Sources and Patterns of Aggression in the Social Structure of the Western World," in *Essays in Sociological Theory* (New York: Free Press, 1964), pp. 298–322.
17. For an excellent review of Parsonian theory in this area, see Stanford M. Lyman, *The Black American in Sociological Thought: A Failure of Perspective* (New York: Putnam, 1972), pp. 145–69.
18. Herbert Blumer, "Race Prejudice as a Sense of Group Position," *Pacific Sociological Review* 1 (1958): 3–7.
19. John Dollard, "Hostility and Fear in Social Life," *Social Forces* 17 (1938): 15–26.
20. Muzafer Sherif, *The Robbers Cave Experiment: Intergroup Conflict and Cooperation* (Middletown, CT: Wesleyan University Press, 1988).
21. See John Higham, *Strangers in the Land: Patterns of American Nativism, 1850–1925* (New Brunswick, NJ: Rutgers University Press, 2002).
22. Paula D. McClain et al., "Black Americans and Latino Immigrants in a Southern City: Friendly Neighbors or Competitors?" *Du Bois Review: Social Science Research on Race* 4 (2007): 97–117.
23. Roger Waldinger, "Black/Immigrant Competition Reassessed: New Evidence from Los Angeles," *Sociological Perspectives*, 40 (1997): 365–86.
24. See Geoff MacDonald, Paul R. Nail, and David A. Levy, "Expanding the Scope of the Social Response Context," *Basic and Applied Social Psychology* 26 (2004): 77–92.
25. John Dollard, *Caste and Class in a Southern Town* (New York: ACLS Humanities E-Book, 2008). Originally published in 1937.
26. Thomas Pettigrew, "Regional Differences in Anti-Negro Prejudice," *Journal of Abnormal and Social Psychology* 59 (1959): 28–36.
27. Jeanne Watson, "Some Social and Psychological Situations Related to Change in Attitude," *Human Relations* 3 (1950): 15–56.
28. Joanne R. Smith and Winnifred R. Louis, "Do as We Say and as We Do: The Interplay of Descriptive and Injunctive Group Norms in the Attitude-Behaviour Relationship," *British Journal of Social Psychology* 47 (2008): 647–66.
29. Christian S. Crandall, Amy Eshleman, and Laurie O'Brien, "Social Norms and the Expression and Suppression of Prejudice: The Struggle for Internalization," *Journal of Personality and Social Psychology* 82 (2002): 359–78.
30. Jenessa R. Shapiro and Steven L. Neuberg, "When Do the Stigmatized Stigmatize? The Ironic Effects of Being Accountable to (Perceived) Majority Group Prejudice-Expression Norms," *Journal of Personality and Social Psychology* 95 (2008): 877–98.
31. See Charles Stangor, "The Study of Stereotyping, Prejudice, and Discrimination Within Social Psychology," pp. 2–4, in Todd D. Nelson (ed.), *Handbook of Prejudice, Stereotyping, and Discrimination* (New York: Psychology Press, 2009).
32. Elliot Aronson, *The Social Animal*, 10th ed. (New York: Worth, 2007), p. 197.
33. Jason K. Clark, Duane T. Wegener, Pablo Briñol, and Richard E. Petty, "Discovering That the Shoe Fits: The Self-Validating Role of Stereotypes," *Psychological Science* 20 (2009): 846–52.
34. See Janet B. Ruscher, *Prejudiced Communication: A Social Psychological Perspective* (New York: Guilford Press, 2001), pp. 20–26.

35. David J. Schneider, *The Psychology of Stereotyping* (New York: Guilford Press, 2005).
36. Brian Mullen, Drew Rozell, and Craig Johnson, "Ethnophaulisms for Ethnic Immigrant Groups: Cognitive Representation of 'The Minority' and 'The Foreigner,' " *Group Processes and Intergroup Relations* 3 (2000): 5–24.
37. Brian Mullen, "Ethnophaulisms for Ethnic Immigrant Groups," *Journal of Social Issues* 57 (2001): 457–75.
38. See Giselinde Kuipers, *Good Humor, Bad Taste: The Sociology of the Joke* (New York: Walter de Gruyter, 2006).
39. Lois Leveen, "Only When I Laugh: Textual Dynamics of Ethnic Humor," *MELUS* 21 (1996): 29–55.
40. U.S. Commission on Civil Rights, *Window Dressing on the Set: Women and Minorities in Television* (Washington, D.C.: U.S. Government Printing Office, 1977); *Window Dressing on the Set: An Update*, 1979.
41. Travis L. Dixon, "Crime News and Racialized Beliefs: Understanding the Relationship between Local News Viewing and Perceptions of African Americans and Crime," *Journal of Communication* 58 (March 2008): 106–25; and Dixon, "Network News and Racial Beliefs: Exploring the Connections between National Television News Exposure and Stereotypical Perceptions of African Americans," *Journal of Communication* 58 (June 2008): 321–37.
42. Dennis J. Ganahl, Thomas J. Prinsen, and Sara Baker Netzley, "A Content Analysis of Prime Time Commercials: A Contextual Framework of Gender Representation," *Sex Roles* 49 (2003): 545–51.
43. Jennifer J. Henderson and Gerald J. Baldasty, "Race, Advertising, and Prime-Time Television," *Howard Journal of Communications* 14 (2003): 97–112.
44. Melinda Messineo, "Does Advertising on Black Entertainment Television Portray More Positive Gender Representations Compared to Broadcast Networks?" *Sex Roles* 59 (2008): 752–64.
45. Shannon N. Davis, "Sex Stereotypes in Commercials Targeted toward Children: A Content Analysis," *Sociological Spectrum* 23 (2003): 407–25.
46. Mark P. Orbe, "Representations of Race in Reality TV: Watch and Discuss," *Critical Studies in Media Communication* 25 (2008): 345–52.
47. Meera E. Deo et al., "Missing in Action: 'Framing' Race on Prime-Time Television," *Social Justice* 35 (2008): 145–62.
48. Martha M. Lauzen, David M. Dozier, and Nora Horan, "Constructing Gender Stereotypes through Social Roles in Prime-Time Television," *Journal of Broadcasting & Electronic Media* 52 (2008): 200–14.
49. Children Now, "Media Impacts Children's Self-Image & How They See Others." Accessed at http://www.childrennow.org/index.php/learn/media_messages_about_race_class_gender/ [December 29, 2010].
50. Matt Sienkiewicz and Nick Marx, "Beyond a Cutout World: Ethnic Humor and Discursive Integration in *South Park*," *Journal of Film and Video* 61 (2009): 5–18.
51. Scott Coltrane and Melinda Messineo, "The Perpetuation of Subtle Prejudice: Race and Gender Imagery in 1990s Television Advertising," *Sex Roles* 42 (2000): 363–89.
52. Dana E. Mastro and Susannah R. Stern, "Representations of Race in Television Commercials: A Content Analysis of Prime-Time Advertising," *Journal of Broadcasting & Electronic Media* 47 (2003): 638–47.
53. Jean Kilbourne, *Can't Buy My Love* (New York: Touchstone Books, 2001).
54. Gina M. Wingood, Ralph J. DiClemente, Jay M. Bernhardt, Kathy Harrington, Susan L. Davies, Allysa Robillard, and Edward W. Hook, III, "A Prospective Study of Exposure to Rap Music Videos and African American Female Adolescents' Health," *American Journal of Public Health* 93 (2003): 437–9.
55. Thomas F. Pettigrew and Linda R. Tropp, "A Meta-Analytic Test of Intergroup Contact Theory," *Journal of Personality & Social Psychology* 90 (2006): 751–83.

56. Thomas F. Pettigrew, "Generalized Intergroup Contact Effects on Prejudice," *Personality and Social Psychology Bulletin*, 23 (1997): 173–85; and Pettigrew, "Intergroup Contact Theory," *Annual Review of Psychology* 49 (1998): 65–85.

57. Elliot Aronson and Neal Osherow, "Cooperation, Prosocial Behavior, and Academic Performance: Experiments in the Desegregated Classroom," *Applied Social Psychology Annual* 1 (1980): 163–96.

58. Iain Walker and Mary Crogan, "Academic Performance, Prejudice, and the Jigsaw Classroom: New Pieces to the Puzzle," *Journal of Community and Applied Social Psychology* 8 (1998): 381–93.

59. See, for example, Biren A. Nagda, Linda R. Tropp, and Elizabeth Levy Paluck, "Looking Back as We Look Ahead: Integrating Theory, Research, and Practice on Intergroup Relations," *Journal of Social Issues* 62 (2006): 439–51; and Ludwin E. Molina and Michele A. Wittig, "Relative Importance of Contact Conditions in Explaining Prejudice Reduction in a Classroom Context: Separate and Equal?" *Journal of Social Issues* 62 (2006): 489–509.

60. Vincent N. Parrillo, *Diversity in America*, 3d ed. (Thousand Oaks, Calif.: Pine Forge Press, 2009), pp. 145–48.

61. U.S. Department of Defense, *Demographics 2008: Profile of the Military Community* (Arlington, Va.: Military Homefront, 2008), p. iii.

62. See Mark E. Engberg, "Improving Intergroup Relations in Higher Education: A Critical Examination of the Influence of Educational Interventions on Racial Bias," *Review of Educational Research* 74:4 (2004): 473–524.

63. See Elizabeth L. Paluck and Donald P. Green, "Prejudice Reduction: What Works? A Review and Assessment of Research and Practice," *Annual Review of Psychology* 60 (2009): 339–67.

# Chapter 5

1. See Jesus Hernandez, "Redlining Revisited: Mortgage Lending Patterns in Sacramento 1930-2004," *International Journal of Urban and Regional Research* 33 (2009): 291–313; Gary A. Dymski, "Racial Exclusion and the Political Economy of the Subprime Crisis," *Historical Materialism* 17 (2009): 149–79.

2. The Prejudice Institute, "What Is Ethnoviolence?" Accessed at http://www.prejudiceinstitute.org/ethnoviolenceFS.html [December 29, 2010].

3. Robert K. Merton, "Discrimination and the American Creed," in Robert M. MacIver (ed.), *Discrimination and National Welfare* (New York: Harper, 1949), pp. 99–126.

4. Stokely Carmichael and Charles Hamilton, *Black Power*, reprint ed. (New York: Vintage Books, 1992).

5. See John R. Logan, *Separate and Unequal: The Neighborhood Gap for Blacks and Hispanics in Metropolitan America*, Lewis Mumford Center, October 15, 2002. Accessed at http://www.eric.ed.gov/PDFS/ED471515.pdf [December 29, 2010].

6. See, for example, Roberto M. Fernandez, "Race, Spatial Mismatch, and Job Accessibility: Evidence from a Plant Relocation," *Social Science Research* 37 (2008): 953–75; and Robert L. Wagmiller, "Male Nonemployment in White, Black, Hispanic, and Multiethnic Urban Neighborhoods, 1970–2000," *Urban Affairs Review* 44 (2008): 85–125.

7. Richard D. Alba, John R. Logan, and Brian J. Stults, "How Segregated Are Middle-Class African Americans?" *Social Problems* 27 (2000): 543–58.

8. See, for example, Juan Manuel Falomir-Pichastor, Daniel Muñoz-Rojas, Federica Invernizzi, and Gabriel Mugny, "Perceived In-Group Threat as a Factor Moderating the Influence of In-Group Norms on Discrimination against Foreigners," *European Journal of Social Psychology* 34 (2004): 135–53.

9. John Rawls, *A Theory of Justice*, rev. ed. (Cambridge, Mass.: Belknap Press, 1999).

10. Joseph Tussman and Jacobus tenBroek, "The Equal Protection of the Laws," *California Law Review* 37 (September 1949): 341–81.

11. Stanford M. Lyman, "The Race Question and Liberalism: Casuistries in American Constitutional Law," *International Journal of Politics, Culture and Society* 5 (1991): 183–247.

12. Steven M. Cahn, *The Affirmative Action Debates*, 2d ed. (New York: Routledge, 2002).

13. Terry H. Anderson, *The Pursuit of Fairness: A History of Affirmative Action* (New York: Oxford University Press, 2005).

14. Quoted in Ian Lopez, *White by Law*, rev. ed. (New York: New York University Press, 2006), p. 124.

15. David R. Colburn, Charles E. Young, and Victor M. Yellen. (2008). *Admissions and Public Higher Education in California, Texas, and Florida: The Post-Affirmative Action Era.* Inter-Actions: UCLA Journal of Education and Information Studies, Vol. 4, Issue 1, Article 2. Accessed at http://www.escholarship.org/uc/item/35n755gf [December 29, 2010].

16. Quoted in Derrick A. Bell, *Silent Covenants: Brown v. Board of Education and the Unfilled Hopes for Racial Reform* (New York: Oxford University Press, 2005), p. 149.

17. J. Edward Kellough, *Understanding Affirmative Action: Politics, Discrimination, and the Search for Justice* (Washington, DC: Georgetown University Press, 2006), pp. 132–38.

18. Tim J. Wise, *Affirmative Action: Racial Preference in Black and White* (New York: Routledge, 2005), p. 164.

19. Linda Chavez, "Court Abandons Colorblind Society," *Human Events* 59 (June 30, 2003): 1–2; Chavez, "No Thanks to Affirmative Action," *The American Prospect* 13 (2002): 34-35; Thomas Sowell, "How 'Affirmative Action' Hurts Blacks," *Forbes* 160 (October 6, 1997): 64.

20. All poll results accessed at www.pollingreport.com/race.htm [December 29, 2010].

21. Brent Berry and Eduardo Bonilla-Silva, "'They Should Hire the One with the Best Score': White Sensitivity to Qualification Differences in Affirmative Action Hiring Decisions," *Ethnic and Racial Studies* 31 (2008): 215–42.

22. Sam Howe Verhovek, "In Poll, Americans Reject Means but Not Ends of Racial Diversity," *New York Times* (December 14, 1997), p. A1.

23. See Stephanie Geiger-Oneto and Scott Phillips, "Driving While Black: The Role of Race, Sex, and Social Status," *Journal of Ethnicity in Criminal Justice* 1 (2003): 1–25.

24. Human Rights Watch, *Decades of Disparity: Drug Arrests and Race in the United States*, 2009. Accessed at www.hrw.org/sites/default/files/reports/us0309web_1.pdf [December 29, 2010].

25. "Transportation." Accessed at www.pollingreport.com/transpor.htm [December 29, 2010].

26. Department of Justice, *Racial Profiling Fact Sheet* (June 17, 2003). Accessed at www.justice.gov/opa/pr/2003/June/racial_profiling_fact_sheet.pdf [December 29, 2010].

27. Patricia Y. Warren and Amy Farrell, "The Environmental Context of Racial Profiling," *The ANNALS of the American Academy of Political and Social Science* 623 (2009): 52–63.

28. *American* Civil Liberties Union, "The Persistence of Racial Profiling in Rhode Island: A Call to Action," 2007. Accessed at www.aclu.org/pdfs/racialjustice/riracialprofilingreport.pdf [December 29, 2010].

# Chapter 6

1. See Brent Simpson and Michael W. Macy, "Power, Identity, and Collective Action in Social Exchange," *Social Forces* 82 (2004): 1373–1409; Laura S. Billings et al., "Race-Based Social Judgment by Minority Perceivers," *Journal of Applied Social Psychology* 30 (February 2000): 221–40; Connie M. Kane, "Differences in Family of Origin Perceptions among African American, Asian American, and Hispanic American College Students," *Journal of Black Studies* 29 (September 1998): 93–105.

2. See, for example, Devon Johnson, "Racial Prejudice, Perceived Injustice, and the Black-White Gap in Punitive Attitudes," *Journal of Criminal Justice* 36 (2008): 198–206; A. E. Taslitz (ed.), "The New Data: Over-Representation of Minorities in the Criminal Justice System," *Law and Contemporary Problems* 66 (Summer 2003): 1–298; Rebecca A. Anderson and Amy

L. Otto, "Perceptions of Fairness in the Justice System: A Cross-Cultural Comparison, *Social Behavior and Personality* 31 (2003): 557–63; Marvin D. Free, Jr., "Race and Presentencing Decisions in the United States: A Summary and Critique of the Research," *Criminal Justice Review* 27 (2002): 203–32; Jody Clay-Warner, "Perceiving Procedural Injustice: The Effects of Group Membership and Status," *Social Psychology Quarterly* 64 (2001): 224–38; Saundra D. Westervelt and John A. Humphrey (eds.), *Wrongly Convicted Perspectives on Failed Justice* (New Brunswick, N.J.: Rutgers University Press, 2001).

3. Clifford R. Shaw and Henry D. McKay, "Juvenile Delinquency and Urban Areas," *The Chicago School Criminology*, Vol. 6 (New York: Routledge, 2004). Originally published in 1942.

4. Robert Agnew et al., "Socioeconomic Status, Economic Problems, and Delinquency," *Youth & Society* 40 (2008): 159–81; Per-Olof H. Wikstrom et al., "Do Disadvantaged Neighborhoods Cause Well-Adjusted Children to Become Adolescent Delinquents?" *Criminology* 38 (November 2000): 1109–42; Matthew R. Lee, "Community Cohesion and Violent Predatory Victimization," *Social Forces* 79 (December 2000): 683–706.

5. Dana L. Haynie, Harald E. Weiss, and Alex Piquero, "Race, the Economic Maturity Gap, and Criminal Offending in Young Adulthood," *Justice Quarterly* 25 (2008): 595–622; and Ronald L. Simons and Phyllis A. Gray, "Perceived Blocked Opportunity as an Explanation of Delinquency among Lower-Class Black Males: A Research Note," *Journal of Research in Crime and Delinquency* 26 (1989): 90–101.

6. See Adrienne Frang and Finn-Aage Esbensen, "Race and Gang Affiliation: An Examination of Multiple Marginality," *Justice Quarterly* 24 (2007): 600–28; Paul R. Vowell and David C. May, "Another Look at Classic Strain Theory: Poverty Status, Perceived Blocked Opportunity, and Gang Membership as Predictors of Adolescent Violent Behavior: *Sociological Inquiry* 70 (2000): 42–60.

7. John P. Hoffmann and Mikaela J. Dufur, "Family and School Capital Effects on Delinquency: Substitutes or Complements?" *Sociological Perspectives* 51 (2008): 29–62; Patricia H. Jenkins, "School Delinquency and School Commitment," *Sociology of Education* 68 (1995): 221–39.

8. See Donna K. Nagata and Yuzuru J. Takeshita, "Psychological Reactions to Redress: Diversity among Japanese Americans Interned during World War II," *Cultural Diversity & Ethnic Minority Psychology* 8 (2002): 41–59, for a study on acceptance by ex-internees decades later after government redress.

9. Tern A. Winnick and Mark Bodkin "Stigma, Secrecy, and Race: An Empirical Examination of Black and White Incarcerated Men," *American Journal of Criminal Justice* 34 (2009): 131–50; and Tally Moses, "Self-Labeling and Its Effects among Adolescents Diagnosed with Mental Disorders," *Social Science & Medicine* 68 (2009): 57–78.

10. Kurt Lewin, *Resolving Social Conflicts* (Washington, DC: American Psychological Association, 1997), p. 375.

11. Gordon W. Allport, *The Nature of Prejudice*. 25th anniversary ed. (New York: Basic Books, 1979), pp. 152–53.

12. Chol Yoo Hyung and Richard M. Lee, "Does Ethnic Identity Buffer or Exacerbate the Effects of Frequent Racial Discrimination on Situational Well-Being of Asian Americans?" *Journal of Counseling Psychology* 55 (2008): 63–74; and Richard M. Lee, "Resilience against Discrimination: Ethnic Identity and Other-Group Orientation as Protective Factors for Korean Americans," *Journal of Counseling Psychology* 52 (2005): 36–44.

13. Andrea J. Romero and Robert E. Roberts, "The Impact of Multiple Dimensions of Ethnic Identity on Discrimination and Adolescents' Self-Esteem," *Journal of Applied Social Psychology* 33 (2003): 2288–305; and J. R. Porter and R. E. Washington, "Minority Identity and Self-Esteem," *Annual Review of Sociology* 19 (1993): 139–61.

14. Gunnar Myrdal, *An American Dilemma* (New York: McGraw-Hill, 1964), pp. 25–28; originally published by Harper, 1944.

15. Allport, *The Nature of Prejudice*, p. 160.

16. Robert E. Park, "Human Migration and the Marginal Man," *American Journal of Sociology* 33 (May 1928): 891; see also Everett V. Stonequist, *The Marginal Man* (New York: Scribner, 1937).

17. See Rutledge Dennis (ed.), *Marginality, Power, and Social Structure, Vol. 12: Issues in Race, Class, and Gender Analysis* (Greenwich, CT: JAI Press, 2005).

18. See Adam Weisberger, "Marginality and Its Directions," *Sociological Forum* 7 (1992): 425–26.

19. Hubert M. Blalock, Jr., *Toward a Theory of Minority Group Relations* (New York: Perigee, 1973), pp. 79–84.

20. Edna Bonacich, "A Theory of Middleman Minorities," *American Sociological Review* 38 (1973): 583–94.

21. Edna Bonacich and John Modell, *The Economic Basis of Ethnic Solidarity* (Berkeley: University of California Press, 1981), p. 30.

22. Norman Pounds, *The Medieval City* (Santa Barbara, CA: Greenwood Press, 2005); and William E. Deal, *Handbook to Life in Medieval and Early Modern Japan* (New York: Oxford University Press, 2007).

23. See John J. Macionis and Vincent N. Parrillo, *Cities and Urban Life*, 5th ed. (Upper Saddle River, N.J.: Prentice Hall, 2010), pp. 40–43.

24. See Allport, *The Nature of Prejudice*, pp. 53–54.

25. Deuteronomy 2:32–35; 3:1, 3–4, 6–7.

26. Dirk Moses, *Colonialism and Genocide* (New York: Routledge, 2008), Chapters 4–5; and Benjamin Madley, "Patterns of Frontier Genocide, 1803–1910: The Aboriginal Tasmanians, the Yuki of California, and the Herero of Namibia," *Journal of Genocide Research* 6 (2004): 167–92.

27. See F. James Davis, *Who Is Black?: One Nation's Definition* (University Park, PA: Penn State University Press, 2001), p. 92; and Winthrop D. Jordan, *White over Black: American Attitudes toward the Negro, 1550–1812*, reissue ed. (Chapel Hill: University of North Carolina Press, 1995).

28. For a discussion of Mexican American lynchings, see William D. Carrigan and Clive Webb, "The Lynching of Persons of Mexican Origin or Descent in the United States, 1848 to 1928," *Journal of Social History* 37 (2003): 411–38; on black lynchings, see Gregory N. Price, William A. Darity, Jr., and Alvin E. Headen, Jr., "Does the Stigma of Slavery Explain the Maltreatment of Blacks by Whites: The Case of Lynchings," *The Journal of Socio-Economics* 37 (2008): 167–93.

29. See Colin M. Tatz, *With Intent to Destroy: Reflections on Genocide* (New York: Norton, 2003).

30. Southern Poverty Law Center, "Active U.S. Hate Groups." Accessed at http://www.splcenter.org/get-informed/hate-map [July 13, 2010].

31. Federal Bureau of Investigation, "2009 Hate Crime Statistics." Accessed at www.fbi.gov/ucr/hc2009/index.html [December 29, 2010].

32. Edna Bonacich, "A Theory of Ethnic Antagonism: The Split Labor Market," *American Sociological Review* 37 (1972): 554.

33. Ibid.

34. Cliff Brown, "The Role of Employers in Split Labor Markets: An Event-Structure Analysis of Racial Conflict and AFL Organizing, 1917–1919," *Social Forces* 79 (2000): 653–81.

35. Kenneth Hudson, "The New Labor Market Segmentation: Labor Market Dualism in the New Economy," *Social Science Research* 36 (2007): 286–312.

# Chapter 7

1. Vincent N. Parrillo, "Asian Americans in American Politics," in Joseph S. Roucek and Bernard Eisenberg (eds.), *America's Ethnic Politics* (Westport, Conn.: Greenwood Press, 1982), pp. 89–112.

2. Jose Itzigsohn, "Immigration and the Boundaries of Citizenship: The Institutions of Immigrants' Political Transnationalism,"*International Migration Review* 34 (2000): 1126–54.

3. Daisuke Akiba, "Ethnic Retention as a Predictor of Academic Success: Lessons from the Children of Immigrant Families and Black Children," *Clearing House* 80 (2007): 223–5.

4. Cynthia Feliciano, "Education and Ethnic Identity Formation among Children of Latin American and Caribbean Immigrants," *Sociological Perspectives* 52 (2009): 135–58.

5. Mary C. Sengstock, "Social Change in the Country of Origin as a Factor in Immigrant Conceptions of Nationality," *Ethnicity* 4 (1977): 61–64.

6. See Pratyusha Tummala-Narra, "The Immigrant's Real and Imagined Return Home," *Culture & Society* 14 (2009): 237–52.

7. Marcus L. Hansen, "The Third Generation in America," *Commentary* 14 (1952): 492–500.

8. Marcus L. Hansen, "The Third Generation," in Oscar Handlin (ed.), *Children of the Uprooted* (New York: Harper & Row, 1966), pp. 255–71.

9. Peter Skerry, "Do We Really Want Immigrants to Assimilate?" *Society* 37 (2000): 57–62.

10. Sean Valentine "Self Esteem, Cultural Identity, and Generation Status as Determinants of Hispanic Acculturation," *Hispanic Journal of Behavioral Sciences* 23 (November 2001): 459–68.

11. Alejandro Portés and Dag MacLeod, "What Shall I Call Myself? Hispanic Identity Formation in the Second Generation," *Ethnic and Racial Studies* 19 (July 1996): 523–47.

12. Nazli Kibria, "The Construction of 'Asian American': Reflections on Intermarriage and Ethnic Identity among Second-Generation Chinese and Korean Americans," *Ethnic and Racial Studies* 20 (July 1997): 523–44.

13. See Paul Spickard, *Japanese Americans: The Formation and Transformations of an Ethnic Group*, rev. ed. (New Brunswick, NJ: Rutgers University Press, 2009).

14. See Mark Ellis and Jamie Goodwin-White, "1.5 Generation Internal Migration in the U.S.: Dispersion from States of Immigration?" *International Migration Review* 40 (2006): 899–926.

15. S. Karthick Ramakrishnan, "Second Generation Immigrants? The '2.5 Generation' in the United States," *Social Science Quarterly* 85 (2004): 380–99.

16. Rosemary Salomone, "Transnational Schooling and the New Immigrants: Developing Dual Identities in the United States," *Intercultural Education* 19 (2008): 383–93.

17. See, for example, Zeynep Aycan and Rabindra N. Kanungo, "Impact of Acculturation on Socialization Beliefs and Behavioral Occurrences among Indo-Canadian Immigrants," *Journal of Comparative Family Studies* 29 (1998): 451–67.

18. See Mimi Kim, "The Political Economy of Immigration and the Emergence of Transnationalism," *Journal of Human Behavior in the Social Environment* 19 (2009): 675–89.

19. Thomas Faist, "Transnationalization in International Migration: Implications for the Study of Citizenship and Culture," *Ethnic & Racial Studies* 23 (2000): 189–222.

20. U.S. Office of Immigration Statistics, "Naturalizations in the United States: 2009" (April 2010), Table 1, p. 2.

21. William L. Yancey, Eugene P. Ericksen, and Richard N. Juliani, "Emergent Ethnicity: A Review and Reformulation," *American Sociological Review* 41 (1976): 391–403.

22. Ibid., p. 393.

23. Stanley Lieberson and Mary C. Waters, "The Location of Ethnic and Racial Groups in the United States," *Sociological Forum* 2 (1987): 780–810.

24. U.S. Office of Immigration Statistics, *Yearbook of Immigration Statistics: 2008* (Washington, DC: U.S. Government Printing Office, 2006), Table 4.

25. Pew Research Center, "Comings & Goings: Migration Flows in the U.S." Accessed at http://pewsocialtrends.org/maps/migration/ [December 29, 2010].

26. Marc J. Perry and Jason P. Schachter, "Migration of Natives and the Foreign Born: 1995 to 2000," *Census 2000 Special Reports* (August 2003), Table 1, p. 3.

27. Robert E. Park, "The Urban Community as a Spatial Pattern and a Moral Order," in Ernest W. Burgess (ed.), *The Urban Community* (Chicago: University of Chicago Press, 1926), pp. 3–18.

28. John Iceland, *Where We Live Now: Immigration and Race in the United States* (Berkeley: University of California Press, 2009).

29. Richard D. Alba, *Ethnic Identity: The Transformation of White America* (New Haven, Conn.: Yale University Press, 1990).

30. Richard D. Alba, *Italian Americans: Into the Twilight of Ethnicity* (Englewood Cliffs, N.J.: Prentice Hall, 1985), pp. 159–75.

31. See Herbert J. Gans, "Symbolic Ethnicity and Symbolic Religiosity: Towards a Comparison of Ethnic and Religious Acculturation,"*Ethnic and Racial Studies* 17 (1994): 577–92.

32. Philip Martin and Elizabeth Midgley, "Immigration: Shaping and Reshaping America," *Population Bulletin* 61:4 (December 2006), p. 19.

33. "Immigration." Accessed at www.pollingreport.com/immigration.htm [December 29, 2010].

34. Steven A. Camarota, "Immigrant Job Gains and Native Job Losses 2000 to 2004," Center for Immigration Studies. Accessed at www.cis.org/articles/2005/sactestimony050405.html [December 29, 2010].

35. George J. Borjas and Leonard F. Katz, "The Evolution of the Mexican-American Workforce in the United States," National Bureau of Economic Research, NBER Working Paper No. 11281 (April 2005).

36. David Card, "Is the New Immigration Really So Bad?" *The Economic Journal* 115 (2005): 300–23; Tyler Cowen and Daniel M. Rothschild, "Don't Bad-Mouth Unskilled Immigrants," *Reason* 38:4 (2006): 42–4.

37. Tamar Jacoby, "Immigration Nation," *Foreign Affairs* 85:6 (2006): 50–65.

38. Ibid.

39. Philip Martin and Elizabeth Midgley, "Immigration in America 2010," *Population Bulletin Update* (June 2010), p. 2.

40. Tyler Cowen and Daniel M. Rothschild, "Don't Bad-Mouth Unskilled Immigrants."

41. "Immigration." Accessed at www.publicagenda.com/citizen/issueguides/immigration/publicview/redflags and at www.pollingreport.com/immigration.htm [December 29, 2010].

42. "Immigration." Accessed at www.pollingreport.com/immigration.htm [December 29, 2010].

43. U.S. Citizenship and Immigration Services, *About Us.* Accessed at www.uscis.gov/portal/site/uscis [December 29, 2010].

44. Jeffrey S. Passel and D'Vera Cohn, "A Portrait of Unauthorized Immigrants in the United States," Pew Hispanic Center (April 14, 2009), pp. i–ii.

45. Ibid., p. 21.

46. Office of Immigration Statistics, "Immigration Enforcement Actions: 2008," *Annual Report* (July 2009), p. 3.

47. Philip Martin, "The Battle over Unauthorized Immigration to the United States," Population Reference Bureau (April 11, 2006): 1.

48. Quoted in W. C. Smith, *Americans in the Making* (New York: Appleton-Century, 1939), p. 39.

49. Maurice R. Davie, *World Immigration* (New York: Macmillan, 1936), p. 36.

50. Carl Wittke, *We Who Build America*, rev. ed. (Cleveland: Cast Western Reserve University Press, 1967), pp. 196–199; James S. Olson, *The Ethnic Dimension in American History* (New York: St. Martin's Press, 1979), pp. 103–6.

51. Hyon B. Shin and Rosalind Bruno, "Language Use and English-Speaking Ability: 2000," *Census 2000 Brief* [October 2003].

52. U.S. Department of Education, National Center for Education Statistics, *The Condition of Education: 2009* (Washington, DC: U.S. Government Printing Office, 2009), p. 18.

53. Michael Fix, "Immigrant Children, Urban Schools, and the No Child Left Behind Act," Migration Policy Institute (November 2005).

54. Data derived from the National Center for Education Statistics and the Center for Applied Linguistics, "ESL and Bilingual Education." Accessed at www.mindplay.com/esl.html [December 29, 2010]; *The Condition of Education: 2009*, Table A-8-1, p. 138.

55. See Vickie W. Lewelling, "Official English and English Plus: An Update," *ERIC Digest.* Accessed at www.cal.org/resources/digest/lewell01.html [December 29, 2010].

56. See Kellie Rolstad, Kate S. Mahoney, and Gene V. Glass, "The Big Picture: A Meta-Analysis of Program Effectiveness Research on English Language Learners," *Educational Policy* 19 (2005): 572–94, and "Weighing the Evidence: A Meta-Analysis of Bilingual Education in Arizona," *Bilingual Research Journal* 29 (2005): 43–67.

57. See, for example, Carolyn Huie Hofstetter, "Effects of a Transitional Bilingual Education Program: Findings, Issues, and Next Steps," *Bilingual Research Journal* 28 (2004): 355–77; Linda Jacobson, "Prop. 227 Seen as Focusing on 'Wrong Issue,'" *Education Week* (March 1, 2006), pp. 18–20.

58. See, for example, Christine Rossell, "Teaching English through English," *Educational Leadership* 62 (2005): 32–6.

59. See "LULAC History—All for One and One for All." Accessed at www.lulac.org/about/history/ [December 29, 2010].

60. U.S. English, Accessed at www.us-english.org/view/3 [December 29, 2010].

61. Rasmussen Reports, "84% Say English Should Be America's Official Language." Accessed at www.rasmussenreports.com/public_content/lifestyle/general_lifestyle/may_2009/84_say_english_should_be_america_s_official_language [December 29, 2010].

62. Public Agenda, "A Place to Call Home: What Immigrants Say Now about Life in America." Accessed at www.publicagenda.com/pages/immigrants-2009-topline [December 29, 2010].

63. Shirin Hakimzadeh and D'Vera Cohn, "English Usage among Hispanics in the United States," Pew Hispanic Center, November 29, 2007.

64. Rubén G. Rumbaut and Alejandro Portes, *Ethnicities: Children of Immigrants in America* (Berkeley: University of California Press, 2001).

65. Rubén G. Rumbaut, Douglas S. Massey, and Frank D. Bean, "Linguistic Life Expectancies: Immigrant Language Retention in Southern California," *Population and Development Review* 32 (2006): 447–60.

66. Hyon B. Shin with Rosalind Bruno, "Language Use and Speaking Ability: 2000," U.S. Census Bureau, *Census 2000 Brief Supplementary Survey*, Table PO35.

67. See Barry R. Chiswick and Paul W. Miller, "A Test of the Critical Period Hypothesis for Language Learning," *Journal of Multilingual and Multicultural Development* 29 (2008): 16–29,

68. Vincent N. Parrillo, *Diversity in America*, 3d ed. (Los Angeles: Pine Forge Press, 2009), pp. 157–8.

69. See, for example, Joseph Barndt, *Understanding and Dismantling Racism: The Twenty-First Century Challenge to White America* (Minneapolis: Fortress Press, 2008), pp. 55–65.

70. Anne Phillips, *Multiculturalism without Culture* (Princeton, NJ: Princeton University Press, 2009), p. 6.

71. David A. Hollinger, *Postethnic America: Beyond Multiculturalism*, rev. ed. (New York: Basic Books, 2006).

72. Jeffrey S. Passel and D'Vera Cohn, "U.S. Population Projections: 2005-2050," Pew Research Center (February 11, 2008). Accessed at http://pewhispanic.org/files/reports/85.pdf [December 29, 2010].

73. U.S. Census Bureau, "National Population Projections," (Washington, DC: U.S. Government Printing Office, 2008).

74. U.S. Census Bureau, *Statistical Abstract of the United States: 2010*, Table 60.

75. Ibid.

76. Michael W. Firmin and Stephanie Firebaugh, "Historical Analysis of College Campus Interracial Dating," *College Student Journal* 42 (2008): 882–8; Derek A. Kreager, "Guarded Borders: Adolescent Interracial Romance and Peer Trouble at School," *Social Forces* 87 (2008): 887–910.

77. Christie D. Batson, Zhenchao Qian, and Daniel T. Lichter, "Interracial and Intraracial Patterns of Mate Selection among America's Diverse Black Populations," *Journal of Marriage and Family* 68 (2006): 658–72.

78. Yuanting Zhang and Jennifer Van Hook, "Marital Dissolution among Interracial Couples," *Journal of Marriage and Family* 71 (2009): 95–107.
79. George A. Yancey, "Experiencing Racism: Differences in the Experiences of Whites Married to Blacks and Non-Black Racial Minorities,"*Journal of Comparative Family Studies* 38 (2007):197–213.
80. Adam B. Troy, Jamie Lewis-Smith, and Philippe Laurenceau, "Interracial and Intraracial Romantic Relationships: The Search for Differences in Satisfaction, Conflict, and Attachment Style," *Journal of Social and Personal Relationships* 23 (2006): 665–80.
81. Suzanne Model and Gene Fisher, "Black-White Unions: West Indians and African Americans Compared," *Demography* 38 (2001): 177–85.
82. George Yancey, "Who Interracially Dates: An Examination of the Characteristics of Those Who Have Interracially Dated," *Journal of Comparative Family Studies* 33 (2002): 179–90.
83. U.S. Bureau of the Census, "Selected Population Profile in the United States," *2008 American Community Survey*, Table S0201.
84. Mireya Navarro, "Beyond Black & White," *New York Times* (May 5, 2008), pp. A22–23.
85. Julie M. Ahnallen, Karen L. Suyemoto, and Alice S. Carter, "Relationship between Physical Appearance, Sense of Belonging and Exclusion, and Race/Ethnic Self-Identification among Multiracial Japanese European Americans," *Cultural Diversity & Ethnic Minority Psychology* 12 (2006): 673–86.
86. Jamie Mihoko Doyle and Grace Kao, "Are Racial Identities of Multiracials Stable? Changing Self-Identification and Single and Multiple Race Individuals," *Social Psychological Quarterly* 70 (2007): 405–23.
87. Haya El Nasser, "Fewer Americans Call Themselves Multiracial," *USA Today* (May 4, 2007), p. 1A.
88. See, for example, Maria P.P. Root (ed.), *The Multiracial Experience: Racial Borders as the New Frontier* (Los Angeles: Sage Publications, 1996).
89. Sam Roberts, "Census Figures Challenge Views of Race and Ethnicity," *New York Times* (January 22, 2010), p. A13.

# Immigration, 1820–2009

Immigrants by Region and Selected Country of Last Residence:
Fiscal Years 1820–2009

| Region and Country of Last Residence[1] | 1820 to 1829 | 1830 to 1839 | 1840 to 1849 | 1850 to 1859 |
|---|---|---|---|---|
| Total | 128,502 | 538,381 | 1,427,337 | 2,814,554 |
| Europe | 99,272 | 422,771 | 1,369,259 | 2,619,680 |
| Austria-Hungary[2,3,4] | — | — | — | — |
| Austria[2,4] | — | — | — | — |
| Hungary[2] | — | — | — | — |
| Belgium | 28 | 20 | 3,996 | 5,765 |
| Bulgaria[5] | — | — | — | — |
| Denmark | 173 | 927 | 671 | 3,227 |
| France[7] | 7,694 | 39,330 | 75,300 | 81,778 |
| Germany[3,4] | 5,753 | 124,726 | 385,434 | 976,072 |
| Greece | 17 | 49 | 17 | 32 |
| Ireland[8] | 51,617 | 170,672 | 656,145 | 1,029,486 |
| Italy | 430 | 2,225 | 1,476 | 8,643 |
| Netherlands | 1,105 | 1,377 | 7,624 | 11,122 |
| Norway-Sweden[9] | 91 | 1,149 | 12,389 | 22,202 |
| Norway[9] | — | — | — | — |
| Sweden[9] | — | — | — | — |
| Poland[3] | 19 | 366 | 105 | 1,087 |
| Portugal[10] | 177 | 820 | 196 | 1,299 |
| Romania | — | — | — | — |
| Russia[3,11] | 86 | 280 | 520 | 423 |
| Spain[12] | 2,595 | 2,010 | 1,916 | 8,795 |
| Switzerland | 3,148 | 4,430 | 4,819 | 24,423 |
| United Kingdom[8,13] | 26,336 | 74,350 | 218,572 | 445,322 |
| Other Europe | 3 | 40 | 79 | 4 |
| Asia | 34 | 55 | 121 | 36,080 |
| China | 3 | 8 | 32 | 35,933 |
| India | 9 | 38 | 33 | 42 |
| Japan | — | — | — | — |
| Turkey | 19 | 8 | 45 | 94 |
| Other Asia | 3 | 1 | 11 | 11 |
| America | 9,655 | 31,905 | 50,516 | 84,145 |
| Canada and Newfoundland[15,16] | 2,297 | 11,875 | 34,285 | 64,171 |
| Mexico[16,17] | 3,835 | 7,187 | 3,069 | 3,446 |
| Caribbean | 3,061 | 11,792 | 11,803 | 12,447 |
| Central America | 57 | 94 | 297 | 512 |
| South America | 405 | 957 | 1,062 | 3,569 |
| Other America[20] | — | — | — | — |
| Africa | 15 | 50 | 61 | 84 |
| Egypt | — | — | — | — |
| Liberia | 1 | 8 | 5 | 7 |
| South Africa | — | — | — | — |
| Other Africa | 14 | 42 | 56 | 77 |
| Oceania | 3 | 7 | 14 | 166 |
| Australia | 2 | 1 | 2 | 15 |
| New Zealand | — | — | — | — |
| Other Oceania | 1 | 6 | 12 | 151 |
| Not Specified[20,21] | 19,523 | 83,593 | 7,366 | 74,399 |

(*Continued*)

See footnotes at end of table.

**Immigrants by Region and Selected Country of Last Residence:
Fiscal Years 1820–2009    (*Continued*)**

| Region and Country of Last Residence[1] | 1860 to 1869 | 1870 to 1879 | 1880 to 1889 | 1890 to 1899 |
|---|---|---|---|---|
| Total | 2,081,261 | 2,742,137 | 5,248,568 | 3,694,294 |
| Europe | 1,877,726 | 2,251,878 | 4,638,677 | 3,576,411 |
| Austria-Hungary[2,3,4] | 3,375 | 60,127 | 314,787 | 534,059 |
| Austria[2,4] | 2,700 | 54,529 | 204,805 | 268,218 |
| Hungary[2] | 483 | 5,598 | 109,982 | 203,350 |
| Belgium | 5,785 | 6,991 | 18,738 | 19,642 |
| Bulgaria[5] | — | — | — | 52 |
| Denmark | 13,553 | 29,278 | 85,342 | 56,671 |
| France[7] | 35,938 | 71,901 | 48,193 | 35,616 |
| Germany[3,4] | 723,734 | 751,769 | 1,445,181 | 579,072 |
| Greece | 51 | 209 | 1,807 | 12,732 |
| Ireland[8] | 427,419 | 422,264 | 674,061 | 405,710 |
| Italy | 9,853 | 46,296 | 267,660 | 603,761 |
| Netherlands | 8,387 | 14,267 | 52,715 | 29,349 |
| Norway-Sweden[9] | 82,937 | 178,823 | 586,441 | 334,058 |
| Norway[9] | 16,068 | 88,644 | 185,111 | 96,810 |
| Sweden[9] | 24,224 | 90,179 | 401,330 | 237,248 |
| Poland[3] | 1,886 | 11,016 | 42,910 | 107,793 |
| Portugal[10] | 2,083 | 13,971 | 15,186 | 25,874 |
| Romania | — | — | 5,842 | 6,808 |
| Russia[3,11] | 1,670 | 35,177 | 182,698 | 450,101 |
| Spain[12] | 6,966 | 5,540 | 3,995 | 9,189 |
| Switzerland | 21,124 | 25,212 | 81,151 | 37,020 |
| United Kingdom[8,13] | 532,956 | 578,447 | 810,900 | 328,759 |
| Other Europe | 9 | 590 | 1,070 | 145 |
| Asia | 54,408 | 134,128 | 71,151 | 61,285 |
| China | 54,028 | 133,139 | 65,797 | 15,268 |
| India | 50 | 166 | 247 | 102 |
| Japan | 138 | 193 | 1,583 | 13,998 |
| Turkey | 129 | 382 | 2,478 | 27,510 |
| Other Asia | 63 | 248 | 1,046 | 4,407 |
| America | 130,292 | 345,010 | 524,826 | 37,350 |
| Canada and Newfoundland[15,16] | 117,978 | 324,310 | 492,865 | 3,098 |
| Mexico[16,17] | 1,957 | 5,133 | 2,405 | 734 |
| Caribbean | 8,751 | 14,285 | 27,323 | 31,480 |
| Central America | 70 | 173 | 279 | 649 |
| South America | 1,536 | 1,109 | 1,954 | 1,389 |
| Other America[20] | — | — | — | — |
| Africa | 407 | 371 | 763 | 432 |
| Egypt | 4 | 29 | 145 | 51 |
| Liberia | 43 | 52 | 21 | 9 |
| South Africa | 35 | 48 | 23 | 9 |
| Other Africa | 325 | 242 | 574 | 363 |
| Oceania | 187 | 9,996 | 12,361 | 4,704 |
| Australia | — | 8,930 | 7,250 | 3,098 |
| New Zealand | — | 39 | 21 | 12 |
| Other Oceania | 187 | 1,027 | 5,090 | 1,594 |
| Not Specified[20,21] | 18,241 | 754 | 790 | 14,112 |

**Immigrants by Region and Selected Country of Last Residence:**
**Fiscal Years 1820–2009** (*Continued*)

| Region and Country of Last Residence[1] | 1900 to 1909 | 1910 to 1919 | 1920 to 1929 | 1930 to 1939 |
|---|---|---|---|---|
| **Total** | **8,202,388** | **6,347,380** | **4,295,510** | **699,375** |
| Europe | 7,572,569 | 4,985,411 | 2,560,340 | 444,399 |
| Austria-Hungary[2,3,4] | 2,001,376 | 1,154,727 | 60,891 | 12,531 |
| Austria[2,4] | 532,416 | 589,174 | 31,392 | 5,307 |
| Hungary[2] | 685,567 | 565,553 | 29,499 | 7,224 |
| Belgium | 37,429 | 32,574 | 21,511 | 4,013 |
| Bulgaria[5] | 34,651 | 27,180 | 2,824 | 1,062 |
| Czechoslovakia[6] | — | — | 101,182 | 17,757 |
| Denmark | 61,227 | 45,830 | 34,406 | 3,470 |
| Finland | — | — | 16,922 | 2,438 |
| France[7] | 67,735 | 60,335 | 54,842 | 13,761 |
| Germany[3,4] | 328,722 | 174,227 | 386,634 | 119,107 |
| Greece | 145,402 | 198,108 | 60,774 | 10,599 |
| Ireland[8] | 344,940 | 166,445 | 202,854 | 28,195 |
| Italy | 1,930,475 | 1,229,916 | 528,133 | 85,053 |
| Netherlands | 42,463 | 46,065 | 29,397 | 7,791 |
| Norway-Sweden[9] | 426,981 | 192,445 | 170,329 | 13,452 |
| Norway[9] | 182,542 | 79,488 | 70,327 | 6,901 |
| Sweden[9] | 244,439 | 112,957 | 100,002 | 6,551 |
| Poland[3] | — | — | 223,316 | 25,555 |
| Portugal[10] | 65,154 | 82,489 | 44,829 | 3,518 |
| Romania | 57,322 | 13,566 | 67,810 | 5,264 |
| Russia[3,11] | 1,501,301 | 1,106,998 | 61,604 | 2,463 |
| Spain[12] | 24,818 | 53,262 | 47,109 | 3,669 |
| Switzerland | 32,541 | 22,839 | 31,772 | 5,990 |
| United Kingdom[8,13] | 469,518 | 371,878 | 341,552 | 61,813 |
| Yugoslavia[14] | — | — | 49,215 | 6,920 |
| Other Europe | 514 | 6,527 | 22,434 | 9,978 |
| Asia | 299,836 | 269,736 | 126,740 | 19,231 |
| China | 19,884 | 20,916 | 30,648 | 5,874 |
| Hong Kong | — | — | — | — |
| India | 3,026 | 3,478 | 2,076 | 554 |
| Iran | — | — | 208 | 198 |
| Israel | — | — | — | — |
| Japan | 139,712 | 77,125 | 42,057 | 2,683 |
| Jordan | — | — | — | — |
| Korea | — | — | — | — |
| Philippines | — | — | — | 391 |
| Syria | — | — | 5,307 | 2,188 |
| Taiwan | — | — | — | — |
| Turkey | 127,999 | 160,717 | 40,450 | 1,327 |
| Vietnam | — | — | — | — |
| Other Asia | 9,215 | 7,500 | 5,994 | 6,016 |

(*Continued*)

## Immigrants by Region and Selected Country of Last Residence: Fiscal Years 1820–2009    (*Continued*)

| Region and Country of Last Residence[1] | 1900 to 1909 | 1910 to 1919 | 1920 to 1929 | 1930 to 1939 |
|---|---|---|---|---|
| Total | 8,202,388 | 6,347,380 | 4,295,510 | 699,375 |
| America | 277,809 | 1,070,539 | 1,591,278 | 230,319 |
| Canada and Newfoundland[15,16] | 123,067 | 708,715 | 949,286 | 162,703 |
| Mexico[16,17] | 31,188 | 185,334 | 498,945 | 32,709 |
| Caribbean | 100,960 | 120,860 | 83,482 | 18,052 |
| Cuba | — | — | 12,769 | 10,641 |
| Dominican Republic | — | — | — | 1,026 |
| Haiti | — | — | — | 156 |
| Jamaica[18] | — | — | — | — |
| Other Caribbean[18] | 100,960 | 120,860 | 70,713 | 6,229 |
| Central America | 7,341 | 15,692 | 16,511 | 6,840 |
| Belize | 77 | 40 | 285 | 193 |
| Costa Rica | — | — | — | 431 |
| El Salvador | — | — | — | 597 |
| Guatemala | — | — | — | 423 |
| Honduras | — | — | — | 679 |
| Nicaragua | — | — | — | 405 |
| Panama[19] | — | — | — | 1,452 |
| Other Central America | 7,264 | 15,652 | 16,226 | 2,660 |
| South America | 15,253 | 39,938 | 43,025 | 9,990 |
| Argentina | — | — | — | 1,067 |
| Bolivia | — | — | — | 50 |
| Brazil | — | — | 4,627 | 1,468 |
| Chile | — | — | — | 347 |
| Colombia | | | | 1,027 |
| Ecuador | — | — | — | 244 |
| Guyana | — | — | — | 131 |
| Paraguay | — | — | — | 33 |
| Peru | — | — | — | 321 |
| Suriname | — | — | — | 25 |
| Uruguay | — | — | — | 112 |
| Venezuela | — | — | — | 1,155 |
| Other South America | 15,253 | 39,938 | 38,398 | 4,010 |
| Other America[20] | — | — | 29 | 25 |
| Africa | 6,326 | 8,867 | 6,362 | 2,120 |
| Egypt | — | — | 1,063 | 781 |
| Ethiopia | — | — | — | 10 |
| Liberia | — | — | — | 35 |
| Morocco | — | — | — | 73 |
| South Africa | — | — | — | 312 |
| Other Africa | 6,326 | 8,867 | 5,299 | 909 |
| Oceania | 12,355 | 12,339 | 9,860 | 3,306 |
| Australia | 11,191 | 11,280 | 8,404 | 2,260 |
| New Zealand | — | — | 935 | 790 |
| Other Oceania | 1,164 | 1,059 | 521 | 256 |
| Not Specified[20,21] | 33,493 | 488 | 930 | — |

**Immigrants by Region and Selected Country of Last Residence: Fiscal Years 1820–2009** (*Continued*)

| Region and Country of Last Residence[1] | 1940 to 1949 | 1950 to 1959 | 1960 to 1969 | 1970 to 1979 |
|---|---|---|---|---|
| Total | 856,608 | 2,499,268 | 3,213,749 | 4,248,203 |
| Europe | 472,524 | 1,404,973 | 1,133,443 | 825,590 |
| Austria-Hungary[2,3,4] | 13,574 | 113,015 | 27,590 | 20,387 |
| Austria[2,4] | 8,393 | 81,354 | 17,571 | 14,239 |
| Hungary[2] | 5,181 | 31,661 | 10,019 | 6,148 |
| Belgium | 12,473 | 18,885 | 9,647 | 5,413 |
| Bulgaria[5] | 449 | 97 | 598 | 1,011 |
| Czechoslovakia[6] | 8,475 | 1,624 | 2,758 | 5,654 |
| Denmark | 4,549 | 10,918 | 9,797 | 4,405 |
| Finland | 2,230 | 4,923 | 4,310 | 2,829 |
| France[7] | 36,954 | 50,113 | 46,975 | 26,281 |
| Germany[3,4] | 119,506 | 576,905 | 209,616 | 77,142 |
| Greece | 8,605 | 45,153 | 74,173 | 102,370 |
| Ireland[8] | 15,701 | 47,189 | 37,788 | 11,461 |
| Italy | 50,509 | 184,576 | 200,111 | 150,031 |
| Netherlands | 13,877 | 46,703 | 37,918 | 10,373 |
| Norway-Sweden[9] | 17,326 | 44,224 | 36,150 | 10,298 |
| Norway[9] | 8,326 | 22,806 | 17,371 | 3,927 |
| Sweden[9] | 9,000 | 21,418 | 18,779 | 6,371 |
| Poland[3] | 7,577 | 6,465 | 55,742 | 33,696 |
| Portugal[10] | 6,765 | 13,928 | 70,568 | 104,754 |
| Romania | 1,254 | 914 | 2,339 | 10,774 |
| Russia[3,11] | 605 | 453 | 2,329 | 28,132 |
| Spain[12] | 2,774 | 6,880 | 40,793 | 41,718 |
| Switzerland | 9,904 | 17,577 | 19,193 | 8,536 |
| United Kingdom[8,13] | 131,794 | 195,709 | 220,213 | 133,218 |
| Yugoslavia[14] | 2,039 | 6,966 | 17,990 | 31,862 |
| Other Europe | 5,584 | 11,756 | 6,845 | 5,245 |
| Asia | 34,532 | 135,844 | 358,605 | 1,406,544 |
| China | 16,072 | 8,836 | 14,060 | 17,627 |
| Hong Kong | — | 13,781 | 67,047 | 117,350 |
| India | 1,692 | 1,850 | 18,638 | 147,997 |
| Iran | 1,144 | 3,195 | 9,059 | 33,763 |
| Israel | 98 | 21,376 | 30,911 | 36,306 |
| Japan | 1,557 | 40,651 | 40,956 | 49,392 |
| Jordan | — | 4,899 | 9,230 | 25,541 |
| Korea | 83 | 4,845 | 27,048 | 241,192 |
| Philippines | 4,099 | 17,245 | 70,660 | 337,726 |
| Syria | 1,179 | 1,091 | 2,432 | 8,086 |
| Taiwan | — | 721 | 15,657 | 83,155 |
| Turkey | 754 | 2,980 | 9,464 | 12,209 |
| Vietnam | — | 290 | 2,949 | 121,716 |
| Other Asia | 7,854 | 14,084 | 40,494 | 174,484 |

(*Continued*)

## Immigrants by Region and Selected Country of Last Residence: Fiscal Years 1820–2009     (*Continued*)

| Region and Country of Last Residence[1] | 1940 to 1949 | 1950 to 1959 | 1960 to 1969 | 1970 to 1979 |
|---|---|---|---|---|
| Total | 856,608 | 2,499,268 | 3,213,749 | 4,248,203 |
| America | 328,435 | 921,610 | 1,674,172 | 1,904,355 |
| Canada and Newfoundland[15,16] | 160,911 | 353,169 | 433,128 | 179,267 |
| Mexico[16,17] | 56,158 | 273,847 | 441,824 | 621,218 |
| Caribbean | 46,194 | 115,661 | 427,235 | 708,850 |
| Cuba | 25,976 | 73,221 | 202,030 | 256,497 |
| Dominican Republic | 4,802 | 10,219 | 83,552 | 139,249 |
| Haiti | 823 | 3,787 | 28,992 | 55,166 |
| Jamaica[18] | — | 7,397 | 62,218 | 130,226 |
| Other Caribbean[18] | 14,593 | 21,037 | 50,443 | 127,712 |
| Central America | 20,135 | 40,201 | 98,560 | 120,374 |
| Belize | 433 | 1,133 | 4,185 | 6,747 |
| Costa Rica | 1,965 | 4,044 | 17,975 | 12,405 |
| El Salvador | 4,885 | 5,094 | 14,405 | 29,428 |
| Guatemala | 1,303 | 4,197 | 14,357 | 23,837 |
| Honduras | 1,874 | 5,320 | 15,078 | 15,651 |
| Nicaragua | 4,393 | 7,812 | 10,383 | 10,911 |
| Panama[19] | 5,282 | 12,601 | 22,177 | 21,395 |
| Other Central America | — | — | — | — |
| South America | 19,662 | 78,418 | 250,754 | 273,608 |
| Argentina | 3,108 | 16,346 | 49,384 | 30,303 |
| Bolivia | 893 | 2,759 | 6,205 | 5,635 |
| Brazil | 3,653 | 11,547 | 29,238 | 18,600 |
| Chile | 1,320 | 4,669 | 12,384 | 15,032 |
| Colombia | 3,454 | 15,567 | 68,371 | 71,265 |
| Ecuador | 2,207 | 8,574 | 34,107 | 47,464 |
| Guyana | 596 | 1,131 | 4,546 | 38,278 |
| Paraguay | 85 | 576 | 1,249 | 1,486 |
| Peru | 1,273 | 5,980 | 19,783 | 25,311 |
| Suriname | 130 | 299 | 612 | 714 |
| Uruguay | 754 | 1,026 | 4,089 | 8,416 |
| Venezuela | 2,182 | 9,927 | 20,758 | 11,007 |
| Other South America | 7 | 17 | 28 | 97 |
| Other America[20] | 25,375 | 60,314 | 22,671 | 1,038 |
| Africa | 6,720 | 13,016 | 23,780 | 71,408 |
| Egypt | 1,613 | 1,996 | 5,581 | 23,543 |
| Ethiopia | 28 | 302 | 804 | 2,588 |
| Liberia | 37 | 289 | 841 | 2,391 |
| Morocco | 879 | 2,703 | 2,880 | 1,967 |
| South Africa | 1,022 | 2,278 | 4,360 | 10,002 |
| Other Africa | 3,141 | 5,448 | 9,314 | 30,917 |
| Oceania | 14,262 | 11,353 | 23,630 | 39,980 |
| Australia | 11,201 | 8,275 | 14,986 | 18,708 |
| New Zealand | 2,351 | 1,799 | 3,775 | 5,018 |
| Other Oceania | 710 | 1,279 | 4,869 | 16,254 |
| Not Specified[20,21] | 135 | 12,472 | 119 | 326 |

**Immigrants by Region and Selected Country of Last Residence:
Fiscal Years 1820–2009** (*Continued*)

| Region and Country of Last Residence[1] | 1980 to 1989 | 1990 to 1999 | 2000 to 2009 |
|---|---|---|---|
| Total | 6,244,379 | 9,775,398 | 10,299,430 |
| Europe | 668,866 | 1,348,612 | 1,348,904 |
| Austria-Hungary[2,3,4] | 20,437 | 27,529 | 33,929 |
| Austria[2,4] | 15,374 | 18,234 | 21,151 |
| Hungary[2] | 5,063 | 9,295 | 12,778 |
| Belgium | 7,028 | 7,077 | 8,157 |
| Bulgaria[5] | 1,124 | 16,948 | 40,003 |
| Czechoslovakia[6] | 5,678 | 8,970 | 18,691 |
| Denmark | 4,847 | 6,189 | 6,049 |
| Finland | 2,569 | 3,970 | 3,970 |
| France[7] | 32,066 | 35,945 | 44,932 |
| Germany[3,4] | 85,752 | 92,207 | 122,373 |
| Greece | 37,729 | 25,403 | 16,841 |
| Ireland[8] | 22,210 | 65,384 | 15,642 |
| Italy | 55,562 | 75,992 | 28,329 |
| Netherlands | 11,234 | 13,345 | 17,351 |
| Norway-Sweden[9] | 13,941 | 17,825 | 19,382 |
| Norway[9] | 3,835 | 5,211 | 4,599 |
| Sweden[9] | 10,106 | 12,614 | 14,783 |
| Poland[3] | 63,483 | 172,249 | 117,921 |
| Portugal[10] | 42,685 | 25,497 | 11,479 |
| Romania | 24,753 | 48,136 | 52,154 |
| Russia[3,11] | 33,311 | 433,427 | 167,152 |
| Spain[12] | 22,783 | 18,443 | 17,695 |
| Switzerland | 8,316 | 11,768 | 12,173 |
| United Kingdom[8,13] | 153,644 | 156,182 | 171,979 |
| Yugoslavia[14] | 16,267 | 57,039 | 131,831 |
| Other Europe | 3,447 | 29,087 | 290,871 |
| Asia | 2,391,356 | 2,859,899 | 3,470,835 |
| China | 170,897 | 342,058 | 591,711 |
| Hong Kong | 112,132 | 116,894 | 57,583 |
| India | 231,649 | 352,528 | 590,464 |
| Iran | 98,141 | 76,899 | 76,755 |
| Israel | 43,669 | 41,340 | 54,081 |
| Japan | 44,150 | 66,582 | 84,552 |
| Jordan | 28,928 | 42,755 | 53,550 |
| Korea | 322,708 | 179,770 | 209,758 |
| Philippines | 502,056 | 534,338 | 545,463 |
| Syria | 14,534 | 22,906 | 30,807 |
| Taiwan | 119,051 | 132,647 | 92,657 |
| Turkey | 19,208 | 38,687 | 48,394 |
| Vietnam | 200,632 | 275,379 | 289,616 |
| Other Asia | 483,601 | 637,116 | 745,444 |

(*Continued*)

**Immigrants by Region and Selected Country of Last Residence:**
**Fiscal Years 1820–2009** *(Continued)*

| Region and Country of Last Residence[1] | 1980 to 1989 | 1990 to 1999 | 2000 to 2009 |
|---|---|---|---|
| Total | 6,244,379 | 9,775,398 | 10,299,430 |
| America | 2,695,329 | 5,137,743 | 4,442,226 |
| Canada and Newfoundland[15,16] | 156,313 | 194,788 | 236,349 |
| Mexico[16,17] | 1,009,586 | 2,757,418 | 1,704,166 |
| Caribbean | 790,109 | 1,004,687 | 1,053,969 |
| Cuba | 132,552 | 159,037 | 271,742 |
| Dominican Republic | 221,552 | 359,818 | 291,492 |
| Haiti | 121,406 | 177,446 | 203,827 |
| Jamaica[18] | 193,874 | 177,143 | 172,523 |
| Other Caribbean[18] | 120,725 | 131,243 | 114,385 |
| Central America | 339,376 | 610,189 | 591,130 |
| Belize | 14,964 | 12,600 | 9,682 |
| Costa Rica | 25,017 | 17,054 | 21,571 |
| El Salvador | 137,418 | 273,017 | 251,237 |
| Guatemala | 58,847 | 126,043 | 156,992 |
| Honduras | 39,071 | 72,880 | 63,513 |
| Nicaragua | 31,102 | 80,446 | 70,015 |
| Panama[19] | 32,957 | 28,149 | 18,120 |
| South America | 399,862 | 570,624 | 856,593 |
| Argentina | 23,442 | 30,065 | 47,955 |
| Bolivia | 9,798 | 18,111 | 21,921 |
| Brazil | 22,944 | 50,744 | 115,404 |
| Chile | 19,749 | 18,200 | 19,792 |
| Colombia | 105,494 | 137,985 | 236,570 |
| Ecuador | 48,015 | 81,358 | 107,977 |
| Guyana | 85,886 | 74,407 | 70,373 |
| Paraguay | 3,518 | 6,082 | 4,623 |
| Peru | 49,958 | 110,117 | 137,614 |
| Suriname | 1,357 | 2,285 | 2,363 |
| Uruguay | 7,235 | 6,062 | 9,827 |
| Venezuela | 22,405 | 35,180 | 82,087 |
| Other South America | 61 | 28 | 87 |
| Other America[20] | 83 | 37 | 19 |
| Africa | 141,990 | 346,416 | 759,742 |
| Egypt | 26,744 | 44,604 | 81,564 |
| Ethiopia | 12,927 | 40,097 | 87,207 |
| Liberia | 6,420 | 13,587 | 23,316 |
| Morocco | 3,471 | 15,768 | 40,844 |
| South Africa | 15,505 | 21,964 | 32,221 |
| Other Africa | 76,923 | 210,396 | 494,590 |

## Immigrants by Region and Selected Country of Last Residence:
### Fiscal Years 1820–2009  (*Continued*)

| Region and Country of Last Residence[1] | 1980 to 1989 | 1990 to 1999 | 2000 to 2009 |
|---|---|---|---|
| Total | 6,244,379 | 9,775,398 | 10,299,430 |
| Oceania | 41,432 | 56,800 | 65,793 |
| Australia | 16,901 | 24,288 | 32,728 |
| New Zealand | 6,129 | 8,600 | 12,495 |
| Other Oceania | 18,402 | 23,912 | 20,570 |
| Not Specified[20,21] | 305,406 | 25,928 | 211,930 |

— Represents zero or not available.

[1] Data for years prior to 1906 refers to country of origin; data from 1906 to 2006 refer to country of last residence.

[2] Data for Austria and Hungary not reported separately for all years during 1860 to 1869, 1890 to 1899, 1900 to 1909.

[3] From 1899 to 1919, data for Poland included in Austria-Hungary, Germany, and the Soviet Union.

[4] From 1938 to 1945, data for Austria included in Germany.

[5] From 1899 to 1910, data included Serbia and Montenegro.

[6] Currently includes Czech Republic and Slovak Republic.

[7] From 1820 to 1910, data included Corsica.

[8] Prior to 1926, data for Northern Ireland included in Ireland.

[9] Data for Norway and Sweden not reported separately until 1869.

[10] From 1820 to 1910, data included Cape Verde and Azores Islands.

[11] From 1820 to 1920, data refer to the Russian Empire. Between 1920 and 1990 data refer to the Soviet Union. From 1991 to present, the data refer to the Russian federation, Armenia, Azerbaijan, Belarus, Georgia, Kazakhstan, Kyrgyzstan, Moldova, Russia, Tajikistan, Ukraine, and Uzbekistan.

[12] From 1820 to 1910, data included the Canary Islands and Balearic Islands.

[13] Since 1925, data for United Kingdom refer to England, Scotland, Wales, and Northern Ireland.

[14] Currently includes Bosnia-Herzegovina, Croatia, Macedonia, Slovenia, Serbia, and Montenegro.

[15] Prior to 1911, data refer to British North America. From 1911, data include Newfoundland.

[16] Land arrivals not completely enumerated until 1908.

[17] No data available for Mexico from 1886 to 1893.

[18] Data for Jamaica not reported separately until 1953. Prior to 1953, Jamaica was included in British West Indies.

[19] From 1932 to 1972, data for the Panama Canal Zone included in Panama.

[20] Included in "Not Specified" until 1925.

[21] Includes 32,897 persons returning in 1906 to their homes in the United States.

*Note:* From 1820 to 1867, figures represent alien passenger arrivals at seaports; from 1868 to 1891 and 1895 to 1897, immigrant alien arrivals; from 1892 to 1894 and 1898 to 2006, immigrant aliens admitted for permanent residence; from 1892 to 1903, aliens entering by cabin class were not counted as immigrants. Land arrivals were not completely enumerated until 1908. For this table, fiscal year 1843 covers 9 months ending September, 1843; fiscal years 1832 and 1850 cover 15 months ending December 31 of the respective years; and fiscal year 1868 covers 6 months ending June 30, 1868.

*Source:* U.S. Department of Homeland Security.